AMERICAN HUMOR

CONTRIBUTORS

PETER M. BRIGGS,
ASSOCIATE EDITOR

JOSEPH BOSKIN

JOSEPH DORINSON

ALAN GRIBBEN

M. THOMAS INGE

LAWRENCE E. MINTZ

NANCY WALKER

STEPHEN J. WHITFIELD

American Humor

ARTHUR POWER DUDDEN, EDITOR

NEW YORK OXFORD

OXFORD UNIVERSITY PRESS

1987

Oxford University Press

Oxford   New York   Toronto
Delhi   Bombay   Calcutta   Madras   Karachi
Petaling Jaya   Singapore   Hong Kong   Tokyo
Nairobi   Dar es Salaam   Cape Town
Melbourne   Auckland

and associated companies in
Beirut   Berlin   Ibadan   Nicosia

Copyright © 1987 by Arthur Power Dudden

Published by Oxford University Press, Inc.,
200 Madison Avenue, New York, New York 10016

Oxford is a registered trademark of Oxford University Press.

Library of Congress Cataloging-in-Publication Data
American Humor.
Some essays previously published in the American quarterly
spring 1985, v. 37, no. 1.
1. American wit and humor—History and criticism
I. Dudden, Arthur Power, 1921-   . II. American quarterly.
PS430.A42   1987   817'.009   86-12869
ISBN 0-19-504212-3 (alk. paper)

All of the essays in this book except one were previously published in substantially
the same form in the *American Quarterly*, Spring 1985, Volume XXXVII, Number 1.
Grateful acknowledgment is hereby given to the American Studies Association and
the American Quarterly for permission to republish this copyrighted material.
The previously unpublished essay is by M. Thomas Inge.

2 4 6 8 9 7 5 3 1

Printed in the United States of America
on acid-free paper

A RATIONAL ANTHEM

My country, 'tis of thee,
Sweet land of felony,
   Of thee I sing—
Land where my fathers fried
Young witches and applied
Whips to the Quaker's hide
   And made him spring.

My knavish country, thee,
Land where the thief is free,
   Thy laws I love;
I love thy thieving bills
That tap the people's tills;
I love thy mob whose will's
   All laws above.

Let Federal employees
And rings rob all they please,
   The whole year long.
Let office-holders make
Their piles and judges rake
Our coin. For Jesus' sake
   Let's *all* go wrong!

Ambrose Bierce

Acknowledgments

Grateful appreciation goes to the late Brownlee Sands Corrin of Goucher College for his innovative approaches to the study of American humor, to Bruce Kuklick and Richard R. Beeman and Janice Radway, Editors in turn, and to Nicole Cawley-Perkins and Shirley T. Wajda, Managing Editors in turn, of *American Quarterly*. A special note of appreciation must also go to Peter M. Briggs of Bryn Mawr College for his wise counsel and generous assistance.

Bryn Mawr College   *Arthur Power Dudden*
August 1986

Contents

Introduction:
American Humor

ARTHUR POWER DUDDEN

In 1888 Samuel Langhorne Clemens, William Dean Howells, and Charles Hopkins Clark combined their talents to publish *Mark Twain's Library of Humor*. Howells who was powerfully struck by the richness of the indigenous lode they had uncovered, was led to observe: "Smack of whom it would, it has always been so racy of the soil that the native flavor prevails throughout, and whether Yankee, Knickerbocker, Southern Californian, refined or broad, prose, verse, or newspaper, it was and is always American."[1] Their hefty anthology was "a monument," as Clarence Gohdes recognized in his later foreword to the volume on its being reissued, "to the collaboration of the chief American humorist and the first of our great critics to maintain that humor should be a source of pride to all who appraise the contribution of the United States to the world's store of literature."[2] American humor, in spite of the genius of many of its practitioners, has received little serious attention

1. Samuel Langhorne Clemens, William Dean Howells, and Charles Hopkins Clark, eds., *Mark Twain's Library of Humor*, illust. E. W. Kemble, foreword Clarence Gohdes (1888; rpt. New York: Bonanza, 1969), x, xiii.

2. Ibid., x.

from critics or historians.[3] The significance of this compilation of essays stems directly from their sin of omission.

Yet comic literature and styles of performance from the first century or so of American independence asserted themselves clearly enough. England's satirical models traveled to the American colonies and flourished, as Peter Briggs demonstrates for us, in the midst of rising revolutionary sentiments and subsequent quarrels over the politics of the young republic. Regional folkways, dialects, and ebullient democracy sponsored Yankee, frontiersman, Dutchman, Quaker, southwestern, and immigrant drolleries or stereotypes thereafter. Religion, politics, and customs of rural, village, or wilderness life interposed themselves between the races and sexes to supply grist for humor's native mills. Self-appointed wits began to earn money by comic lecturing and writing before 1840. A decade or two later Artemus Ward, Josh Billings, and Petroleum Vesuvius Nasby would lead the way to celebrity status for themselves and their kind. It would remain for Mark Twain, in Alan Gribben's view, to establish the importance of American humor permanently, and to help bring about the emphasis on political, ethnic, and even feminist humor that has pervaded America in the twentieth

---

3. Whether or not humor has been considered too elusive or trivial to take seriously in its own terms, like the popular culture of which it is both a part and a partaker, is unclear. Some scholars have pursued American humor's native strains (though not among the truly Native Americans, the Indians) for indications of the frontier nation's cultural emergence. Others have used humor as evidence to discover the covert traits of American character for the identical purpose of distinguishing the civilization of the United States from that of Europe.

The pioneer studies of American humor were Jeanette Reid Tandy's *Crackerbox Philosophers on American Humor and Satire* (New York: Columbia Univ. Press, 1925); Constance Rourke's *American Humor: A Study of the National Character* (New York: Harcourt, Brace, 1931); Walter Blair's *Native American Humor (1800–1900)*, rev. ed. (1937; rpt. San Francisco: Chandler, 1960); and Blair's *Horse Sense in American Humor from Benjamin Franklin to Ogden Nash* (Chicago: Univ. of Chicago Press, 1942). M. Thomas Inge, *The Frontier Humorists: Critical Views* (Hamden, Conn.: Archon, 1975) affords a convenient set of appraisals. The leading modern syntheses are Norris W. Yates, *The American Humorist: Conscience of the Twentieth Century* (Ames: Iowa State Univ. Press, 1964); and Jesse Bier, *The Rise and Fall of American Humor* (New York: Holt, Rinehart and Winston, 1968); Walter Blair and Hamlin Hill, *America's Humor from Poor Richard to Doonesbury* (New York: Oxford Univ. Press, 1978); and Blair and Raven I. McDavid, Jr., eds., *The Mirth of a Nation: America's Great Dialect Humor* (Minneapolis: Univ. of Minnesota Press, 1983) continue the pioneer tradition for the greater part. Blair and Hill's *American Humor*, however, indicates

century. Such humor was usually an outgrowth of publicly debated issues or controversial institutions, as Arthur Dudden, Joseph Boskin, Joseph Dorinson, and Nancy Walker spell out in their essays, and has increasingly and almost invariably become disbelieving if not contentious in tone. Since Will Rogers, in fact, American humor's older genialities have come to be outweighed by the belligerent stridencies of recent times. The gentle readers of modern American humor, if there are any left, must beware of its vulgarity and violence in ethnic, political, or sexual forms. Contemporary humorists are more often than not working beyond the fringes of social respectability.

The components of alienated and self-detached humor were always present. These included the skeptical, the sardonic, the mocking, even the deliberately cruel. Such humor was frequently racist or sexist. Its political effects were anarchistic, its style tough and enduring. Nasby's racist neighbors are recognizable today. Twain's uncovering of the corruptible, smug self-satisfaction inflating the nation's village elites, in "The Man Who Corrupted Hadleyburg," and his ridicule of mankind's pretentions to godliness, in *The Mysterious Stranger*, reflect the maturing of his artistry, not the tragedy of his decline. Ambrose Bierce and

---

newer possibilities for analysis (379–87). The sources for the works listed above were almost exclusively literary, except for the final chapter of Blair and Hill's book and for Bier's ample gleanings from stage, screen, radio, television, and the performing clubs. Rourke's, Blair's, and Bier's books and judgments have been extraordinarily influential for a long time, and deservedly so. Yet in Rourke's case one might well wonder why her book on the American character could not have been a study of American humor as titled. The fruits should have been at least as ripe for plucking. Humor was invariably a less elusive concept for investigation than the national character of a polyglot people.

To approach the contemporary range of humor studies, see *American Humor: An Interdisciplinary Newsletter*, which seeks to present a multidisciplinary perspective and bibliography. Volumes 1–3 (Spring 1974–1976) have been published in a hard-bound edition by AMS Press, New York. See, for an outstanding example of its contents, Brownlee Sands Corrin. "An Annotated Audio-Videography of Socio-Political Wit, Humor, and Satire," *American Humor*, 2 (Fall 1975), 3–60. See also *Studies in American Humor* (Southwest Texas State University); the newsletter entitled *Humor Events and Possibilities* from the *Workshop Library on World Humour* published in Washington, D.C.; WHIM (Western Humor and Irony Membership) at Arizona State Univ. in Tempe; also the programs, tape recordings, and other emanations from the First, Second, Third, Fourth, Fifth, and Sixth International Conferences on Humor. For a breezy, yet thoughtful, appreciation of American humor, see Peter DeVries, "Perelmania," *New Yorker*, 13 Aug. 1984, 88–91.

H. L. Mencken followed Nasby and Twain's latterday lead. So, to varying degrees, would Ring Lardner, Mort Sahl, Lenny Bruce, and even James Thurber as time went by. Laugh with Kurt Vonnegut if you will, but you must never overlook the terrible interruptions of his firestorm nightmares. The primary function of such humor is antithetical, explains Jesse Bier, in that "It is filled with skepticism, cruelty, and derogation, a means of perspective between exaltation and destruction."[4] American humor doesn't follow a formula, yet it separates itself cleanly from serious protest writings and systematic revolutionary doctrines. It attacks society's follies and fools indiscriminately, revealing in the process those shadowy highlights and lowlights between pretensions and achievements. One gains from American humor's acidic strain a sense of the nation's true history, in the movement of humor from its early American formulations toward its contemporary manifestations.

Throughout the twentieth century America's humor has migrated to new arenas to take advantage of opportunities afforded by new sponsors and media. The comic strips reduced American humor to a daily prescription, M. Thomas Inge recounts, while ethnic comedians and silent movies spectacularly widened its horizons and, as Larry Mintz explains, its roles. Mass circulation of newspapers, periodical magazines, the stages of vaudeville and burlesque, the standup comics of nightclubs, the talking motion pictures, radio programs, and, ultimately, television have steadily converted humor into a multinational business enterprise with manifold models and outlets. The talented Will Rogers mastered most of these possibilities before he died, while political humor matured with him to become American humor's mainstream. In the Watergate case, Stephen Whitfield suggests, American political humor demoted Richard Nixon himself from a tragicomic president into a comic figure of archetypical lineaments.

What's so funny about American humor?—this is the paramount question. Yet as important as this question is, the answer is not often susceptible to academic analysis, for humor has a tendency to evaporate in the heat of critical examination. Humor will also vanish if its intended thrusts are no longer timely. As the *New Yorker*'s E. B. White once observed: "Humor can be dissected, as a frog can, but the thing dies in the process and the innards are discouraging to any but the pure

4. Bier, *Rise and Fall of American Humor*, 29–30, and passim.

scientific mind."[5] It is debatable whether any intellectual treatment of humor seeking to preserve its flavor can avoid becoming a celebration instead of an analysis. Divorced from all of its incentives for laughing, American humor, like any other topic, abruptly becomes sober. Example and analysis must contend in dramatic tension to sustain the context from which laughter springs. We should bear in mind that criticism of humor is a less well-developed genre than the criticism of fiction or nonfiction, drama or poetry. Criticism of humor is defined more often than not by highly personal tastes, that is, by gut reactions rather than by any widely accepted evaluative or analytical standards. What strikes one individual as hilarious can bore or disgust another. Humor's vulnerability became painfully evident in a 1984 report by Jean Civikly and Ann L. Darling, two specialists in speech communication, which indicated that a teacher's use of humor in the classroom would be received defensively by the students, most likely "with suspicion and hostility." Whether or not the playing of canned laughter would have eased the tension, the report did not say.[6]

Another obstacle to any serious appreciation of American humor was that it could be barbed, disconcerting, intimidating, or even downright vicious. Christopher Morley observed in 1933 that:

> There has always been something *sui generis* in the American comic spirit, though I don't know that it has ever been recognizably defined. A touch of brutality perhaps? Anger rather than humor? Various words rise to the mind—*sardonic, extravagant, macabre*—we reject each one, yet the mere fact that it suggests itself points to some essential hardness or sharpness of spirit.[7]

---

5. E. B. White, Pref., in E. B. White and Katharine S. White, eds., *A Subtreasury of American Humor* (1941; rpt. New York: Modern Library, 1948), xvii. For some accounts of recent directions, see: Jan Hoffman, "She Who Laughs Last: Women Comics Cut Loose," *Village Voice*, 9–15 Sept. 1981, 1, 39–43; "Is Nothing Sacred: the Low Art of Parody—Spoofing for Fun and Profit," *Newsweek* (25 April 1983), 64–70; Julia Klein, "The New Stand-up Comics"; and Mary Kay Blakely, "Kate Clinton on the Feminist Comedy Circuit," both in *Ms.*, (Oct. 1984), 116–28.

6. *The Chronicle of Higher Education* (11 July 1984), 25.

7. Christopher Morley, Foreword, in William Murrell, *A History of American Graphic Humor* (New York: Whitney Museum of American Art, 1933), I, ix. For the predisposition to violence, see Thomas L. Hartshorne, "Recent Interpretations of the American Character," *American Studies International*, 16 (Winter 1975), 13–14.

More often than not American humor was no casual laughing matter, considering its destructive features, say from Petroleum Vesuvius Nasby to Lenny Bruce. The American people equipped native humorists with both targets and weapons at the same time. Jesse Bier argues that the conformist strivings of Americans are a consequence of the country's pluralism, the struggle to hold the society together against its centrifugal forces. A further consequence of the culture's centripetal tendencies is seen in the popular effort to uphold the faith in progress and to thwart fanaticism by ostentatiously encouraging dissent or even attack. "Humor has accepted that challenge with alternate glee and rage," Bier contends, "and it has pushed its peculiarly heightened prerogatives in America to the further limits."[8]

Other sources of light illuminate this position. The opposition of wit to authority has generally been apparent to psychologists, biologists, sociologists, and anthropologists, who substantially agree with each other that humor relieves hostilities and aggressions through individual or communal outbursts of merriment.[9] For this reason Thomas Hobbes, in his *Leviathan*, thought that much of the passion called laughter was cowardly, albeit outwardly aggressive, "a sign of pusillanimity," he decided, by which the fainthearted and mean-spirited experience a sudden glory in applauding themselves joyously at the defects of others.[10] Mark Twain, on the other hand, celebrated humor as mankind's supreme weapon, though it was employed too seldom, he believed. "Against the assault of laughter nothing can stand," his mysterious stranger proclaims, but quickly adds: "You are always fussing and fighting with other weapons. Do you ever use that one? No, you leave it lying and rusting. As a race, do you ever use it at all? No, you lack sense and the courage."[11]

8. Bier, *Rise and Fall of American Humor*, 1.

9. Ibid., 1–31, 214, and passim; A. A. Brill, "Wit: Its Technique and Tendencies," ch. 5 of *Basic Principles of Psychoanalysis* (1949;1 rpt. New York: Washington Square Press, 1960), 105–27; Melville Jacobs, "Humor and Tragedy," ch. 10 of *Pattern in Cultural Anthropology* (Homewood, Ill.: Dorsey Press, 1964), 240–52. For a new attempt to destroy previous theories of laughter (including Freud's), see John Morreall, *Taking Laughter Seriously* (Albany: State Univ. of New York Press, 1983).

10. Thomas Hobbes, *Leviathan* (1651), ed. A. R. Waller (Cambridge: Cambridge Univ. Press, 1935), Part I "Of Man," ch. 6.

11. Samuel Langhorne Clemens [Mark Twain], *The Mysterious Stranger* (1916; rpt. New York: Harper and Brothers, 1950), 131–32.

Malcolm Muggeridge, onetime editor of *Punch* magazine, helped us to realize that humor must occasionally be offensive or insulting in order to emphasize the grotesque disparity between intention and performance. "By its nature humor is anarchistic," Muggeridge stated, "and implies when it does not state, criticism of existing institutions, beliefs, and functionaries." Inevitably, he postulated, "All great humor is in bad taste!" In Muggeridge's definition, sizeable segments of America's humor were great indeed.[12] This point of view was not without dispute. James Thurber, choosing Will Rogers as his example, decided that "as a people we have always preferred the gentle to the sharp."[13] Eugene Field's caustic burlesques of children's primers are usually overlooked in favor of his later, more popular, bedtime stories and poems in a sentimental vein.[14] And many critics have faulted the older Mark Twain for turning—as they see it—into an embittered aberration of the youthful and lighthearted Samuel Clemens, a charge that has similarly been directed at Bierce and Mencken.[15]

There is a need to investigate American humor more systematically and intensely in all of its rich variety than literary scholars or American Studies disciplinarians have managed to do so far. It is not enough to leave the field to popular culture studies or the enthusiasts of the American Humor Studies Association. What are American humor's characteristics? How have these evolved and expressed themselves? Which characteristic(s), if any, is or are distinctively American, or perhaps even uniquely so? Do the necessary cross-cultural comparisons sustain any possible claim for national uniqueness (especially if it is true, as is customarily asserted, that humor is relished universally by all of the earth's peoples)? These questions and the issues they generate are too important to treat lightly or scarcely at all.

To indicate some directions for improving and expanding American humor studies, we offer you this set of essays. We have purposely

12. Malcolm Muggeridge, "America Needs a PUNCH," *Esquire* (April 1958), 59–61.

13. James Thurber, "State of the Nation's Humor," *New York Times Magazine* (7 Dec. 1958), 26, and from comments attributed to Thurber on a television program as cited in an editorial, "Thurber on Milk," in the *Philadelphia Inquirer* (25 March 1959), 22. See also Thurber's "The Future, if Any, or Where Do We Non-go from Here?" *Harper's* (Dec. 1961), 40–45.

14. Eugene Field, *The Complete Tribune Primer* (Boston: Mutual Book, 1901), 45, 93.

15. However, see Blair and Hill, *America's Humor*, 379–87.

emphasized the trends of the most recent half century or so to compensate for their neglect to date. We advance no claim to comprehensiveness, but coherence and cogency will become evident throughout the following pages. Even the controversies and disparate viewpoints arising out of contemporary criticism of American humor have been incorporated. Whatever may be missing from the ensuing pages is more than likely lacking not from oversight but by intention. This inquiry originated, as all humor studies should, with the age-old problem set forth in Ecclesiastes II: "I said of laughter, '*It is* mad'; and of mirth, 'What doeth it?'"

AMERICAN HUMOR

English Satire and Connecticut Wit

PETER M. BRIGGS

Qui transtulit sustinet ("He who carried across, sustains").
—Colonial (and later state) motto of Connecticut

There was laughter on these shores, of course, before there were scribes to record it, and for this reason any study of early American humor is likely to begin with notions easier to suppose than to demonstrate. Europeans met Indians in solemn conclave, and then each party went home with their own people to mock the dress, burlesque the manners, and parrot the mispronunciations of the other. Between decks of the Mayflower children whispered together, making foolish faces and mimicking the solemnity of their parents. Near New Amsterdam English travelers mocked Dutchmen, and the Dutch in their turn ridiculed the English. In the South children had to be taught not to snicker at the great man's funny-sounding name, General Oglethorpe. Everywhere older settlers tested the gullibility of newcomers by telling tall tales; new arrivals laughed uncertainly and looked forward to the day when they would possess the humorous self-assurance of older settlers. And, as with every great venture, things went wrong—it was rainy and muddy, or snowy and cold, or hot and dusty; mosquitoes were everywhere, or chiggers, or flies; crops failed or were eaten by pests; guns misfired and

3

wagons broke; food spoiled and neighbors gossiped; children died, wives complained, and men got drunk—and people laughed ruefully at all these things because there was little else to be done.

In a sense, then, there is no identifiable beginning to a native tradition of American humor. By the same token we should recognize that nearly all of the early American humor that we do possess now is belated humor, humor that had to wait until people had the time, detachment, and inclination to write it down, along with the expectation of an audience to share it. Recording humor in a literary form changes its nature, of course; gone are the immediacy, spontaneity, and all the theatrical effects of personal delivery; in their place come the formal conventions of literary humor—the careful control of perspective and tone and pace, the building and shaping of audience expectations, the artful contrivance of economy, irony, and wit, the licensed improprieties of the professed humorist, and so on.[1] To formalize humor in literature, then, is naturally a conservative gesture in a double sense: it preserves materials by setting them apart from the world of ephemera; and it performs this act of preservation by accomodating new materials to older cultural forms and conventions. (There are many more new jests in the world than there are new ways of telling them.) The higher one aspires as a humorist—for example, if one would be a formal verse satirist rather than a mere jokester—the more one is likely to be inspired yet circumscribed, challenged yet embarrassed by what has already been done well by one's predecessors in the humorous tradition.

Hence, there is another kind of belatedness in humor, a self-conscious awareness of one's debt to honored predecessors for the basic tools of one's trade, an indebtedness that may extend from fundamental conventions to bits of felicitous phrasing that the later humorist is anxious to revive or unwilling to forego. New literary opportunities and old literary obligations are often simultaneous and coincident; and, just as Dante was conducted by the shade of Virgil, so the latter-day humorist is likely to find his work prompted and shaped and haunted by the spectres of Juvenal and Horace, Rabelais and Cervantes, Swift

---

1. For a provocative survey of the oral tradition in American humor and of the difficulties of accommodating colloquial origins and conventional literary forms, see Walter Blair, "'A Man's Voice, Speaking': A Continuum in American Humor," included in Harry Levin, ed., *Veins of Humor,* Harvard English Studies 3 (Cambridge: Harvard Univ. Press, 1972), 185–204.

and Pope. Significantly, the shade of Virgil finally left Dante in Purgatory.

My subject, then, is the simultaneous newness and oldness of early American satirical humor, and the rich possibilities and subtle difficulties of accommodating the new with the old that American humorists encountered as they sought the right combination of "European-ness" and "American-ness," local color and general significance, personal idiosyncrasy and a representative voice. My principal examples are drawn from the works of John Trumbull, a Yale graduate (class of 1767) and a member of that loosely connected circle of poets—Timothy Dwight, Joel Barlow, David Humphreys, Lemuel Hopkins—generally known as the Connecticut Wits. Trumbull was not the first American literary humorist (George Alsop, Ebenezer Cook, Benjamin Franklin, William Byrd II, Dr. Alexander Hamilton, and others came earlier),[2] but he was one of the most accomplished, and he also aspired higher than most, which meant that he confronted more directly the problem of combining the new and the old in an attempt to establish America as an appropriate setting for traditional kinds of literary humor. By now several generations of critics have concluded that Trumbull was basically a secondary figure in the development of American poetry and satire, a precocious poet whose early works suggested a literary promise that was never fulfilled in mature works, and there is no need here to challenge this assessment. Yet Trumbull is an enjoyable poet just as he stands, and there is useful instruction even in the works of secondary poets. Trumbull's struggles to domesticate his muse provide a clear instance of some of the general difficulties of cultural transmission and the particular difficulties and ambivalences of realizing America and American-ness in a literary form.

Seen from a sufficient philosophical distance, the rise of learning and the arts in America seemed natural, even inevitable. The translation of

---

2. For sympathetic accounts of Alsop, Cook, and Hamilton, see the pertinent chapters in J.A. Leo Lemay's *Men of Letters in Colonial Maryland* (Knoxville: Univ. of Tennessee Press, 1972). For discussion of Byrd and a broad survey of the development of a satiric tradition in the South, see Richard Beale Davis, *Intellectual Life in the Colonial South, 1585–1763* (Knoxville: Univ. of Tennessee Press, 1978), III, 1344–1400. Geroge F. Horner offers a persuasive account of Franklin's assimilation of the *Spectator* type of essay to American contexts in "Franklin's *Dogood Papers* Re-examined," *Studies in Philology*, 37 (1940), 501–23.

the fruits of older cultures westward to be renewed in younger and flourishing cultures was a well-established literary convention, and, insofar as one subscribed to this convention, the matter of carrying English culture to her colonies in North America seemed a simple and straightforward one, as direct and predictable as the westward movement of the sun.[3] In a poem originally titled "America, or the Muse's Refuge: A Prophecy" (written 1726, published 1752) George Berkeley celebrated the future glory of America and particularly her fugitive muse:

> There shall be sung another golden age,
> The rise of Empire and of Arts,
> The Good and Great inspiring epic Rage,
> The wisest Heads and noblest Hearts.

Berkeley concluded his prophecy with the most famous lines he ever wrote: "Westward the Course of Empire takes its Way. . . . Time's noblest Offspring is the last."[4] He sought to support his hopeful vision with constructive action, projecting the establishment of a colonial college in Bermuda, and, when that project failed for want of funding, sending books to Harvard and both books and monies to Yale. (John Trumbull would later hold a Berkeley scholarship as a graduate student at Yale.) Others in England shared Berkeley's hope for an American golden age, even after the Bermuda project failed. As late as 1774, almost on the eve of the Revolution, Horace Walpole could write of America's prospects with undimmed enthusiasm:

> The next Augustan age will dawn on the other side of the Atlantic. There will, perhaps, be a Thucydides at Boston, a Xenophon at New York, and, in time, a Virgil at Mexico, and a Newton at Peru. At last, some curious traveller from Lima will visit England and give a description of the ruins of St. Paul's.[5]

---

3. See Rexmond C. Cochrane, "Bishop Berkeley and the Progress of Arts and Learning: Notes on a Literary Convention," *Huntington Library Quarterly*, 17 (1953–54), 229–49.

4. *The Works of George Berkeley*, ed. A.A. Luce and T.E. Jessop (London: Thomas Nelson and Sons, 1948–57), VII, 373.

5. Letter from Walpole to Horace Mann, 1774, quoted in Cochrane, "Bishop Berkeley," 245.

Not surprisingly, matters looked somewhat different, if one stood on the opposite shores of the Atlantic. American colonists would gladly have embraced a native Thucydides or a village Virgil, but none raised his voice, and the resistless wave of European culture moving westward seemed more likely to overwhelm than to encourage the early signs of a distinctively American culture. By the middle of the eighteenth century American colonials were dependable importers of English culture— poetry, plays, and novels, of course, but also music, prints, paintings, theological works, instructional books, and so on. They had the money to pay for such cultural imports, but seemingly little prospect for repaying English culture in kind. The most they could hope was that their evident provincialism would not last forever, that at some indefinite future time, America might beget artists who would prove that colonial culture represented—not exactly something new, but a legitimate *extension* of English culture. For the present, however, there was little to be done beyond learning a graceful acceptance of provincial status. In 1728 Mather Byles, a Harvard graduate and a Congregational minister at Boston, nephew to Cotton Mather and himself a sometime poet, wrote a humble yet enthusiastic letter of admiration to Alexander Pope. The attitude he struck in presenting himself to Pope combines self-consciousness with a certain desperate grace; turning from a celebration of Pope's works, Mather felt it necessary to apologize for himself and his compatriots:

> . . . [S]uffer me in Justice to my Native Countrey, to assert our *Taste* for the polite Studies, at the same Time that I am obliged to acknowledge our *Unskilfullness* in them. . . . [W]e can *relish*, what we are unable to *produce*, and *admire* where we can by no means *imitate*.[6]

Pope sent Byles a copy of his translation of the *Odyssey* as an encouragement to colonial letters.

There were also more general grounds for wondering whether American culture would ever realize the golden hopes that Europeans had so easily pinned upon it. In fact, even Europeans were of two minds about

---

6. *The Correspondence of Alexander Pope*, ed. George Sherburn (Oxford: Clarendon Press, 1956), II, 528. On the more general topic of Pope's popularity in America and his influence on early American poetry, see Agnes Marie Sibley, *Alexander Pope's Prestige in America, 1725–1835* (New York: King's Crown Press, 1949), esp. chs. 1 and 4.

America.[7] In his *Recherches philosophiques sur les Américains*, published in 1768, Cornelius DePauw, a French natural scientist, lent an unhelpful hand to American cultural confidence when he wondered rather pointedly whether America really possessed all the promise that others attributed to it. He argued on quasi-scientific grounds that America's climate was naturally unwholesome and perverse: American conditions caused European plants and domestic animals to become stunted and unhealthy, while noxious native plants and wild animals thrived; America was naturally a land of small crops and large weeds, stunted livestock and large mosquitoes.[8] The possible analogy between blighted American nature and dwarfish American culture was obvious to contemporary observers, and although it is doubtful that DePauw's arguments ever persuaded a single American *not* to write a poem, play, or whatever, still the currency of such ideas suggests the deep ambivalence that many American colonials, still taking many of their cues from European attitudes, must have felt toward their own cultural endeavors.

Viewed against this doubt-filled background, the early career of John Trumbull seems oddly smooth and straightforward, unimpeded by his colonial status and circumstances.[9] An extraordinarily precocious child who aspired early to become a poet, Trumbull studied privately with his father, a minister, and passed the entrance examinations for Yale College at the age of seven. For obvious reasons Trumbull's parents did not wish him actually to matriculate at that time, so their quick-witted and somewhat bookish son spent the next six years at home, reading and broadening his preparation for college. Not surprisingly, young Trumbull did well as an undergraduate at Yale, then as a graduate student, then as a tutor. The Yale curriculum at the time paid little heed to

7. See Gilbert Chinard, "Eighteenth Century Theories on America as a Human Habitat," *Proceedings of the American Philosophical Society*, 91 (1974), 27–57; and Henry Steele Commager and Elmo Giordanetti, *Was America a Mistake? An Eighteenth-Century Controversy* (New York: Harper and Row, 1967), passim.

8. Commager and Giordanetti, *Was America a Mistake?*, 75–102.

9. Standard accounts of Trumbull's literary career are to be found in the following: Moses Coit Tyler, *The Literary History of the American Revolution* (New York: G.P. Putnam's Sons, 1897), chs. 9 and 20; Alexander Cowie, *John Trumbull: Connecticut Wit* (Chapel Hill: Univ. of North Carolina Press, 1936); Leon Howard, *The Connecticut Wits* (Chicago: Univ. of Chicago Press, 1943), chs. 2 and 6; and Victor E. Gimmestad, *John Trumbull* (New York: Twayne, 1974).

postclassical literature, a shortcoming that Trumbull would presently satirize, but he himself found time to become quite thoroughly versed in modern letters through independent reading.[10] In 1769, when he was still only nineteen, Trumbull collaborated with Timothy Dwight (who was seventeen) to launch a series of mildly satirical familiar essays, "The Meddler" papers, modeled loosely on Addison and Steele's *Spectator* papers, which appeared in *The Boston Chronicle*. In 1772-73, while he was serving as a tutor at Yale, Trumbull showed his independent-mindedness and self-confidence by publishing the first of the two poems for which he is remembered, *The Progress of Dulness*, which satirized among other things contemporary educational attitudes at Yale. Here was a writer unwilling to be circumscribed by the austere pieties of provincial life.

The three parts of *The Progress of Dulness* describe satirically the careers of three representative colonial types. In Part I Trumbull presents Tom Brainless, a farm boy who grows up to become first a dull and empty-headed scholar, then a tyrannical schoolmaster, and at last a provincial preacher who urges his dozing congregation toward salvation with the help of bold dogmatism and secret plagiarism. Part II presents Dick Hairbrain, son of a colonial farmer turned squire, who uses his opportunity to attend college to launch a career as a wit, fop, and debauché. In the final part Trumbull describes Miss Harriet Simper, a pretty girl who, through the efforts of her mother and other relatives, grows up to become a colonial coquette, doomed after countless fashionable flirtations and a frustrated love affair with Dick Hairbrain to settle down to a dull marriage with Tom Brainless. *The Progress of Dulness* is usually described as a satire of contemporary educational attitudes and practices (which it certainly is), but it also implies a broader indictment of colonial society as ill-educated, pretentious, short-sighted, complacent, and shallow. The satire itself is a well-managed one: witty, controlled, and multifaceted, quite an accomplished performance for a satirist of twenty-three.

My interest here, however, is not so much in *The Progress of Dulness* as a promising individual performance, but rather in its satirical genealogy, its evident indebtedness to some of the prevailing traditions of

10. In *The Connecticut Wits,* ch. 1, Leon Howard surveys the important changes in the Yale curriculum between 1763 and 1778 and assesses the various Wits' reactions to that curriculum.

English satire. In fact, Trumbull's poem can be read as a composite of elements borrowed from the English satirists whom he most admired. The syntax, tone, and basic narrative structure of the poem are derived from Swift's various "Progress" poems—"The Progress of Love," "The Progress of Beauty," "The Progress of Poetry"—all of which explore a general theme by tracing the particular misadventures of a burlesque anti-hero or heroine. Trumbull's rough meter is Butlerian or Swiftian, as is also his tendency to include long lists of unlovely satiric particulars. Trumbull's informality of address and his affection for asides to the reader may be Swiftian, or they may derive from Charles Churchill, whose works were much admired in America by 1770. The poet's main theme, the prevalence of Dulness in the colonies, is clearly traceable to Pope's *Dunciad*, but in the various parts of his poem Trumbull borrows from other poems of Pope as diverse as *The Rape of the Lock, An Essay on Man*, and the *Epistle on the Characters of Women*. Modern scholars have also noted echoes from Waller, Dryden, Etherege, Prior, Gay, and others.[11] Indeed, no small part of the art of Trumbull's poem is his easy and unobtrusive conflation of materials from such heterogeneous resources into a form that has its own energy and coherence.

Still, many of Trumbull's borrowings are too obvious to be hidden. Clearly they represent implicit tributes to earlier satirists, but they also serve the poet as an economical way of orienting his own satire and of making it more resonant and generally significant. For example, he portrays Tom Brainless as a preacher struggling to put together a credible sermon—

> Round him much manuscript is spread,
> Extracts from living works, and dead,
> Themes, sermons, plans of controversy,
> That hack and mangle without mercy,
> And whence, to glad the reader's eyes,
> The future dialogue shall rise [I, 337–42].[12]

—a passage that clearly recalls Pope's energetic description of Colley Cibber struggling to rise through desperation and plagiarism into creativity:

11. For brief but substantial discussion of the full range of Trumbull's poetical debts, see Gimmestad, *John Trumbull*, 19–25, 60–67, 90, and 139ff.

12. Unless otherwise noted, quotations of Trumbull are taken from *The Satiric Poems of John Trumbull*, ed. Edwin T. Bowden (Austin: Univ. of Texas Press, 1962).

> Round him much Embryo, much Abortion lay,
> Much future Ode, and abdicated Play;
> Nonsense precipitate, like running lead,
> That slip'd thro' Cracks and Zig-zags of the Head;
> . . .
> Next o'er his Books his eyes began to roll,
> In pleasing memory of all he stole, . . [B *Dunciad* I, 121–24, 127–28].[13]

In effect, Tom Brainless's lack of comprehension, wit, and substance is tied by allusion to a much longer tradition of dull, stolen hackwork, and Grub Street reaches across the ocean to embrace an American divine.

More generally speaking, Trumbull's entire presentation of Tom Brainless stands as an extended allusion to *The Dunciad*: Tom's rise through education to dull, dogmatic mediocrity recapitulates in miniature many of the abuses of learning satirized by Pope—the self-pleased wanderings of muddle-headed dullards whose notions of learning dissociate it from any ideas of natural order or human usefulness. Yet there is no *conspiracy* against civilization in *The Progress of Dulness*: Tom Brainless is a cultivated fool, but not a threat to any larger notion of civilization. To be sure, Trumbull was not an Alexander Pope, and his poem lacks the intensity, the seriousness, and the scope of Pope's poem; the story of Tom Brainless is not an American *Dunciad*. Yet it should be pointed out that a part of the relative lack of significance of Tom's story has little to do with Trumbull's abilities or aspirations. The American colonies in 1772 simply did not possess an intellectual, social, and political establishment that was or even, I dare say, could have been imagined to be comparable to Britain's—no capital, no court, no Parliament, no Prime Minister, no Oxford or Cambridge, not even a Grub Street or Smithfield or Drury Lane. The presence of such a backdrop of all-encompassing, integrated, and sinister cultural power is an important grounding to the satire in *The Dunciad*: Pope was writing about a society—really, a civilization—that could at least be conceived to operate, and to degenerate, as an integrated whole.[14] Since America was not

---

13. Quotations of Pope's poetry are taken from the Twickenham edition of *The Poems of Alexander Pope*, ed. John Butt et al. (New Haven: Yale Univ. Press, 1939–69), and follow the notation conventions of that edition.

14. For a persuasive account of the metaphors and parallels that unify and amplify *The Dunciad*, see Aubrey L. Williams, *Pope's Dunciad: A Study of Its Meaning* (London: Methuen, 1955), passim.

similarly centralized and integrated, Trumbull was forced by simple circumstance to employ metaphors of cultural decline in more restricted and less resonant ways. To put the matter plainly, Pope himself could not have written an American *Dunciad* at the time. More of this hereafter.

If the story of Tom Brainless springs principally from *The Dunciad*, the stories of Dick Hairbrain and Miss Harriet Simper derive from *The Rape of the Lock*. Both Dick and Harriet are foolish young things, trying out their self-centered pretensions and vanities upon the colonial social scene: Dick learns of up-to-date skepticism and stylish vices, while Harriet toys with foppish lovers and dotes upon the latest London fashions. Pope's Belinda, inevitably, provides the appropriate model and point of reference for comparable vanities and follies in Dick and Harriet, and Trumbull repeatedly recalls small details from Belinda's world in order to dramatize theirs. Trumbull even half-replicates Pope's sylphs, surrounding Harriet first with a cloud of trifling delusions— "Chamaeleons thus, whose colors airy As often as Coquettes can vary, Despise all dishes rich and rare, And diet wholly on the air . . ." (III, 141-44)—and then later with a "powder'd swarm of bowing Lovers": "No lamp expos'd in nightly skies E'er gather'd such a swarm of flies . . ." (III, 400, 403-04). The overall lesson that Trumbull finds in Dick Hairbrain's foppish and debauched career is really a "male" version of the famous moral that Pope's Clarissa tries to explain to Belinda after the loss of her lock (*Rape of the Lock* V, 19-34). Here is Trumbull's version:

> But oh, since youth and years decay,
> And life's vain follies fleet away,
> Since Age has no respect for Beaus,
> And Death the gaudy scene must close,
> Happy the Man, whose early bloom
> Provides for endless years to come;
> That learning seeks, whose useful gain
> Repays the course of studious pain,
> Whose fame the thankful age shall raise,
> And future times repeat its praise;
> Attains that heart-felt peace of mind,
> To all the will of heav'n resign'd, . . [II, 531-42]

Again, one grants that Trumbull was not as fine a poet as Pope; his writing is less polished and resonant, and his tetrameter couplets lack the tautness, complexity, and balance so consistently characteristic of Pope's pentameter verse. Nonetheless, it is clear that Trumbull was engaged in a basically similar enterprise.

To appreciate the full (though intermittent) artfulness of Trumbull's poem, however, it is necessary to dwell, not on passages where he latched onto one particular model and sought to "translate" it to American circumstances, but on those passages where he deftly combined different resources to highlight his own subject. Consider, for example, his portrayal of Dick Hairbrain, returned from a European grand tour with all his affectations intact:

> As fire electric draws together
> Each hair and straw and dust and feather,
> The travell'd Dunce collects betimes
> The levities of other climes;
> And when long toil has giv'n success,
> Returns his native land to bless,
> A Patriot-fop, that struts by rules,
> A Knight of all the shire of fools [II, 403-10]

The burlesque simile is characteristically Swiftian or Butlerian, but it may also recall Pope's depiction of the "needy Poet" in *The Dunciad* as a "vile straw that's blown about the streets, . . . now loose, now fast, And carry'd off in some Dog's tail at last" (B III, 289-92). Certainly Trumbull's whole portrait of Dick Hairbrain as grand tourist glances at Pope's depiction of "young Aeneas," ". . . saunter[ing] Europe round, And gather[ing] ev'ry Vice on Christian ground" (B *Dunciad* IV, 311-312). Finally Trumbull's description of young Dick as "Knight of all the shire of fools" echoes Dryden's description of Sir Fopling Flutter, another grand tourist, in his epilogue to Etherege's *Man of Mode*:

> True Fops help Nature's work, and go to school,
> To file and finish god-a'mighty's fool.
> Yet none Sir *Fopling* him, or him can call;
> He's Knight o' th' Shire, and represents ye all.[15]

In other words, Trumbull has marshalled a whole tradition of fops and fools who stand just behind his presentation of Dick and serve to amplify its meaning.

15. *The Poems of John Dryden*, ed. James Kinsley (Oxford: Clarendon Press, 1958), I, 159.

More generally speaking, Trumbull can be seen thinking through his satiric situation, his characters, his themes, his strategies, in terms of the achievements of his English predecessors in satire. This is good neoclassical practice, of course, and much the same thing that Pope or Churchill had done before him; satirists strengthen their works by the implicit insistence that such works do not stand alone, that they are parts of an honorable tradition. At the same time, however, this continual recollection of English predecessors suggests cumulatively a reluctance or an inability on Trumbull's part to imagine a distinctively American kind of satire, a new set of satiric norms and metaphors to go with a new setting for satire. (What exactly does "knight of the shire" mean in a land with no knights and in one where the term 'shire' was rapidly falling into disuse?) Obviously it was neither possible nor even desireable for Trumbull to invent a wholly new complement of satiric devices to reestablish satire on a new continent—new satire would inevitably continue to reflect its ancestors, even if those ancestors were an ocean away—and the poet was, after all, writing for an audience that had grown up on English kinds of satire. Nonetheless, it does not seem as if Trumbull's notions of satire have in any significant way been expanded or augmented by removal to America, and in some ways they clearly have been diminished by distance. In fact, there is little in *The Progress of Dulness* that is distinctively American: the satirist's heroes and heroine are definitely provincial, borrowing their thoughts and tastes from a world they conceive as more sophisticated than theirs, but for the most part they could be inhabitants of *any* province—a Cornish coquette, a Scottish preacher, an Irish fop. Their American-ness is subsumed in general provincialness.[16] More significantly, it is clear that Trumbull's ideas of wit and satire are still basically London-centered; Connecticut and its local peculiarities are impediments to be overlooked, not resources for a new, strongly rooted American satire. In short, Trumbull wrote a rather good satire, but he was failing in important ways to "imagine" the literary potential of an American setting.

16. In *John Trumbull*, 61–72, Victor Gimmestad argues persuasively that there is quite a bit of topical reference in the poem; however, only a reader with a very specialized knowledge of New Haven history would be prepared to recognize topical allusions. Virtually all readers of *The Progress of Dulness* since 1772 (and probably most contemporary readers as well) have been forced to construe Trumbull's characters as representative types.

Trumbull dealt more directly with American materials in his more mature satire *M'Fingal,* published in parts in 1776 and 1782. Basically this poem tells the story of an American Tory, Squire M'Fingal, who seeks to discredit or subvert the efforts of American patriots to assert political independence from Britain: M'Fingal, defeated first in argument, then in a drunken brawl among enflamed partisans, finally becomes the victim of revolutionary zeal as he is tarred and feathered by vengeful patriots. Trumbull's mock-heroic poem is ostensibly an imitation of Butler's *Hudibras,* but Trumbull himself admitted that he had more often followed Swift and Churchill as models than Butler.[17] A modern reader might be most struck by the number of Miltonic parodies that are sprinkled throughout the poem. Again, Trumbull was clearly thinking through his satiric situation in terms of the achievements of honored predecessors.

Still, *M'Fingal* does deal directly with subject matters and settings that are contemporary and distinctively American. M'Fingal attends a real town meeting,[18] real troops march on a real Boston Common, and the various arguments in the poem between patriots and loyalists are based upon recent political events within the colonies. Yet even here there is a parodox. Consider as an instance M'Fingal's first glimpse of the Liberty pole in the town square which he and his Tory companions subsequently seek to pull down:

> When sudden met his angry eye,
> A pole, ascending thro' the sky,
> Which num'rous throngs of Whiggish race
> Were raising in the market-place;
> Not higher school-boys kites aspire,
> Or royal mast or country spire,

17. Quoted (506–7) in Bruce Ingham Granger's more general assessment of Butler's place in the development of American satire, "Hudibras in the American Revolution," *American Literature,* 27 (1955–56), 499–508.

18. In a letter to John Adams, dated 14 Nov. 1775, Trumbull stated that he drew his satirical picture of a town meeting "from the life," but the form of his statement today seems unintentionally paradoxical: "The Picture of the Townmeeting is drawn from the life, with as proper lights, shades & Colouring as I could give it, & is I fancy no bad likeness" (quoted in Gimmestad, *John Trumbull,* 88). Once again Trumbull is trying to express the immediacy of a real event by the paradoxical expedient of viewing it through a lens provided by an older, more established artistic form—in this case, the formal portrait.

> Like spears at Brobdignagian tilting,
> Or Satan's walking-staff in Milton;
> And on its top the flag unfurl'd
> Waved triumph o'er the prostrate world,
> Inscribed with inconsistent types
> Of liberty and thirteen stripes [III, 5-16].

Obviously the subject matter is local, particular, and American, but what is more interesting is Trumbull's method of imagining the Liberty pole—high as a royal mast, a Brobdignagian spear, Satan's walking-staff. It could be argued that Trumbull is writing from M'Fingal's point of view and that these English-derived metaphors are really artful reflections of the hero's Tory outlook. Yet it seems more likely, here as elsewhere, that Trumbull is revealing in himself a certainToryism of the imagination, showing an ongoing figurative and imaginative indebtedness to English culture even as he and his fellow patriots celebrated political independence from England.

One further instance of this phenomenon in *M'Fingal* should confirm the point. Toward the end of the satire, M'Fingal, like many of his epic predecessors, is granted a vision of the future. Unwillingly, he sees the rout of his fellow Tories, the triumphs of the patriots, and the eventual rise of a new and independent nation. His vision concludes with a prophecy of America's future greatness:

> To glory, wealth and fame ascend,
> Her commerce rise, her realms extend;
> Where now the panther guards his den,
> Her desart forests swarm with men,
> Her cities, tow'rs and columns rise,
> And dazzling temples meet the skies;
> Her pines descending to the main,
> In triumph spread the watry plain,
> Ride inland lakes with fav'ring gales,
> And croud her ports with whit'ning sails;
> Till to the skirts of western day,
> The peopled regions own her sway [IV, 1033-44].

It is tempting to read Trumbull's apotheosis of America as an anticipation of Americans' nineteenth-century assertion of their "manifest destiny"—and perhaps it is—but it should also be pointed out that Trumbull's vision is a fairly close imitation of Pope's celebration of *English* destiny at the end of *Windsor Forest* (particularly ll. 375–90). Aiming to describe an American future, Trumbull is once again swept unwillingly back into an English past.[19]

To a significant extent, then, the newly independent Americans were forced to laugh at their British brethren with borrowed laughter, at least in their fledgling literature, and to assert their independence with cultural forms derived from the very people against whom they rebelled. (Recall that "Yankee Doodle," which American revolutionaries enthusiastically adopted as a kind of unofficial national anthem, had earlier been a marching tune used by British soldiers. And, when George Washington arrived at New York to be inaugurated as first president of the new republic, he was greeted by a mixed chorus singing a patriotic ode written by an American, one Samuel Low; the tune for the ode was a borrowed one, however—the music of "God Save the King.")[20] John Trumbull and his fellow Wits, like many other Americans of the revolutionary generation, were saddled with all the implicit contradictions that accompanied a successful political revolution that was not, and not even *intended* to be, a cultural revolution. The business of establishing political independence from Britain was a relatively easy matter compared with the more subtle, ambivalent, and tortuous task of establishing some sort of imaginative independence.

It is an unpleasing and ultimately unprofitable task simply to dwell upon the derivative qualities of Trumbull's satiric verse or to trace similar signs of poetic belatedness in the works of the other Connecticut

19. Trumbull also echoed *Windsor Forest* repeatedly in his early ode, "Prospect of the Future Glory of America," the conclusion to his *Essay on the Use and Advantages of the Fine Arts,* delivered as a Master's degree oration at the Yale commencement in September 1770. See Trumbull's *Poetical Works*, 2 vols. (Hartford: Samuel G. Goodrich, 1820), II, 157–61. *Windsor Forest* evidently made a similar impression on the imagination of Trumbull's fellow patriot, friend, and legal mentor, John Adams. When Adams visited Windsor in 1783, he was almost willing to overlook the castle for the forest, and specifically Pope's vision of the forest: "I must confess that all the pomps and pride of Windsor did not occupy my thoughts so much as the Forest, and comparing it with what I remembered of Pope's Windsor Forest" (quoted in Sibley, *Pope's Prestige*, 19).

20. Kenneth Silverman, *A Cultural History of the American Revolution* (New York: Thomas Y. Crowell, 1976), 275–77, 289–91, 606.

Wits. Let us just assume the conclusions toward which such musings might lead: that the Connecticut Wits were not as talented, polished, or persistent as their greatest predecessors in English satire; that the Wits were overvalued in their own time, largely for patriotic reasons; and that the Wits have been faintly praised by modern critics, partly because of earlier overpraising, but more because the Wits had little lasting impact upon the development of English or American satire. (Of course, the Wits were imitating satiric models that were already somewhat out of date, even at the time they wrote, and their efforts coincided with the relative decline in popularity of satire and other neoclassical kinds of "wit" in England.) Still, Trumbull and his fellow Wits are often enjoyable in themselves, and they are critically interesting insofar as their relative lack of success reveals something both about the nature of satire and about the processes of cultural transmission.

What, then, might be learned from their example?

First, something about the inevitable tension between theory and practice in satire. In theory the Wits should have been more successful than they were: the rise of satire in American newspapers before and during the Revolution suggests an audience eager for and responsive to satire,[21] and the Wits could claim for themselves not only personal energy and precocious ability, but, thanks to the Revolution, great issues and occasions for satire as well. Moreover, satire *should* do well in unsettled times—recall that most participants in the Revolution and its aftermath learned to fear American anarchy as much as English oppression[22]—simply because satire is well suited to the needs of writers (and readers) who know what they are against, though not necessarily what they are for. Unfortunately, however, theory cuts the other way as well. Revolutionists generally believe (or pretend to believe) in new beginnings for individuals and for societies; satirists, mindful of the persistence of human vices and follies, seldom if ever trust notions of new beginnings. The Wits were at least partially caught, then, between

21. See Bruce Ingham Granger, *Political Satire in the American Revolution, 1763–1783* (Ithaca: Cornell Univ. Press, 1960), passim. For an interestingly opposite perspective (still mostly satirical) on the Revolution, see James C. Gaston, *London Poets and the American Revolution* (Troy, N.Y.: Whitson, 1979).

22. Trumbull's third (and last) major satire. *The Anarchiad*, a rather uneven work written in 1786–87 in collaboration with Lemuel Hopkins, Joel Barlow, and David Humphreys, was a pro-Federalist piece of propaganda directed against the anarchic tendencies of American governance under the Articles of Confederation.

their revolutionary patriotism and the skepticism inherent in their chosen vocation. Trumbull's Tories are a loutish bunch, but too often his patriotic Whigs are little better.[23]

Second, the example of the Connecticut Wits suggests something about the imaginative condition of the American colonies. That the American Revolution was a political revolution far more than it was a cultural one is obvious, but some of the consequences of this notion are worth emphasizing. To put the issue bluntly, colonialism implies a state of mind and a state of imagination as well as a political situation, and the state of mind may be far harder to transcend than political constraints. At least initially, the colonial writer is beholden to the mother country and its culture for all the components of his craft—his conventions, his metaphors, the themes and settings that are considered appropriate for art, his very language and its artistic potentialities. A contemporary English satirist whom Trumbull read put the matter succinctly: "No man lives long enough to get rid of his nursery."[24] The Connecticut Wits knew America well, and yet they had a difficult time *imagining* it for literary purposes; to a surprising extent, the territory was theirs, but their imaginations were not. Or to put that matter more forcefully, it is most surprising the extent to which their cultivated imaginations, well stocked with a close knowledge of the best English models, stood between them and those native conditions they might have "realized" in lasting literature. In an oft-quoted letter to his wife Abigail, John Adams explained the necessity of his participation in the Revolution by looking ahead to the longer prospects of his family:

—I must study Politicks and War that my sons may have liberty to study Mathematicks and Philosophy, . . . Geography, natural History, Naval Architecture, navigation, Commerce and Agriculture, in order to give their Children a right to study Painting, Poetry, Musick, Architecture, Statuary, Tapestry and Porcelaine.[25]

23. For a provocative discussion of the pessimistic strain in the satire that grew out of the Revolution, see Lewis P. Simpson, "The Satiric Mode: The Early National Wits," included in Louis D. Rubin, Jr., ed., *The Comic Imagination in American Literature* (New Brunswick: Rutgers Univ. Press, 1973), 49–61.

24. *The Rolliad*, 21st ed. (London: J. Ridgway, 1799), 150. *Criticisms on the Rolliad*, an anti-Tory satire first published in London in 1784, served as an inspiration and structural model for the Wits' *Anarchiad*.

25. Letter of [12?] May 1780: *Adams Family Correspondence*, ed. L.H. Butterfield and Marc Friedlaender (Cambridge: Harvard Univ. Press, 1973), III, 342.

Note that the artistic pursuits are all in the third generation: implicitly Adams knew what others were reluctant to recognize, that a true imaginative revolution might well be the work of generations.

Third, the example of Trumbull and his fellow Wits suggests some lessons about satire, and particularly the portability of satire. In his Preface to *A Tale of a Tub*, Jonathan Swift's hack narrator announces with considerable confidence that

> . . . nothing is so very tender as a *Modern* Piece of Wit, and, . . . apt to suffer so much in the Carriage. Some things are extreamly witty *to day*, or *fasting*, or *in this place*, or *at eight a clock*, or *over a Bottle*, or *spoke by Mr.* What d'y'call'm, or *in a Summer's Morning*: Any of which, by the smallest Transposal or Misapplication, is utterly annihilate. Thus, *wit* has its Walks and Purlieus, out of which it may not stray the breadth of a Hair, upon peril of being lost.[26]

To be sure, Swift's Hack is not exactly an authority on this or any other matter, and clearly Swift is making fun of the notion that all wit is merely local and transitory. Still, the Hack may have a point, though for reasons of which he cannot quite conceive. Consider the case of John Trumbull. Although Trumbull was not as fine a poet as Pope, still he could write down a fool or knave in a manner nearly as devastating as Pope's—and yet his fools and knaves do not seem to *matter* as Pope's did.[27] Why not? The fact is that satire depends for its force, richness, and resonance upon an imaginative context as well as a circumstantial one, and that imaginative context was far thinner in America than in London. Consider the simple matter of geography: the business of carrying the Smithfield muses to the ear of kings (B *Dunciad* I, 2) was really quite different from carrying a rumor of impending dullness from New Haven to Hartford (formerly Suckiaug), with stops at Middletown and Wethersfield.[28] Pope was writing satire within a frame of reference

26. Jonathan Swift, *A Tale of a Tub*, ed. A.C. Guthkelch and D. Nichol Smith (Oxford: Clarendon Press, 1958), 43.

27. At least once, Trumbull attempted "characters" and a Moral Essay directly "in the manner of Pope": see *Poetical Works* (1820), II, 181–84.

28. It was a later generation of "Connecticut Wits" typified by Mark Twain and Charles Dudley Warner who learned to find humor in the incongruity and sheer improbability of American place-names. In their novel *The Gilded Age: A Tale of Today* (1873), for example, their speculator-protagonist, Colonel Beriah Sellers, projects a possible railroad through rural Missouri: from St. Louis to Slouchburg, Doodle-

that was not only well established but also celebrated—Grub Street and St. Paul's, Smithfield and St. Stephen's—and that well-known geography implies an important dimension of the meaning of his satire. Trumbull had no such substructure to rely upon. Moreover, Pope could build upon an imaginative landscape that accompanied the geographical one, and Trumbull could not. A new Belinda floating on the Housatonic or the Quinnipiac simply could not mean what that former Belinda floating on the Thames had meant. The Thames implied an open-ended set of imaginative associations—mythical Trojans, Romans, Britons; Elizabeth I meeting Leicester, battles and treasons and trysts; poetry by Spenser, Drayton, Milton, Dryden, and a hundred others. The accumulation of these associations forms the basis of Belinda's significance, both real and imaginary. The Housatonic, on the other hand, simply implied an unknown river with a rather exotic name, and nothing that a new Belinda could say or do would much alter its imaginative associations. What is true of Pope's geography in *The Rape of the Lock* or *The Dunciad* is also true in other realms of reference: lords and lapdogs, sylphs and sycophants, mayors and madams—all find their true significance in relation to one another and in relation to a whole, elaborately encoded vision of English "civilization." Clearly Pope enriched and focused existing associations by raising them to satiric intensity, and therein lies much of the greatness of his works, but he was not forced—as Trumbull often was—to postulate those underlying designs and relationships before embellishing them. My general point is a simple one: great satire is most often characterized by economy, intensity, and resonance, and these virtues are not wholly within the individual satirist's power. The satirist must have the talent and the wit to make the most of what he is given in the way of imaginative context, but if he is given little, there is little that he can make of it, whatever his talents. In short, transporting satire may remove it from those contexts, real and imaginary, which did not create but rather *permitted* its most fundamental virtues.

This notion of the imaginative context of satire has another implication worth considering. A Popean kind of satire makes appeal most

ville, Brimstone, Belshazzar, Catfish, Babylon, Bloody Run, Hail Columbia, Hark-from-the-Tomb; then across the Columbus River (formerly Goose Run), bypassing Hawkeye, to Napoleon (formerly Stone's Landing); then on to Hallelujah and Corruptionville (". . . patriotic?—why, they named it after Congress itself"). See *The Gilded Age*, ch. 27.

often for its positive values to historical ideals, not abstract ones, and most of history, both literary and civic, was an ocean away, as far as Americans were concerned. This oceanic remove from history does not necessarily eliminate the possibility of historical resonance in satire or elsewhere, but it makes any such resonance a much more distant one. (The very fact that the American experiment could be considered alternatively as a fulfillment of past history or as an escape from it implies the underlying tentativeness of all contemporary statements of its historical relationships.) Moreover, an Alexander Pope was able to write satire upon the basis of some notion, real or imagined, of historical and moral order, social coherence, metaphysical balance *betrayed*: satire was a sad record and consequence of the falling away from a coherent and integrated order, civilized in its parts, beautiful and sanctified as a whole.[29] Americans in 1776 or 1789 were much more in the position of discovering and asserting that their culture *had* a true center, a coherence, an order, a teleology—and to such labors a satirist need not apply. By nature conservative and skeptical, satire is best suited to charting known territories and traditional values, not to imagining new ones.

John Trumbull and his fellow Wits seem to mark the stretching-thin of an older English tradition of satiric humor more clearly than they signal a new beginning for American satire. Still, their example was not without influence: a significant number of later writers—Washington Irving and Oliver Wendell Holmes, Sr., provide ready instances—continued to seek to embrace and assert the cosmopolitan ease and urbanity that they admired in their greatest British predecessors. Yet the true beginnings of a more distinctively American kind of literary satire lie elsewhere—and that "elsewhere" is, of course, another story, the story of an oral and quasi-oral satiric humor that grew out of promotional literature and tall tales, and the literary impersonation of rustic earthiness and crackerbarrel wisdom and humor. This alternative tradition of humor and satire had fewer literary pretensions—in fact, it often seemed to pride itself on its lack of "refinement"— and therefore was

29. For an important essay on this subject, see Earl Miner, "In Satire's Falling City," included in H. James Jensen and Malvin R. Zirker, Jr., eds., *The Satirist's Art* (Bloomington: Indiana Univ. Press, 1972), 3–27.

less haunted by European literary precedents. This new humor was a boisterous child, energetic, brash, familiar and plain-spoken, irreverent, insistently uninhibited—and, as we all know, that energetic native child eventually grew up to become Mark Twain. Of course, Twain possessed more historical distance from European origins than the Wits had, and he was not one to be daunted by British predecessors or circumscribed by European precedents. Yet it *is* worth recalling how many times over the course of his career Twain brought European characters, social institutions, codes of expression and behavior, particularly English ones, into his own works, seemingly just to make fun of them. To be sure, Twain was jauntily American, and he played the role to the hilt. Yet he seems also to have felt the need for a wise caution, running up to twist the lion's tail one more time, just to make sure that that lion was *still* dead.

The Importance of
Mark Twain

ALAN GRIBBEN

Mark Twain is the only writer we have recognized as an author of immortal American prose after having branded him a "humorist." When in 1956 Floyd Stovall explained the selection process that included Mark Twain (along with Poe, Emerson, Hawthorne, Thoreau, Melville, Whitman, and James) among the eight authors who deserved landmark bibliographical essays sponsored by the American Literature Group of the Modern Language Association, he could assume that "doubtless most readers will agree that at this time and for the purposes of this volume they are the most important American writers."[1] If one adds two figures considered and then omitted—Howells and Dickinson—Twain's uniqueness is still evident. As a consequence of this reputation for humor, Twain's literary accomplishments were never taken for granted; in the beginning Howells, Brander Matthews, William Lyon Phelps, and others had to insist upon Twain's stature as a major American novelist. Yet even during Samuel Clemens's lifetime, encouraging signs of his rising status began to appear.

1. *Eight American Authors: A Review of Research and Criticism*, ed. Floyd Stovall (New York: W.W. Norton, 1956), vi.

In an era when universities bestowed honorary degrees less freely than some perhaps do today, three schools conferred doctorates on Clemens; the first of these, Yale University in 1901, produced a richly symbolic event: there sat Samuel Clemens, self-educated, a product of a rough-and-tumble border state and the strike-it-rich Far West, receiving the highest distinction awarded by a university whose curriculum had seemed conservative to the colonial poet John Trumbull. The cultural revolution betokened by this ceremony was probably no more apprehended by those in attendance than was the equally suggestive fact that Clemens had felt compelled to make his adoptive home the New England city where Trumbull and the Connecticut Wits had flourished. Inasmuch as Twain had found Connecticut—and the western regions where he had resided previously—to be suitable settings for his literature, the American literary independence, now completed attained, was merely being solemnized at this Yale proceeding, as it later would be in similar ceremonies at the University of Missouri (1902) and at Oxford University (1907).[2]

Other tributes arrived as well. Professor Richard Burton declared in 1904 that Clemens was the "one living writer of indisputable genius" in the United States. That same year Clemens was among the first seven individuals selected by secret ballot for membership in the American Academy of Arts and Letters. The other six honorees—including authors William Dean Howells, Edmund Clarence Stedman, and John Hay—have never again been accorded that degree of public esteem, nor have most of those whom these seven people then elected, such as Thomas Bailey Aldrich and Charles Eliot Norton.[3] In 1899, Brander Matthews had classed Twain with Cervantes and Molière, and this sort of accolade, over the objections of certain dissenters in each succeeding

2. More than fifty years ago Vernon Louis Parrington discerned Twain's importance in this regard: "Here at last was . . . a native writer thinking his own thoughts, using his own eyes, speaking his own dialect—everything European fallen away, the last shred of feudal culture gone, local and western yet continental. . . . Yet in spite of a rare vein of humor, . . . he made his way slowly to polite recognition. For years he was regarded by authoritative critics as little more than a buffoon, an extravagant fun-maker with a broad streak of western coarseness." See *The Beginnings of Critical Realism in America, 1860–1920* (New York: Harcourt, Brace and World, 1930), 86.

3. Larzer Ziff discusses some of the ironies of this election ceremony in *The American 1890's: Life and Times of a Lost Generation* (New York: Viking Press, 1966), 345–47.

decade, has gained many adherents. During Clemens's lifetime, Matthew Arnold, John Nichol, and Henry James were among the skeptics regarding his mounting reputation, but their reservations were balanced by the enthusiasm of commentators like Joel Chandler Harris, who in 1908 called Mark Twain "our greatest writer of fiction," and Howells, who termed him, memorably, the Lincoln of our literature. As Jay B. Hubbell has noted, *Adventures of Huckleberry Finn* and Twain's other works found admirers as eminent as Robert Louis Stevenson, Thomas Hardy, Andrew Lang, and George Bernard Shaw.[4]

Nevertheless, Mark Twain's literary stature has suffered, from time to time, *because* of his predilection for comic forms. In 1920, most notably, Van Wyck Brooks led his historic attack on Twain's credentials and achievements, though ensuing testimonials from authors, critics, teachers, and readers elevated Twain to a towering position among the masters of American literature. In the category of humor, indeed, his supremacy today is essentially unassailable, yet Jay B. Hubbell correctly observes that

> for the literary critic Mark Twain poses two special problems. First, he was a great humorist, and Brooks and other critics with little taste for humor have had great difficulty in assessing the value of his books. In the second place, Mark Twain was and still is enormously popular, and this disturbs the modern critics who seem to value only those writers whom they regard as alienated from society. This . . . is a main reason why they have made so much of his pessimism.[5]

For those who harbor ambivalent feelings about Twain's mass popularity in the United States, then and now, a redeeming virtue is Twain's apparent vitalness to American writers. Demonstrably he bequeathed to the twentieth century a style of prose that speaks to us almost contemporarily, less impeded by outmoded linguistic locutions than that of any other humorist—or of virtually any writer, for that matter—of his day. His flexible voice even now comes through as vibrantly as though he were dictating those autobiographical recollections to us instead of to Albert Bigelow Paine and the stenographer Miss Hobby. That modulated voice emerged effectively in his works again and again,

4. Jay B. Hubbell, *Who Are the Major Writers? A Study of the Changing Literary Canon* (Durham, N.C.: Duke Univ. Press, 1972), 144.

5. Ibid., 144.

until eventually he came to believe that this narrative device alone was everything literature was about, that he could dispense with setting, dialect, manners, character development, even plot. He would progressively experiment with eliminating these other elements, one by one, in stories like "The Man That Corrupted Hadleyburg" (1899) and "The $30,000 Bequest" (1904), culminating in the enchanting *talk* of his Autobiographical Dictations, often faulted for their formlessness, but which can best be viewed as a reversion to Twain's earliest, favored form—a series of newspaper-type topical sketches and occasional columns, each perfectly intact and self-contained.

Yet in spite of the distinctive "oral" style that Twain developed for his prose, he has never been the target of parodies like those that have mimicked the rhetoric of Poe, Cooper, Whitman, James, Crane, Hemingway, and Faulkner. Like these writers, Twain can momentarily seem windy, excitable, or pompous. Yet in the main, he succeeded in finding a sense of balance, forging a flexible style that conveys subtlety and density of meaning as well as the disarming fluidity of ordinary conversational speech. One of the less memorable of Twain's paragraphs in the least admired of his travel narratives, *Following the Equator* (1897), can still illustrate the suppleness of his delivery:

> In England any person below the heir who is caught with a rabbit in his possession must satisfactorily explain how it got there, or he will suffer fine and imprisonment, together with extinction of his peerage; in Bluff [,New Zealand], the cat found with a rabbit in its possession does not have to explain—everybody looks the other way; the person caught noticing would suffer fine and imprisonment, with extinction of peerage. This is a sure way to undermine the moral fabric of a cat. Thirty years from now there will not be a moral cat in New Zealand. Some think there is none there now. . . . All governments are more or less shortsighted: in England they fine the poacher, whereas he ought to be banished to New Zealand. New Zealand would pay his way, and give him wages.[6]

Hyperbole, anthropomorphism, the occasional idiomatic expression, and a jab at English law are evident in passages like this one. However, its ultimate effectiveness stems from the impression it delivers of a

6. Mark Twain, *Following the Equator* (Hartford, Conn.: American Publishing, 1897), 285–86.

likable persona's actual speech, daringly punctuated with semicolons and structured around parallel phrases, then artfully frozen in print. Such paragraphs do not simply fool us, as Hemingway's dialogues and monologues succeed in doing, into erroneously supposing that people actually speak English that way (most excerpts from Hemingway's novels and short stories sound wooden and clumsy when read aloud, despite the verisimilitude they appear to exude on the page). In Twain's case, the majority of his tales and essays can be read orally without embarrassment to the reader; people may not talk in such carefully crafted units of punctuation and equipoise, but the rhythms and diction are harmoniously suited to the context and subject matter.

Many of Mark Twain's verbal effects, of course, depended upon his skill in creating the form of address for one dominant speaker. Twain tinkered with vernacular approaches over and over again, often finding his way to workable combinations of story and tone, and once managing to invent a boy's monologue that ensured his place in all studies of fictional narrative. He always had an affection for this "aural" element in literary works, rehearsing oral readings of Robert Browning's verse monologues and Rudyard Kipling's ballads; his own fiction featured loquacious figures like Simon Wheeler, Uncle Mumford, Colonel Sellers, and even King Leopold. In *A Tramp Abroad* (1880), the comic model for travelers like Paul Theroux, which helps them chuckle at inconveniences and teaches them to acknowledge and cherish their inescapable attitudes of cultural superiority, the narrator gives the impression of an oral manner. To fully savor Twain's joke in chapter twenty-five of that work, however, a reader needs to review a typical account of chamois-hunting that appeared in Twain's day; then the subversive nature of Twain's assault on what Henry Nash Smith has variously termed "genteel bombast," "bookish phrases," "clichés of refinement and ideality," and "decadent high culture of the nineteenth century" also comes into focus.[7] The following description appeared in a Philadelphia periodical a little more than a decade before Twain wrote *A Tramp Abroad*; I quote only a few sentences:

---

7. Henry Nash Smith, *Mark Twain: The Development of a Writer* (Cambridge: Harvard Univ. Press/Belknap Press, 1962), 16, 17, 41; Smith, *Democracy and the Novel: Popular Resistance to Classic American Writers* (New York: Oxford Univ. Press, 1978), 119.

The most courageous inhabitants of the Alps take a particular pleasure in looking for and killing the chamois in the wilds of the highest
mountains. Great courage, presence of mind and perseverance is wanted
in chamois hunting. With the thick-soled shoes, the iron-tipped stick, the
pointed hat, ornamented with a chamois beard, and the double-barrel
rifle, the hunter starts in the evening . . . to surprise the chamois at their
pasturages. . . . Often thick fogs come up, so that he can see but a few
feet ahead; or a furious tempest breaks out, that threatens to precipitate
the hunter into the abyss. It is no wonder that chamois-hunters lose their
lives in falling down a gap in the ice, or a precipice; and, nevertheless,
other inhabitants of the Alps undertake this dangerous chase.[8]

Twain's version of these heroics in *A Tramp Abroad*, a book that is
currently undervalued and often out of print, comically expatiates on
the vermin that infested his Swiss hotels:

A great deal of romantic nonsense has been written about the Swiss
chamois and the perils of hunting it, whereas the truth is that even
women and children hunt it, and fearlessly; indeed, everybody hunts it;
the hunting is going on all the time, day and night, in bed and out of it. It
is poetic foolishness to hunt it with a gun; very few people do that. . . .
The romancers always dress up the chamois hunter in a fanciful and
picturesque costume, whereas the best way to hunt this game is to do it
without any costume at all. . . . The creature is a humbug in every way,
and everything which has been written about it is sentimental exaggeration. It was no pleasure to me to find the chamois out, for he had been
one of my pet illusions; all of my life it had been my dream to see him in
his native wilds some day, and engage in the adventurous sport of
chasing him from cliff to cliff. It is no pleasure to me to expose him,
now, and destroy the reader's delight in him and respect for him, but still
it must be done.[9]

His astonishing series of paired opposites in this passage, his scoffing
attack on stilted "romantic nonsense," his undeterred insistence upon a
mistaken identification, his confusion of mighty exploits with everyday

---

8. "Chamois Hunting in the Alps" [anonymous], *Saturday Night* [Philadelphia],
7 Dec. 1867, 7.

9. Mark Twain, *A Tramp Abroad*, Author's National Ed., 2 vols. (New York:
Harper & Brothers, 1907), I, 245–46.

nuisances—we recognize these as hallmarks of Twain's comic pose. They enabled him to exploit European guides, Turkish coffee, and Turkish baths (*Innocents Abroad*); stagecoach-travel, American Indians, and horse-auctions (*Roughing It*); river-piloting, Walter Scott, and Indian legends (*Life on the Mississippi*), and countless other materials that other writers seldom turned to their advantage.

Yet in terms of most techniques that Twain employed, he was exemplary rather than unprecedented. Certainly "The Celebrated Jumping Frog" (1865), with its easily distracted monologist and his anecdote about the illness of Parson Walker's wife ("it seemed as if they warn't going to save her"), is reminiscent of the Widow Bedott's rambling accounts of her family and neighbors, especially the recollections of her deceased husband Hezekiah:

> Why its an onaccountable fact that when that man died he hadent seen a well day in fifteen year, though when he was married and for five or six year after I shouldent desire to see a ruggeder man than what he was. But the time I'm speakin' of he'd been out o' health nigh upon ten year, and O dear sakes! how he had altered since the first time I ever see him! That was to a quiltin' to Squire Smith's a spell afore Sally was married. I'd no idee then that Sal Smith was a gwine to be married to Sam Pendergrass. She'd ben keepin' company with Mose Hewlitt, for better'n a year, and every body said *that* was a settled thing, and lo and behold! all of a sudding she up and took Sam Pendergrass.[10]

In this hodpodge of gossipy details about health, marriage, and friendship, with its chatty, countrified speech and the earnest, candid tone of address, we are already close to the Pike County dialect of garrulous Simon Wheeler's yarn, and also to Jim Blaine's extravagant efforts to narrate the story of his grandfather's old ram:

> Seth Green was prob'ly the pick of the flock; he married a Wilkerson—Sarah Wilkerson—good cretur, she was—one of the likeliest heifers that was ever raised in old Stoddard, everybody said that knowed her. She could heft a bar'l of flour as easy as I can flirt a flapjack. And spin? Don't mention it! Independent? Humph! When Sile Hawkins come

---

10. Frances Miriam Whitcher, *The Widow Bedott Papers* (1856), rpt. in Walter Blair's *Native American Humor* (1937; rpt. New York: Chandler, 1960), 271–72.

a-browsing around her, she let him know that for all his tin he couldn't trot in harness alongside of *her*.[11]

The comic plight, on the other hand, of the unwilling listener, trapped into hearing details about which he simply has no interest and gradually enmeshed in the spreading web of fact and anecdote, proved a fresh if reliable predicament in Twain's fiction. In its drollest variants he dramatizes the captive hearer's torture with tender solicitude. The offended genteel narrator who "frames" the Simon Wheeler story of "The Celebrated Jumping Frog" indignantly construes the tale as an attempt "to bore me to death with some exasperating reminiscence . . . as long and as tedious as it should be useless to me," and his fate is shared by the Mark Twain character in "About Barbers" (1871), who emphasizes that he merely wants a quick shave so that he can catch a noontime train, then sits in agony while the loose-tongued barber, the prototype for Ring Lardner's dense barber in "Haircut," "lathered one side of my face thoroughly, and was about to lather the other, when a dog-fight attracted his attention, and he ran to the window and stayed and saw it out, losing two shillings on the result in bets with the other barbers, a thing which gave me great satisfaction." That last comment suggests how much Twain comes to detest this prating person who, as it turns out, owns a dog himself, and "strung out an account of the achievements of a six-ounce black and tan terrier of his till I heard the whistles blow for noon, and knew I was five minutes too late for the train. . . . The barber fell down and died of apoplexy two hours later. I am waiting over a day for my revenge—I am going to attend his funeral."[12] In chapter twenty-six of *A Tramp Abroad*, the situation humorously evokes the harangue that Coleridge's Wedding Guest endures: the Washington correspondent Riley pushes a captive "against an iron fence, buttonholed him, fastened him with his eye, like the ancient mariner," and proceeded to unfold the story of a government claim-seeker in the era of Andrew Jackson.[13]

11. Mark Twain, *Roughing It*, ed. Franklin P. Rogers and Paul Baender, The Works of Mark Twain Series (Berkeley: Univ. of California Press, 1972), 345.

12. Mark Twain, "About Barbers," in *Mark Twain's Sketches, New and Old* (Hartford, Conn.: American Publishing, 1875), 259–61.

13. Twain, *A Tramp Abroad*, I, 270.

This habitual gambit of depicting the talkative narrator's audience as victim, thus compelling the reader to reflect that he too has been taken advantage of (even though he has enjoyed the tale), represents one of the comprehensive uses Twain made of the vernacular voices he fashioned. Why he succeeded at this more lastingly and appealingly than his contemporary humorists is still a matter for discussion. In a slightly different connection, Ernest Earnest ascribes Twain's originality of style to the publishing practice for which he was criticized in his own day, and this explanation possibly has relevance here: "One reason that Mark Twain had been able to break new ground in the use of colloquial American English was that he published his books in the subscription press, that is through publishers whose salesmen took orders from door to door. He did this not in order to escape the restrictions of conservative editors but simply because he thought he could make more money. . . . The unsophisticated public who patronized the subscription publishers was less squeamish than the Anglophile editors, critics, and professors of literature." Henry Nash Smith adds: "This [subscription method] was probably a wise decision. It was a way for the writer to free himself from the dominant literary conventions. . . . He was forced to invent a new form and a new style in which to express himself."[14]

It is true that Mark Twain was one of the few humorists to avail himself of the awesome sales apparatus of the subscription-canvassing method. Yet this in itself cannot entirely account for why George Ade's clever fables and stories—even the marvelous "Dubley, '89," that amusing account of an alumnus's inappropriate speech at a dinner of the Beverly alumni—are practically forgotten today, along with the humorous productions of scores of other literary comedians like Petroleum V. Nasby and Robert J. Burdette, while Twain reigns paramount in the field of American comedy. George Ade and the others primarily wrote their materials for specific newspapers (and newspaper syndicates)—the Chicago *Record*, the Toledo *Blade*, and the Burlington *Daily Hawk Eye*—as Twain did at the commencement of his writing career, an arrangement he was eventually able to abandon. When the newspaper wits collected their disparate columns for a publisher, the resulting book often relied on repetitious devices and lacked genuine coherence and development. Bill Nye's *Forty Liars, and Other Lies* (1882), for

---

14. Ernest Earnest, *The Single Vision: The Alienation of American Intellectuals* (New York: New York Univ. Press, 1970), 48–49; Smith, *Democracy and the Novel*, 107.

example, is certainly entertaining in its way. Taking biased aim at Mormons, Ute and Sioux Indians, Chinese, newspaper editors, bandits, and the assassin Guiteau, Nye employs understatement and malapropism to advantage. The preface concedes: "There is a tacit admission . . . by the author that some little trifling falsehoods may have crept into the work, owing to the hurry and rush of preparation. . . . I hope there will be no ill-feeling on the part of those who are mentioned personally. . . , and who are still alive, and comparatively vigorous." A dog story in the book, "Entomologist," divertingly relates for children the adventures of a Thurberian dog that ate fifteen feet of a lariat, obliging his master to buy that article; the dog finally dies after devouring some soft plaster of Paris, leaving a plaster cast of himself ("interior view") and prompting the epitaph, "He bit off more than he could chew." Nye's remark about fashion-plate plug hats is entirely worthy of Twain's exaggerations: "In former years they used to hang a man who wore a plug hat west of the Missouri, but after awhile they found that it was a more cruel and horrible punishment to let him wear it, and chase it over the foot-hills when the frolicsome breeze caught it up and toyed with it, and lammed it against the broad brow of Laramie Peak." All the same, the miscellaneous nature of *Forty Liars*, despite its western flavor of tall tales and "lies," suggests the drawbacks of many such publications.[15]

The fact is, the majority of American humorists—as Joel Chandler Harris proved with *Sister Jane* (1896) and *Gabriel Tolliver* (1902)—were better equipped for the squib, the sketch, the story, or a heterogeneous collection of anecdotes and yarns rather than extended fictional inventions of satire and plot.[16] Fortunately for Twain, he experimented intrepidly with numerous genres, moving from the hoax and burlesque to the travel sketch, the short story, the polemical essay, the monologue, and the novel; he was capable, as it turned out, of adequately (if haltingly) converting his talents for the purpose of lengthier efforts that needed greater control of form. In addition, he wrote voluminously;

---

15. Edgar W. Nye, *Forty Liars, and Other Lies* (Chicago: Belford, Clark, 1882), 6, 199, 223.

16. David E. E. Sloane notes, for example, that "after the Civil War, [Orpheus C.] Kerr, like the others, tried to write sustained fiction. The handful of novels he produced were only modestly successful." When the famous Artemus Ward died, Ward "had not attempted sustained fiction in any form, and the possibilities of American humor in that area remained untapped until the successes of Mark Twain." See *Mark Twain as a Literary Comedian* (Baton Rouge: Louisiana State Univ. Press, 1979), 24, 44.

any minor author of the nineteenth century whose literary estate could successfully lay claim to even one tenth of Twain's writings would instantly be granted new respect and would duly be inserted in classroom textbooks.

Our contemporary fascination with *The Mysterious Stranger* (1916), "The War Prayer" (1923), and other fiction and essays from Mark Twain's later phase—a departure from the taste of anthology editors of previous generations—indicates that modern readers admire Twain's courage in registering his moods and approve of the fact that his religious beliefs, social philosophies, and literary techniques must be studied in terms of different "periods" of his outlook. As a consequence, he seems engagingly honest and complex. The truth is, his late polemics and diatribes have accorded with the temper of our recent angry decades. There is an irony here, because, to take one instance, Samuel Clemens could not bring himself to copyright his favorite philosophical treatise *What Is Man?* (written in 1898, published in 1906) in his own name, let alone sign the title page.[17] It was not that any real harm could come to the distinguished author expressing these deterministic views about human conduct—rather, his misgivings involved the insecurity he often displayed about the public image he had created, that venerated Mark Twain persona he had projected skillfully and infallibly for so many years. Clemens the man was at odds with Twain the image in their final years, and this tension between the private and the public figure, his tragic and comic qualities, has become the dominant issue in Mark Twain commentary ever since. Alice Hegan Rice was shocked and embarrassed in August, 1909, when she visited Richard Watson Gilder and listened to Clemens lambasting the order of the universe; later she wrote, "I have an amusing recollection of Mr. Gilder leading me protectingly into the house on one of those occasions, and whispering, 'Don't listen to that blasphemous and unhappy old man!'"[18] Yet the

---

17. Private secretary Isabel V. Lyon recorded on 9 May 1906: "It was this day that Mr. Clemens gave the Gospel Ms. to Mr. Frank Doubleday to take to start in on the publishing of 250 copies to be printed on the DeVinne press; not to be published in Mr. Clemens's name, not even to be copyrighted in his name." See Lyon's journal in the Humanities Research Center, Univ. of Texas at Austin; text quoted from Laurie Lentz's "Mark Twain in 1906: An Edition of Selected Extracts from Isabel V. Lyon's Journal," *Resources for American Literary Study*, 11 (Spring 1981), 31.

18. Alice Hegan Rice, *The Inky Way* (New York: Appleton-Century, 1940), 80.

disgust of Twain's associates went beyond the pall he could cast on a dinner party. They and his audience at large wanted America's foremost humorist to conclude his life with good cheer—to inspire all of us in our trudging circumstances, to set an example for the properly humorous departure from mortal existence. No doubt they hoped for an upbeat exit such as (the supposedly carefree, but actually crusty) William Saroyan tried to supply in 1981 when he telephoned the Associated Press to report, only slightly in advance, his own demise; with cheeky aplomb, the author of *The Time of Our Life* expressed nonchalant curiosity about the sequence of sensations he was soon to undergo.

Mark Twain's mask trembled a bit toward the end, and he was not uniformly capable of jocular pronouncements. Yet he had the consolation of knowing that he had outstripped his competitors in the field of comedy, had indeed set a new record of longevity for his mass popularity. When he came to assess the reasons behind this phenomenal success, he would attribute it to the impatience with human foibles that he manifested more and more obsessively after 1895. His definitive explanation dates from 1906, when Twain dictated a screed about his fellow humorists that has become well known to literary historians. Glancing through the contents of an anthology of American humor that he had helped compile nearly twenty years earlier, *Mark Twain's Library of Humor,*[19] he concluded on July 13, 1906, that the book was now "a cemetery" and gloated about his own survival in contrast to the literary expiration of his many contemporaries:

> I have had for company seventy-eight other American humorists. Each and every one . . . rose in my time, became conspicuous and popular, and by and by vanished. . . . There is probably not a youth of fifteen years of age in the country whose eye would light with recognition at the mention of any one of the seventy-eight names.

Alluding to Nasby, Ward, Strauss, Derby, Burdette, Perkins, Kerr, O'Brien, Billings, and the Danbury *News* Man, he observed that their "writings and sayings were once in everybody's mouth but are now heard of no more and are no longer mentioned." Then he made the oft-quoted assertion that (in his opinion) accounted for his endurance:

19. *Mark Twain's Library of Humor*, ed. Samuel L. Clemens [also William Dean Howells and Charles Hopkins Clark] (New York: Charles L. Webster, 1888).

Why have they perished? Because they were merely humorists. . . .
Often it is merely an odd trick of speech and of spelling, as in the case of
Ward and Billings and Nasby . . . and presently the fashion passes and
the fame along with it. . . . Humor must not professedly teach, and it
must not professedly preach, but it must do both if it would live forever.
By forever, I mean thirty years. . . . I have always preached. That is the
reason that I have lasted thirty years. . . . I was not writing the sermon
for the sake of the humor. I should have written the sermon just the
same. . . . I am saying these vain things in this frank way because I am a
dead person speaking from the grave.[20]

Like much of Twain's autobiography, this is compelling and revela-
tory and quotable; for one thing, it recalls his declaration made forty
years earlier (in a letter written from San Francisco to Orion and Mollie
Clemens on October 19, 1865) that he had contemplated the prospect of
becoming a preacher, but, lacking "the necessary stock in trade—*i.e.*,
religion," had yielded to "a 'call' to literature, of a low order—i.e.,
humorous."[21] Yet the statement of 1906 is not altogether as true as its
currency today would imply. The volume to which Twain adverts
contains specimens from forty-six authors, not seventy-eight. This is a
minor matter, however; without question the book collected most of the
humorists who were known by the 1880s, and Twain mentally added
others who had appeared on the scene in the succeeding decades. More
significant is the overlooked fact that humorists like Petroleum V.
Nasby, Josh Billings, and even Artemus Ward were undeniably—and
frequently—serious in *their* writings. Whether criticizing draft-dodgers
or ridiculing human avarice, they were scarcely the "phunny phellows"
whom Mark Twain caricatures here. Moreover, Professor Brom Weber
and others have pointed out that the Civil War humorists who elected
to don "dialectal [sic] masks of semiliterates," depending on "quasi-
phonetic misspelling, or eye dialect as it is termed by linguists," were
inventive forerunners of realism because of this convention of "ortho-
graphic rearrangement."[22]

20. *Mark Twain in Eruption*, ed. Bernard DeVoto (New York: Harper and Brothers,
1940), 201–3.
21. Quoted in Justin Kaplan's *Mr. Clemens and Mark Twain: A Biography* (New
York: Simon and Schuster, 1966), 14.
22. See, for instance, Brom Weber, "The Misspellers," in *The Comic Imagination in
American Literature*, ed. Louis D. Rubin, Jr. (New Brunswick, N.J.: Rutgers Univ.
Press, 1973), 128–35.

Then, too, Twain's own writings frequently can be shown to have lacked the moral didacticism that he cites as purportedly essential for durability. Few of his early tales and sketches display examples of such "preaching." How much seriousness are we supposed to discern, for example, in his sketch titled "The Late Benjamin Frankin" (1870), in which the narrator complains that Franklin's maxim about "early to bed and early to rise" brought on his "present state of general debility"? "My parents used to have me up before nine o'clock in the morning sometimes when I was a boy," he avers. "If they had let me take my natural rest where would I have been now? Keeping store, no doubt, and respected by all." In the same sketch he scoffs because Franklin "was always proud of telling how he entered Philadelphia for the first time, with nothing in the world but two shillings in his pocket and four rolls of bread under his arm. But really, when you come to examine it critically, it was nothing. Anybody could have done it."[23] It is similarly difficult to detect the "sermon" in "The Celebrated Jumping Frog," "Jim Wolfe and the Tom-Cats," "Jim Blaine and His Grandfather's Old Ram," "An Encounter with an Interviewer," "Jim Baker's Bluejay Yarn," and dozens of other tales.

The fact is, Mark Twain was thinking in 1906 mainly of the literary works he had been publishing at that time. Perhaps he also had in mind the strident indictments that appeared in *Following the Equator* (1897). He had omitted humor to a dismal extent in "A Dog's Tale" (1903), "The Czar's Soliloquy" (1905), and *What is Man?* (which would be circulated in August 1906). Yet for many years most critics have taken Twain's self-analysis at face-value, principally because of his prestigious ranking in American humor; he is unquestionably preeminent among the humorists whom he names and dismisses. Also, the fervent tone of his professed dedication to "preaching" allays the inclination to look behind his words. Finally, and most important, Twain is conceptualized by teachers and critics primarily in terms of the single novel of his that they most teach and study, *Adventures of Huckleberry Finn* (1885). There Mark Twain did seem to be inculcating lessons about human nature and social behavior; we readers come away from that book feeling that we have learned a good deal more than Huck has concerning our fellow human beings, their gullibility, their greed, and their

<hr/>

23. Mark Twain, "The Late Benjamin Franklin," in *Mark Twain's Sketches, New and Old*, 277.

strivings for fellowship and self-respect. The prominence of this novel has colored our responses to Twain's appraisal of himself in 1906, and the latter credo does not merit the acceptance it has gained. After all, he made these sweeping generalizations about *every* American humorist he knew, and about the *entirety* of his own humor—and these opinions are simply the fond wishes of an elderly author rather than historical truth.

Twain's reflections, however, do raise questions that have engrossed scholars for a number of years. For the most part, those who have given thought to these topics have agreed that Twain *is* superior to his brethren, being possibly the leading humorist whom the United States has produced in any century; but they point out that his favorite ploys—understatement, black dialect, exaggeration, burlesque, incongruity, deadpan vernacular, and others—were used by his contemporaries and those who preceded them. James M. Cox declares of A. B. Longstreet, J. J. Hooper, J. G. Baldwin, T. B. Thorpe, Henry Clay Lewis, and G. W. Harris: "All these humorists might have been forgotten had not Mark Twain, whose whole genius was rooted in the [Southern] tradition, made his way into the dominant culture." M. Thomas Inge adds: "The importance of the work of the group of writers known as the Southwestern Humorists to the mainstream of American literature received only slight critical recognition until it was observed that it furnished a literary background for and influenced much of the writings of Mark Twain."[24] Indeed, these early Southern humorists' fiction is virtually as inaccessible and baffling to most American readers today as an unglossed page of Shakespeare's history plays; the dialects, folkways, costumes, oaths, drinks, and romps of Sut Lovingood, Simon Suggs, and other rustic characters seem as strange and intimidating to many present-day students as the speech and behavior of Prince Hal and Falstaff.[25] Still, ephemeral Southern materials had their place in Mark Twain's development; it has often been pointed out, for example, that Twain's first famous story about the jumping frog was formerly an

24. James M. Cox, "Humor of the Old Southwest," in Rubin, ed., *The Comic Imagination*, 112; M. Thomas Inge, ed., *The Frontier Humorists: Critical Views* (Hamden, Conn.: Archon, 1975), 266.

25. In fact, there has been a recent attempt to salvage nineteenth-century humorous stories by preparing "modernized texts," in *The Mirth of a Nation: America's Great Dialect Humor*, ed. Walter Blair and Raven I. McDavid, Jr. (Minneapolis: Univ. of Minnesota Press, 1983).

oral anecdote in the Old Southwestern tradition of humor, that its "frame" narrator bore resemblances to the gentlemen who introduced stories by Thorpe, Longstreet, and others, and that its dialect rests on perhaps forty years of written dialect humor.[26]

Mark Twain also formed part of an even larger tradition, that of "rural humor," in the company of Josiah Allen's wife (Marietta Holley), the Danbury *News* Man (James Bailey), Robert Burdette, Bill Nye (Edgar W. Nye), Max Adeler (Charles Heber Clark), M. Quad (Charles B. Lewis), and Peck's Bad Boy (George Wilbur Peck). C. Carroll Hollis, admitting that "there is no . . . Rabelais, no Cervantes, . . . except for Mark Twain" among the rural comedians, asks, "Why is it then that Clemens is remembered and Nye and the others forgotten?" He answers that, among other advantages, Mark Twain's subjects did not date so quickly. This point especially is worth noting. Lewis Leary has remarked that much of Oliver Wendell Holmes's "humor is so topical that, unlike his one-horse shay, it failed even to outlive its century," and Louis B. Wright has stressed something that we all know intuitively: "Humor is a very perishable commodity."[27] Mark Twain, however, seems funny without any footnotes supplying the historical, political, and literary contexts (as Charles Neider has repeatedly demonstrated with his scissors-and-paste editions of Twain's writings). Human responses remain the same, even when customs alter; the sexually embarrassed purchaser of kid gloves in Gibraltar ("I was hot, vexed, confused, but still happy; but I hated the other boys for taking such an absorbing interest in the proceedings") is ever amusing for his mortification whenever we readers open chapter seven of *The Innocents Abroad* (1869). Beyond erotic innuendoes, this narrator fully typifies the American reaction to all that is foreign, complicated, and assuredly elegant.

Equally timeless is the anecdote in *Roughing It* about the liar named Markiss whom Mark Twain met on the island of Maui, a man compulsively determined to top every conversationalist's story with the tale of his own smoking chimney, huge tree, fast horse, parsimonious employer, until he acquires such a reputation for mendacity that a coroner's jury refuses to believe Markiss's handwritten suicide note, despite

26. See, for instance, Kenneth S. Lynn, ed., *The Comic Tradition in America: An Anthology* (London: Victor Gollancz, 1958), 335.

27. C. Carroll Hollis, "Rural Humor of the Late Nineteenth Century," Lewis Leary, "Washington Irving," and Louis B. Wright, "Human Comedy in Early America," in Rubin, ed., *The Comic Imagination*, 170, 174, 176, 116, 21.

every evidence that he has hanged himself, and returns a verdict of "death 'by the hands of some person or persons unknown.' " This lying character ruins Mark Twain's stay on the island, he would have us suppose, and indeed every such encounter, abroad or at home, illustrates how easily American naiveté can be taken advantage of; but his narrator is invariably grateful for the educating experience. In Honolulu, to pick an example, he luxuriates in the abundance of edible fruits—oranges, pineapples, bananas, mangoes, guavas, melons:

> Then there is the tamarind. I thought tamarinds were made to eat, but that was probably not the idea. I ate several, and it seemed to me that they were rather sour that year. They pursed up my lips, till they resembled the stem-end of a tomato, and I had to take my sustenance through a quill for twenty-four hours. They sharpened my teeth till I could have shaved with them, and gave them a "wire edge" that I was afraid would stay; but a citizen said "no, it will come off when the enamel does"—which was comforting, at any rate. I found, afterward, that only strangers eat tamarinds—but they only eat them once.[28]

By means of such stratagems, Mark Twain shouldered his way to the forefront of literary comedians, emerging from the main body of those writers boldly and permanently. Yet reasons can be found elsewhere than in his powers of absolute originality. He fared better than the rest by more skillfully blending and utilizing the range of techniques that they were already employing. Twain's writings, not theirs, have become the essential grammar for American comic devices such as the deadpan style and ironic understatement.

What, then, besides Mark Twain's mastery of a new dimension in oral-sounding prose, constitute his chief innovations? First and foremost, Leland Krauth seems correct in singling out the way Twain altered one of the tactics of Old Southwestern humor: "he changed the frame, that structural division between the conventional gentleman narrator and his vulgar heroes which created a separation between the author's world of order, reason, and morality, and the actor's life of disorder, violence, and amorality. Twain eliminated this division."[29]

28. Twain, *Roughing It*, 407.
29. Leland Krauth, "Mark Twain: The Victorian of Southwestern Humor," *American Literature*, 54 (1982), 377.

Krauth is referring to the vernacular voice of Huckleberry Finn, but Henry Nash Smith gives this deduction a wider application:

> The straight character speaks in correct, even pedantic or pompous language which contrasts vividly with the incorrect but highly colored speech of the backwoods character. In Mark Twain's best writing (including of course *Adventures of Huckleberry Finn*) the vernacular spokesman takes over the narrative entirely; the straight character disappears and although his presence can still be felt behind the scenes or beneath the surface, the speech of the vernacular character becomes the only available narrative medium.[30]

Twain tried out composite "voices" in some of his early newspaper sketches; in a piece titled "The Reception at the President's" (1870), for instance, his persona is a voluble Washington visitor from the Nevada sagebrush who, intent upon describing desert scenes and personages to President Ulysses S. Grant, impedes a stately procession at the White House (another case of a storyteller's descent upon a cornered listener). Growing indignant when angry people in the line begin pressing against him from behind, the desert denizen whirls and confronts a hapless man at his rear who is being crushed by the growling mob; in high-toned, stuffy diction he reprimands the innocent, unoffending fellow: "My friend, your conduct grieves me to the heart. A dozen times at least your unseemly crowding has seriously interfered with the conversation I am holding with the President, and if the thing occurs again I shall take my hat and leave the premises." Yet it is the meek-looking man, amazed at such effrontery, who retorts with authentic colloquial speech: "I wish to the mischief you would! Where did you come from anyway, that you've got the unutterable cheek to spread yourself here and keep fifteen hundred people standing waiting half an hour to shake hands with the President?"[31] Later, of course, Twain's creations like Hank Morgan would be able to speak an animated, slangy brand of English while expressing some of the author's intellectual beliefs. This evolution was a significant accomplishment for American humor, and in the

30. Smith, *Democracy and the Novel*, 108. See also Kenneth S. Lynn, *Mark Twain and Southwestern Humor* (Boston: Little, Brown, 1959), 148.

31. Mark Twain, "The Reception at the President's," rpt. in *Mark Twain: Life as I Find It*, ed. Charles Neider (Garden City, N.Y.: Hanover House, 1961), 118.

process Mark Twain capably modified the Old Southern tradition of regional "dialect" until its tone, smoothed and tempered, became "vernacular" instead.[32] For these contributions alone, his works merit special attention. Yet they have other characteristics that have ensured their importance to a later age.

One of these traits is the tremendous *range* of Mark Twain's literary productions. During a career spanning half a century, he tried his hand at numerous categories and subgenres of literature, including detective fiction, scatology, maxims, science fiction, and political pamphlets. The diversity of his enormous canon would have had little lasting effect if these experiments had lacked quality. Every scholar of humor (vainly) makes the point that Twain borrowed nearly every device or trick that our textbooks now glibly give him the credit for inventing, but such quibbles have had no impact on Twain's popularity. College students are aware of the river raftsmen's boasts, if familiar with such folklore at all, through the discarded chapter from *Huckleberry Finn* that became the nucleus of chapter three in *Life on the Mississippi* (1883), with its bragging by Bob and the Child of Calamity:

> Look at me! I take nineteen alligators and a bar'l of whiskey for breakfast when I'm in robust health, and a bushel of rattlesnakes and a dead body when I'm ailing! . . . Whoo-oop! Stand back and give me room according to my strength! Blood's my natural drink, and the wail of the dying is music to my ear![33]

A dozen humorists and local colorists, preceded by anonymous newspaper and magazine sketch-writers, had reported these ritualistic face-offs in comparable detail before. Yet Mark Twain incorporated them into books, books that sold well by subscription. What is more, he gradually assembled these books into a corpus that chronicles a narrator's adventures in four diverse regions of the United States and several parts of Europe. Thus the individual incidents and passages gain magnitude by their inclusion in an epic account of life in the nineteenth century, like the prodigious record of English existence that Charles Dickens left behind.

32. See esp. James M. Cox, *Mark Twain: The Fate of Humor* (Princeton: Princeton Univ. Press, 1966), 167.

33. Mark Twain, *Life on the Mississippi* (Boston: James R. Osgood, 1883), 47.

Too, it must be said that this American, more than most of his fellow humorists, accepted challenges and took risks to overcome circumstances. Imagine Sam Clemens staying behind as a small-town Missouri newspaper editor. Impossible. It is even difficult to envision him as a longtime San Francisco columnist like Ambrose Bierce. That role simply does not fit our idea of his restless temperament. In Hannibal his family's poverty saved him from setting down roots, and imbued him with the aggrandizing wanderlust that helped him contribute an élan to our national scene. Through his travels, he came to embody an intrinsically American characteristic: refusing to be impressed when expected to be—particularly when ushered into the presence of so-called "culture." No one at the time fully apprehended his feat in bridging the West by vanquishing the codes of the East, and doing so more effectively than Bret Harte, as it turned out. Born in Missouri, schooled in the colorful regions of Nevada and California, Twain went east to master the necessary economic and literary formulas. Americans rewarded this venturesomeness by adopting him as a unifying legend for the nation as a whole.

The generations of humorists who succeeded Mark Twain were largely college-educated, and they had often served on the staffs of college humor magazines rather than local newspapers—people like Robert Benchley and Heywood Broun (Harvard), George Ade (Purdue), Alexander Woollcott (Hamilton), Donald Ogden Stewart and Clarence Day (Yale), John Kendrick Bangs (Columbia College), James Thurber (Ohio State), Max Shulman (Minnesota), Frank Sullivan and E.B. White (Cornell), and S.J. Perelman (Brown). University training inevitably led American humor away from the rural or homely styles of Artemus Ward, Petroleum V. Nasby, Orpheus C. Kerr, Josh Billings, Bill Nye, and Robert J. Burdette, though some exceptions (like Finley Peter Dunne, Damon Runyon, Will Rogers, and H. Allen Smith) survived and flourished without the benefits of higher education or ostensibly sophisticated styles. Robert Benchley, however, makes a superb example of the emerging mode that would become dominant, and some of his writings show an affinity with Twain's. There is a Twain-like tone to Benchley's "Ladies Wild," a waggish invective against parlor card games (or, for that matter, *any* games except regular poker): "I became the spoil-sport of the party again, and once or twice I caught them trying to slip the deal past me, as if by mistake. . . . They had finally got it down to a game where everything was wild but the black nines, and everyone was trying for 'low.'"[34] Professor Norris W. Yates notes that

the most important feature of Benchley's humor was a character-type which may be labeled the "Little Man." In the nineteenth century, John Phoenix, Charles Heber Clark, and others sometimes depicted gentle, bewildered fumblers trying unsuccessfully to cope with an environment too big and too complex for them.[35]

Mark Twain's most analogous story in this vein is titled "Playing Courier" (1891). Attempting to arrange all of the details for his family's travel between Geneva and Bayreuth, the narrator stubbornly refuses to employ a courier to assist him. A series of mishaps plagues his efforts, capped finally by his stupid purchase of lottery tickets under the impression that he is buying railway tickets. "I affected to be greatly amused; it is all one can do in such circumstances; it is all one can do, and yet there is no value in it; it deceives nobody, and you can see that everybody around pities you and is ashamed of you." When his family learns that he has additionally lost both their baggage and their hotel rooms, they are openly dismayed.

They would skip over a thousand creditable features to remark upon and reiterate and fuss about just one fact, . . . —the fact that I elected myself courier in Geneva, and put in work enough to carry a circus to Jerusalem, and yet never even got my gang out of town. I finally said I didn't wish to hear any more about the subject, it made me tired.[36]

Few other authors besides James Thurber have employed this sort of understatement so efficaciously in behalf of the "Little Man."

It is conceivable, if Samuel Clemens had somehow lived two decades longer, that he might have joined the set of writers associated with the

34. Robert Benchley, "Ladies Wild," in *A Carnival of Modern Humor*, ed. P. G. Wodehouse and Scott Meredith (New York: Delacorte Press, 1967), 16; previously published in *The Benchley Roundup*, ed. Nathaniel Benchley (New York: Harper and Row, 1938).

35. Norris W. Yates, *Robert Benchley*, TUAS No. 138 (New York: Twayne, 1968), 18–21, also 25. Professor Yates's book supplies a list of the college-educated humorists whom Benchley knew.

36. Mark Twain, "Playing Courier," collected in *The American Claimant and Other Stories and Sketches* (New York: Harper and Brothers, 1898), 505–8.

New Yorker magazine—Benchley, White, Sullivan, Thurber, John O'Hara, Dorothy Parker (and later, Corey Ford, S.J. Perelman, A.J. Liebling, and the others). Would Twain have become a revered member of the Algonquin Hotel crowd, slicing away with scalpel-like wit while seated with George Kaufman at the famous Round Table? Would he have appeared in the pages of the same magazine that today carries Woody Allen's casuals? Quite likely, for Mark Twain was ever alert to the winds of comedic change. Mark Twain became, after all, "Mark Twain"; his legend grew, at his encouragement, and he grew along with it as man and writer. It is exceedingly difficult to live within the confines of expectations harbored by one's public; stage and screen personalities and even novelists like Kurt Vonnegut, Jr., and Norman Mailer, whose private lives are spotlighted relentlessly, can tire of their own aura. Yet Clemens adapted to this excruciating role, thrived in it, and died in the process of adding new dimensions to it. This is an astounding achievement, one that has not yet been adequately appreciated by his biographers.[37] The early hunger for renown by a river-village youth cannot account for the energy that the mature Clemens lavished in shoring up his public image; it is easy to understand why so many sentimental commentators have gushed about the "original" character whom he left behind for future ages. As his image came into focus, Mark Twain knew by instinct what Americans wanted and needed in the way of mythic figures, and he provided one that will evidently last as long as our country.[38] No one else had the diplomacy, talent, audacity, or the desire requisite to leave behind that majestic, white-maned, ingratiating image in our collective mind. For most students and many teachers, Mark Twain embodies what is memorable and noteworthy about the post-Civil War decades of literary realism and our national experience.

Thinking about Twain's importance to American literature and humor, one finds it almost impossible to disagree with commonplaces of literary history that seem in little danger of being overturned. Mark Twain *did* signal the end of the American Romantic era, as survey

37. However, Louis J. Budd's recent book, *Our Mark Twain: The Making of His Public Personality* (Philadelphia: Univ. of Pennsylvania Press, 1983), begins to address this fascinating topic.

38. In 1981, in recognition of this fact, the University of Alabama sponsored a national symposium titled "The Mythologizing of Mark Twain"; the papers delivered there (eight of them published by the Univ. of Alabama Press in 1984 as *The Mythologizing of Mark Twain*) examined various features of Twain's incredibly resilient legend.

works and textbooks announce routinely.[39] Although Mark Twain's collected literary criticism has yet to appear as a volume in the Mark Twain Papers Series, a few of his animadversions against Jane Austen, Sir Walter Scott, George Meredith, and others have made known his jocular attitude about critical principles and his devotion to realistic precepts of his own time. Unfairly but magnificently malicious, and as famous as Hemingway's eulogy to *Huckleberry Finn* in *Green Hills of Africa*, Twain's "Fenimore Cooper's Literary Offences" has become a staple of anthologies and actually helps students sense the buried resentment against preceding Romantic writers that partially motivated Twain and other realist authors. In pieces like this one and in the marginalia in his copies of Bret Harte's works ("One of those brutal California stage-drivers could not be polite to a passenger,—& not one of the guild ever 'sir'd' *anybody*," he groused),[40] Twain revealed himself as a close observer of detail, nuance, and diction—opening the way for less stuffy approaches to essays in literary criticism. He is undoubtedly one of the chief inspirations for the small but welcome band of academic wits—among them, Hamlin Hill, James M. Cox, John Gerber, Jesse Bier, Louis D. Rubin, Jr., Leslie Fiedler (Samuel Clemens Professor of English at SUNY-Buffalo), and John Seelye—who in the 1970s and 1980s could be entertaining in their own right when reading conference papers or writing reviews and articles about American humor. Mark Twain's tone enabled them to realize that unbroken solemnity in discussing humor is simply asking for a pie in the face, or is at least inviting another Woody Allen lampoon in the *New Yorker* about the hilarious obtuseness of pompous professors.

Mark Twain's aggregate influence is immeasurable, but we know at least that his books appeared on the library shelves of some of the most talented younger writers of his period—Stephen Crane and Hamlin Garland, for instance.[41] Jay Hubbell notes that Twain's influence on

39. Lars Åhnebrink declares, typically, that "an obvious manifestation that the old school was vanishing and a new era was about to dawn was exhibited in the parodies and attacks that Mark Twain aimed at romanticism." See *The Beginnings of Naturalism in American Fiction*, in Essays and Studies on American Language and Literature, ed. S. B. Liljegren, No. 9 (New York: Russell and Russell, 1961), 127.

40. Bret Harte's *The Luck of Roaring Camp, and Other Sketches* (Boston: Fields, Osgood, 1870). Sydney J. Krause discusses this marginalia in *Mark Twain as Critic* (Baltimore: Johns Hopkins Univ. Press, 1967), 202–20.

41. James E. Kibler, Jr., "The Library of Stephen and Cora Crane," *Proof*, 1 (1971), 207, 229; Åhnebrink, *The Beginnings of Naturalism*, 103, 144 n. 2.

writers of fiction "is greater than that of any other American writer except Henry James."[42] Scholars have discerned the impact of Mark Twain on the works of Ernest Hemingway, Sherwood Anderson, Thomas Wolfe, F. Scott Fitzgerald, John Steinbeck, and William Faulkner.[43]

If Mark Twain had never existed, if young Sam Clemens had succumbed to an early illness, as his family expected, or had he drowned in the Mississippi River, like several of his boyhood chums, then something in our literature would be tangibly missing, and we would know it. What we professors and students and readers would find lacking would be our linkage point with the nineteenth century, especially with its humor, in the form of an actual man whom we can admire and feel affection toward. Mark Twain is one of our few symbolic means of maintaining the crucial continuity between our past cultural heritage and our present-day attitudes. He is a reference figure for all of us, citizen-readers and artist-comedians, marking the common denomina-

42. Hubbell, *Who Are the Major Writers?*, 144.

43. For Hemingway, see Richard Bridgman, *The Colloquial Style in America* (New York: Oxford Univ. Press, 1966), 129–30, 196–97, 202, 219, 227; Jesse Bier, "A Note on Twain and Hemingway," *Midwest Quarterly*, 21 (1980), 261–65; Michael S. Reynolds, *Hemingway's Reading 1910–1940: An Inventory* (Princeton: Princeton Univ. Press, 1981), 194–95; James D. Brasch and Joseph Sigman, *Hemingway's Library: A Composite Record* (New York: Garland Publishing, 1981), 76–77; among others, see for Anderson, Richard Bridgman, *The Colloquial Style in America*, 152–55, 159–60; G. Thomas Tanselle, "Anderson, Annotated by Brooks," *Notes and Queries* (London), 213 (Feb. 1968), 60–61; *Sherwood Anderson's Memoirs: A Critical Edition*, ed. Ray Lewis White (Chapel Hill: Univ. of North Carolina Press, 1970), 342; Hilbert H. Campbell and Charles E. Modlin, "A Catalog of Sherwood Anderson's Library," in *Sherwood Anderson: Centennial Studies* (Troy, N.Y.: Whitston Publishing Co., 1976), 96–97; also (in the same volume), Walter B. Rideout, "A Borrowing from Borrow," which quotes Anderson's praise for Twain's "honesty" and "wholesome disregard of literary precedent" (p. 162); for Wolfe, Percy H. Boynton, *America in Contemporary Fiction* (Chicago: Univ. of Chicago Press, 1940), 220–21; Andrew Turnbull, *Thomas Wolfe* (New York: Charles Scribner's Sons, 1967), 15, 128, 232, 282; C. Hugh Holman, *The Loneliness at the Core: Studies in Thomas Wolfe* (Baton Rouge: Louisiana State Univ. Press, 1975), 84; for Fitzgerald, Robert Sklar, *F. Scott Fitzgerald: The Last Laöcoon* (New York: Oxford Univ. Press, 1967); for Steinbeck, Robert J. DeMott, *Steinbeck's Reading: A Catalogue of Books Owned and Borrowed* (New York: Garland Publishing, 1984), xxiii, 112–13; for Faulkner, Joseph Blotner, *William Faulkner's Library—A Catalogue* (Charlottesville: Univ. Press of Virginia, 1964), 8, 10, 23; Jesse Bier, *The Rise and Fall of American Humor* (New York: Holt, Rinehart and Winston, 1968), 105, 138, 352.

tor of what we want to perceive to be the American character. As a public speaker and lecturer, indeed, the mature Mark Twain was very possibly our last performing humorist who presented himself as a "general" personage—neither an easterner nor exactly a westerner, the embodiment instead of the entire sum of national regionalism, all parts equal, none predominating. This "generic" persona, so different from Will Rogers's lariat-twirling actor, is equally remote from the ethnic *shtick* of Woody Allen and Richard Pryor or the urban neurosis of Joan Rivers and David Brenner. He has no direct, obvious successors, only his impersonators; the humor of our contemporary nightclubs is fragmented and typecast. The foe of humbug, explicitly rebelling against outworn Romantic forms and themes, he detested high airs and smug complacency—putting him in the progression that has led to the stand-up insults of W.C. Fields as well as Lenny Bruce.

Learning from Artemus Ward and others, Twain mastered discriminative lessons of theatricality and publicity. Among other feats, he contrived his public persona so as to convey the impression of (feigned) laziness, lack of erudition, easy success. If the current generation of nonreading Americans is less familiar than their literate predecessors with the qualities of his lesser works, and sometimes even with his greatest novels, at least he is often quoted from pulpits, in newspaper columns, and at lecterns. He has gained favor with academicians while retaining his hold on the taste of the ordinary reader, something that Poe's fiction accomplished but O. Henry's failed to bring off.

Mark Twain endures because he is greater than any of his possible classifications—crackerbarrel philosopher, literary comedian, world traveler, realist, Naturalist, hoaxer, novelist, vernacular humorist, after-dinner speaker—with which he might be labeled. He did practically everything that was expected of a man of letters in his age, and he generally acquitted himself well in every department. He gave his countrymen pride in themselves, their humor, their literature. And he elevated the station of his calling: among Twain's achievements, one of his grandest was his success in making literary humor seem like a respectable profession. His wealth, his Nook Farm home, his fraternal relations with the influential and the lionized—these and other signs of status laid a benediction on his career so lasting that all subsequent authors of comic sketches, stories, and novels owe him a large debt. He rescued the funnyman from the smudged-print pages of Billings, Phoenix, and Nasby and restored him to the honored tradition of Benjamin

Franklin, Oliver Wendell Holmes, and James Russell Lowell. Moreover, Twain mixed seriousness and comedy so subtly in works like *A Connecticut Yankee in King Arthur's Court* that he himself did not always understand his initial intentions, and he thus educated publishers and reviewers and readers about the deeper possibilities of humor, preparing American audiences for John Cheever, Kurt Vonnegut, Jr., Thomas Berger, John Barth, and others.

American literature would have flourished without Mark Twain's contributions. Yet it would be stuffier, less colorful, less redolent of the river and the West, less alluring. He has given us, along with rich impressions of life on rafts, steamboats, stage coaches, railroad cars, and ocean ships, a reassurance that we are not traveling into some black hole of the future, that we have a renewable and accessible past that guarantees a sane and attainable future. By finding amusement in the writings and speeches of one American figure of the nineteenth century, we assuage disturbing anxieties about our historical and cultural isolation when we contemplate with misgivings the dawning age of computer technology, biological engineering, and galactic transportation. If we can palpably touch the steamboat pilot's wheel with Mark Twain, then our grip on the spaceship controls of the twenty-first century feels surer as we extend our capacity to shuttle a supply of humor into the farther reaches of human history.

The Record of
Political Humor

ARTHUR POWER DUDDEN

"Let's Look at the Record."
Al Smith

In his "Doonesbury" Panels, one Sunday morning early in 1982, comic-strip artist G. B. Trudeau portrayed a Pentagon spokesman explaining to a Senate committee on civil defense that life would still be possible after an all-out nuclear attack. Sixty percent of the economy could be reconstituted within twenty-four months, the general testified, "unless, of course, a disproportionate number of lawyers survive." He continued his testimony:

> We believe that given enough notice we would be able to keep losses down to only twenty million people, which is a whopping 91% survival rate. Moreover, life for the survivors will be quite tolerable. The government would assume the responsibility of distributing fresh water, cheese, grain, and emergency change-of-address cards. Also, every shelter owner will be encouraged to equip his unit with several good books and maybe some post card reproductions of famous paintings.

50

"To preserve civilization as we know it?" a Senator asked the general. "Affirmative," the general advised, "Otherwise you have to start over with a zero-based culture."[1]

Trudeau's readers might manage somehow to find his bemedaled armed forces spokesman amusing, although these same readers could well be driven from laughter to anguish by their apprehension of the arms race escalating between the superpowers. Cleverly Trudeau suggested another, yet closely related problem: the authorities might perceive political humor itself as threatening to the national security and attack it accordingly, most likely on patriotic defensive grounds. This factor could justify comedy publishing entrepreneur Bob Orben's reiterated appeals for politics to be governed by an improved sense of humor, while, at the same time, Orben was endeavoring to encourage better comic materials to flow his way.[2]

Humor on the topic of politics has been a familiar vehicle for popular disdain or even opposition throughout American history. Politics has afforded abundant targets for wits, satirists, and comedians at which to aim their scorn. With almanacs, newspapers, and comic showmen popping up everywhere in the nineteenth century, a widening variety of humorists focused their talents on the indigenous resources at hand to poke fun at foolish or knavish political figures. They realized humor's tactical objectives by attacking extraordinary behavior and individual shortcomings in democracy's political arena. Rarely however, in these formative years, did American political humor overreach its own bounds to decry democracy's ideals or to dispute the people's faith in their capacity to govern themselves.

By the middle of the twentieth century, the gloves were removed, as political humorists regularly directed their wit—and their wrath—at more substantial matters of public policy and personality. Highly paid comic columnists and entertainers would fire off barrages broadside at whatever public scandal or governmentally inspired disaster chanced to

1. G.B. Trudeau, "Doonesbury," *Philadelphia Inquirer* (9 May 1982) Comics Section, 2, Universal Press Syndicate. Within a few months, according to Postal Service officials, "about 2000" emergency change-of-address forms were supplied to each post office, except the very small ones. See the *New York Times* (13 Aug. 1982), A26.

2. Marjorie Hunter, "Q. & A.: Bob Orben," *New York Times* (1 June 1982), A20. See Robert Orben's semimonthly subscription newsletter *Current Comedy* (Wilmington, Del.: Comedy Center).

be provoking the people's indignation at the time. The mass media's outpourings of news and commentary so thoroughly succeeded in concentrating public attention in sporadic moments of stimulated excitement that contemporary political humor has come to assert itself in wave-like crescendos with intervening lulls. It is because these peaks of concentrated frenzy arise from concentrating on particular subjects or topics that contemporary political humor can best be comprehended topically rather than serially or by individual accomplishments, as was characteristic of byegone periods. One development after another chosen by comics and wits to dismember, including the die-hard resistance to the Civil Rights Movement or the Watergate affair, have been spotlighted in comic brilliance. Like the volcano Mount St. Helen's, political humor in the second half of the twentieth century seems to erupt unpredictably and even dangerously. Pinkerton and War Department bunglers were shocking enough a century or so ago, but the CIA and the Pentagon's institutionalized *agents provocateurs* represent something else altogether. Total disbelief is close to becoming political humor's polestar. Nevertheless, contemporary political humor's volatility must not be viewed only as an aberration from past practices. The evolutionary directions it has followed from the older traditions into the past half-century or so continue to define its present characteristics.[3]

Throughout the nineteenth century, the nation's professional humorists were usually eccentric literary personalities or traveling showmen themselves. Seba Smith (1792–1868) wrote as Major Jack Downing from Downingville, Away Down East in the State of Maine, the fictitious confidant of presidents from Andrew Jackson to Franklin Pierce, who combined his keen perceptions of the public's business with a stalwart audacity like Brother Jonathan and eventually Uncle Sam. Charles Farrar Browne (1834–1867) wrote as Artemus Ward, who, though plainly indebted to Jack Downing, exemplified the broad dimensions of an impressario localized only by his semiliterate prattle,

3. Arthur Power Dudden, ed., *The Assault of Laughter: A Treasury of American Political Humor* (South Brunswick, N.J.: A.S. Barnes/Thomas Yoseloff, 1962); Dudden, *Pardon Us, Mr President! American Humor on Politics* (South Brunswick, N.J.: A.S. Barnes, 1975); and Leonard C. Lewin, ed., *A Treasury of American Political Humor* (New York: Delacorte Press, 1964). For a handbook to both British and American examples of note, see Leon A. Harris, *The Fine Art of Political Wit* (New York: E. P. Dutton, 1964).

which he skimmed from the speech patterns of America's rural villages and small towns. David Ross Locke (1833–1888) followed next, expressing his corrosive irony under the pseudonym of Petroleum Vesuvius Nasby. Nasby's bizarre letters told of pretended interventions with Abraham Lincoln and Andrew Johnson against the vindictive tempers of Civil War and Reconstruction times. Samuel Clemens (1835–1910), better known as Mark Twain, castigated legislators, flayed bureaucrats, or ridiculed governmental institutions as furiously as anyone else; politics elicited more of his righteous indignation than his social satire, however, at the price of his sense of humor. American political humor reached new heights in the ruminations of Mr. Martin Dooley, the creation of Finley Peter Dunne (1867–1936). Jack Downing, Artemus Ward, Petroleum Nasby, Mark Twain, and Mr. Dooley developed a glorious tradition. James Russell Lowell (1819–1891) through his characterization and writings of Hosea Bigelow, Charles Henry Smith (1826–1903) through Bill Arp, Henry W. Shaw (1818–1885) through Josh Billings, Robert Henry Newell (1836–1901) through Orpheus C. Kerr [Office Seeker], and Edgar Wilson Nye (1850–1896) through Bill Nye upheld that tradition while attracting their own loyal followings. If the pseudonyms disguised the true authorship, they enhanced the characterizations sought by the authors in their own life-like masquerades of the characters themselves. The dialects and comic typographical devices or spelling blunders veiled the biases behind the humorists' thrusts, while unmistakably pointing out the targets for laughter.[4]

Skepticism always, and cynicism often, bound these comic practitioners together with each other and their audiences. They seemed to expect the worst. Their most telling comic thrusts were less than joyful, often more negative than positive on balance. Democracy itself was still on trial, though the crowd's favorite. Even the comparatively mild Josh Billings bet on the lion over the lamb, when he observed, "The furst law ov natur iz tu steal, the sekund law iz tu hide, and the third iz—to steal

4. For selective access, together with the other anthologies listed in n.3 of the Introduction of this book, see Walter Blair and Raven I. McDavid, Jr., eds., *The Mirth of a Nation: America's Great Dialect Humor* (Minneapolis: Univ. of Minnesota Press, 1983); Kenneth S. Lynn, ed., *The Comic Tradition in America: An Anthology* (New York: Doubleday Anchor, 1958); Louis Untermeyer, ed., *A Treasury of Laughter* . . . (New York: Simon and Schuster, 1946); E. B. White and Katharine S. White, eds., *A Subtreasury of American Humor* (New York: The Modern Library, 1948).

agin."[5] Artemus Ward's ungrudging preference for George Washington over all other statesmen because, "He never slopt over!" is not only persuasive, but it grows still more so with the passage of time. Ward's classic shilly-shally is as convincing as a press conference: "My perlitical sentiments agree with yourn exactly," he ruled. "I know they do, becaws I never saw a man whose didn't."[6] Likewise, Petroleum Vesuvius Nasby identified President Andrew Johnson's Copperhead supporters for him without difficulty, as he and the electioneering Chief Executive together in 1866 went "swingin' round the cirkle" to seek votes for Johnson's favorite Congressional candidates: "I observe in the crowds a large proportion uv red noses, and hats with the tops off. I notice the houses unpainted, with pig pens in front ov em," Nasby noted in recognizing the back country rusticity of the president's supporters. Himself an elastic Democrat, Nasby loved his party not for its principles, but for its elected right to dispense the spoils of office. Johnson could have Nasby and his tattered ilk on easy terms, but he would have to furnish the ammunition to fight the battles. "Will he do it?" asked Nasby, who wanted a postmastership for himself. "That's the question a hundred thousand hungry soles, who hanker even ez I do, are daily askin'."[7]

As for Mark Twain, his growing fury at politics and politicians tended to override his sense of humor. His early political reporting was serious and disciplined for the Virginia City (Nevada) *Territorial Enterprise* (1862–1864). His characterizations of the members of the Third Territorial Legislature were personal yet astutely comic. The Civil War's tragedies most likely steered him toward acidity and savagery. Leo Marx suggests that the growing bitterness in American humor sprang from postbellum despair. Jesse Bier believes that the war resolved too little of the slavery problem while adding the evils of industrial rapacity to an already bloody national history.[8] If true, *The Gilded Age* (1874)

5. Henry Wheeler Shaw (Josh Billings], *Hiz Sayings* (1866; rpt. New York: AMS Press, 1972), 86.

6. Charles Farrar Browne [Artemus Ward], *The Complete Works* . . . (London: John Camden Hotten, 1865), 38, 124.

7. David Ross Locke [Petroleum Vesuvius Nasby], *Swingin' Round the Cirkle* (Boston: Lee and Shepard, 1867), 219.

8. Ivan Benson, *Mark Twain's Western Years* (Stanford: Stanford Univ. Press, 1938), 78–79; Jesse Bier, *The Rise and Fall of American Humor* (New York: Holt, Rinehart, and Winston, 1968), 9; Leo Marx, "Mr. Eliot, Mr. Trilling, and *Huckleberry Finn*," *American Scholar*, 22 (1953), 425.

offers clues to the substance of Twain's despair, while his "Letter Read at a Dinner of the Knights of St. Patrick," in 1876, expressed his wish that he could have St. Patrick on hand "to trim us up for the centennial" by ridding the country of its politicians entirely, as the saint had long ago destroyed all of the reptiles in Ireland. Twain's nostalgic humor turned corrosive from *Tom Sawyer* to *Huckleberry Finn*. His bent for comic truthtelling strengthened his animus against the standard wisdom and moral uplift of patriotic formulas mixed with entrepreneurial deceits. He was ever the man to recognize humbug if it was present, which it patently was in the politics of his time, and to recoil instinctively in genuine alarm. "I have been reading the morning paper," he wrote to William Dean Howells in 1899. "I do it every morning—well knowing that I shall find in it the usual depravities and basenesses and hypocrisies and cruelties that make up civilization and cause me to put in the rest of the day pleading for the damnation of the human race." Twain's anger against public affairs underscored his maxim about the United States: "It is by the goodness of God that in our country we have those three unspeakably precious things: freedom of speech, freedom of conscience, and the prudence never to practice either of them." Increasingly frustrated rather than amused by politics and politicians, he growled to Finley Peter Dunne, Mr. Dooley's creator, "If I could keep my faculty for humor uppermost, I'd laugh the dogs out of the country. But I can't. I get too mad."[9]

Finley Peter Dunne made capital use of the "dogs" who were infuriating Mark Twain, however. Dunne had been given free rein in 1893, when he was only twenty-five years old, to comment editorially on affairs of the day for the Chicago *Evening Post*. He endeavored to expose hollowness and sham in the rich and powerful through the

9. Samuel Langhorne Clemens and Charles Dudley Warner, *The Gilded Age: A Tale of Today* (Hartford, Conn.: American Publishing, 1874), 404–15, and passim; Samuel Langhorne Clemens, "Letter Read at a Dinner of the Knights of St. Patrick," 16 March 1876, *Tom Sawyer Abroad, Tom Sawyer Detective and Other Stories* (New York: Harper and Brothers, 1904), 437–38; Henry Nash Smith and William M. Gibson, eds., *Mark Twain–Howells Letters: The Correspondence of Samuel L. Clemens and William D. Howells, 1872–1910* (Cambridge: Harvard Univ. Press/Belknap Press, 1960), II, 691; Samuel Langhorne Clemens, *Following the Equator: A Journey Around the World* (Hartford, Conn.: American Publishing, 1897), 195; Philip Dunne, ed., *Mr. Dooley Remembers: The Informal Memoirs of Finley Peter Dunne* (Boston: Little, Brown, 1963), 260. Political commentator Garry Wills once regarded *The Gilded Age* as America's best political novel. See *New York Times Book Review* (6 June 1976), 7.

device of saloonkeeper Martin Dooley's conversations with his friends McKenna and Hennessey. Dunne added the immigrants' experiences and an urban flavor of his own invention to the crackerbox tradition of comic political commentary and voluntary advice developed by Major Jack Downing, Hosea Bigelow, Artemus Ward, and Petroleum Vesuvius Nasby. Possessing a keen ear for sidewalk speech, he exploited his talent through a rich vein of satirical, jocose, and waggish humor. His characters expressed themselves in an unreal Irish brogue compounded from all of Erin's dialects and homogenized by many years of living and working in Chicago. Mr. Martin Dooley himself emerged over several months from more than one real-life prototype. Included somewhere in Dooley's ancestry, it is likely, was James McGarry, who presided over a saloon on Dearborn Street, but there were others without doubt, among them Peter Dunne himself.[10] McGarry's exemplary acceptance of the inevitable and his wise rejection of futile protestation grew quickly into Martin Dooley's hallmark. Thus: "His [McGarry's] bartender stuck his head in the door to the back room and asked, 'Is George Babbitt good for a drink?' 'Has he had it?' asked McGarry. 'He has,' said the barkeeper apologetically. 'He is,' answered McGarry resignedly."[11]

Mr. Dooley's greatness still shines. Readers can chuckle today at the confusion in his friend Hennessey's mind, in "The O'Briens Forever," between presidential candidate Williams Jennings Bryan and William J. O'Brien, a welterweight alderman from Chicago's South Side. Meaningless oratory was audited for all time in the exchange between the defeated Dorgan and the victorious O'Brien: " 'Well,' " says Dorgan, 'I can't understand it,' he says. 'I med as manny as three thousan' speeches,' he says. 'Well', says William J. O'Brien, 'that was my majority,' he says. 'Have a drink,' he says."[12] On national affairs, Mr. Dooley merrily held forth on candidates and issues, on "Raypublicans," "Dimmycrats," and populists, on the relationship of marriage and drink to politics, the Supreme Court ("th' supreme court follows th' iliction returns"), the vice presidency ("it isn't a crime exactly"), and senatorial courtesy, which, Dooley decided, rules the Senate in the absence of any

10. Elmer Ellis, *Mr. Dooley's America: A Life of Finley Peter Dunne* (New York: Alfred A. Knopf, 1941), 58–101.

11. Ibid., 66–67.

12. Finley Peter Dunne, "The O'Briens Forever," *Mr. Dooley in the Hearts of His Countrymen* (Boston: Small, Maynard, 1899), 101–6.

other rules.[13] On national affairs, Mr. Dooley's fame will endure for his "book review" of Teddy Roosevelt's self-centered account of the Spanish-American War. "If I was him," said Dooley, "I'd call the book 'Alone in Cubia.' " And in 1904 Mr. Dooley stung Theodore Roosevelt again with his characterization of Roosevelt's election to the presidency in his own right as an "Anglo-Saxon triumph."[14]

Dooley's Irishness was fundamental to all issues, including this one. He was merely employing his insider's insight into politics together with an outsider's grasp of the democratic pretentions and nativistic contradictions of American society. Dooley's eyes always twinkled. Politics was serious business, he realized, but scarcely critical. Politics was a sport to banish dull care. "It's a game iv hope, iv jolly-ye'er-neighbor, a confidence game," he determined. The sweet hope of success is always in the air. "If ye don't win fair, ye may win foul," said Dooley. "If ye don't win, ye may tie an' get the money in th' confusion." In life and politics, laughter was inevitable, yet punishment was inescapable also. Dooley's example brings to mind the pupil about to suffer a thrashing from his tutor. "If you can't be easy, be as easy as you can," he implores.[15]

The political science of the sage of Archey Street was beyond cavil. He once said: "A man that'd expict to thrain lobsters to fly in a year is called a loonytic; but a man that thinks men can be turned into angels be an iliction is called a rayformer—an' remains at large."[16] He loved to recount the "old but niver tiresome" stories of election day in Grover Cleveland's time, such as:

13. Finley Peter Dunne, "A Candidate's Pillory," *Mr. Dooley in the Hearts of His Countrymen,* 107–12; Dunne, "On a Populist Convention," *Mr. Dooley in Peace and in War* (Boston: Small, Maynard, 1899), 197–201; Dunne, "Marriage and Politics," *Mr. Dooley's Philosophy* (New York and London: Harper and Brothers, 1906), 141–47; Dunne, "The Supreme Court's Decisions," *Mr. Dooley's Opinions* (New York: R. H. Russell, 1901), 21–26; Dunne, "The Vice-President" and "Senatorial Courtesy," *Dissertations by Mr. Dooley* (New York and London: Harper and Brothers, 1906), 115–20, 193–95; Dunne, "Drink and Politics," *Mr. Dooley on Making a Will and Other Necessary Evils* (New York: Charles Scribner's Sons, 1919), 43–46.

14. Dunne "A Book Review," *Mr. Dooley's Philosophy,* 13–18; Dunne, "The 'Anglo-Saxon' Triumph," *Dissertations by Mr. Dooley,* 213–18; Ellis, *Mr. Dooley's America,* 206–8. See also Finley Peter Dunne, "Mr. Dooley's Friends: Teddy Roosevelt and Mark Twain," *Atlantic Monthly,* 212 (Sept. 1963), 78.

15. Dunne, "The Candidate," 199.

16. Dunne, "Casual Observations," 255.

Texas give a Dimmycrat majority iv five hundred thousan', but will reopen th' polls if more is nicessary; th' Dimmycats hope, if th' prisint ratio is maintained th' Raypublican victhry in Pinnsylvania will not be unanimous. An' wan candydate rayceives six million votes an' is overwhelmingly defeated, an' th' other rayceives five millyon nine hundherd thousan' and is triumphantly ilicted.[17]

He would have relished the "iliction" of John Fitzgerald Kennedy in 1960, when Chicago's Cook County tabulations powerfully assisted Kennedy to carry Illinois and the White House. "We do make progress," Dooley recognized, "but it's the same kind Julyus Caesar made an' ivry wan has made befure or since, an' in this age iv masheenery we're still burrid be hand."[18]

No less than self-government by the American people was at stake, as these comic writers knew in exposing its shortcomings.

Politics, as defined by Ambrose Bierce, Satan's lexicographer, is: "A strife of interests masquerading as a contest of principles. The conduct of public affairs for private advantage." *A politician*: "An eel in the fundamental mud upon which the superstructure of organized society is reared. When he wriggles he mistakes the agitation of his tail for the trembling of the edifice. As compared with the statesman, he suffers the disadvantage of being alive."[19] "Has the art of politics no apparent utility?" inquired H. L. Mencken. "Does it appear to be unqualifiedly ratty, raffish, sordid, obscene, and low down, and its salient virtuosi a gang of unmitigated scoundrels?" he pressed. "Then let us not forget its high capacity to soothe and tickle the midriff, its incomparable services as a maker of entertainment."[20] Will Rogers joyously greeted each election season in "Cuckooland," his affectionate label for the United States. "Come pretty near having two holidays of equal importance in the same week," Rogers recognized, "Halloween and Election, and of the two Election provides the most fun. On Halloween they put pumpkins on their heads, and on Election they don't have to."[21] Rogers's zest

17. Dunne, "The Candidate," 201–2.

18. Dunne, "Machinery," 218.

19. Ambrose Bierce, *The Devil's Dictionary* in *The Collected Writings . . .* (1946; rpt. New York: Citadel Press, 1960), 328.

20. Henry L. Mencken, Introd., *A Carnival of Buncombe*, ed. Malcolm Moos (Baltimore: Johns Hopkins Univ. Press, 1956), x.

21. Will Rogers, *The Autobiography of Will Rogers*, ed. Donald Day (1944; rpt. Boston: Houghton Mifflin, 1979), 233.

for election season can be shared by recalling the story related by Lyndon Johnson of that possibly apocryphal street-corner campaign speech when Al Smith was being taunted by a heckler: "Tell them all you know, Al. It won't take long!" Al unerringly retaliated: "I'll tell them all we both know, and it won't take any longer!"[22]

Will Rogers, the Oklahoma-born cowboy actor, monologist, news commentator, and top-billed star of stage, radio, and motion pictures, proved to be the last great American political humorist of familiar stripe. Rogers ranks first of all time in income earned and enduring popular fame. His death in 1935 ended the long line of highly successful professional wits, who, from the middle of the nineteeth century onward, had raised political humor to a national forum for skeptical and dissenting viewpoints. Chewing his gum conspicuously while spinning a lariat, Rogers learned to jest casually with audiences. He reached his peak on stage from 1916 to 1925 in Ziegfeld's *Follies*, where, by his own description, he "just played his natchell self," introducing his comic editorials: "Well, all I know is what I read in the papers." In 1922 Rogers began to write humorous commentaries for the *New York Times* and the McNaught syndicate, offering advice on occasion to his country's statesmen, as Jack Downing, Artemus Ward, Bill Arp, and Mr. Dooley did before him. In 1926 he sent home from Europe "Letters of a Self-Made Diplomat to his President," along with a string of cables to CALCOOLWHITEHOUSEWASH, the first of hundreds of his tersely telegraphed opinions on the news of the day intended for the public's consumption.[23]

"Politics is the best show in America," Will Rogers decided. "I love animals and I love politicians and I like to watch both of 'em play either

22. Alvin Shuster, "Jokes with the LBJ Brand," *New York Times Magazine* (13 Sept. 1964), 104.

23. Sponsored by the Will Rogers Memorial Commission, the cowboy philosopher's lifetime output is systematically being reissued in nineteen or more volumes under uniform headings: Series I—*Books,* Series II—*Convention Articles*, Series III—*Daily Telegrams*, Series IV—*Weekly Articles*, Series V—*Radio Broadcasts* (other categories and volumes will be announced in time). Joseph A. Strout, Jr., James M. Smallwood, et al., eds., *The Writings of Will Rogers* (Stillwater: Oklahoma State Univ. Press, 1973–   ). Still useful and readily accessible are Will Rogers, *The Autobiography of Will Rogers*, ed. Donald Day (Boston: Houghton Mifflin, 1949), 37, 75, 363, and passim; Will Rogers, *How We Elect Our Presidents*, ed. Donald Day (Boston: Little, Brown, 1952), passim. See also Bryan B. Sterling, *The Best of Will Rogers* (New York: Crown, 1979).

back home in their native state or after they have been sent to a zoo or to Washington."[24] Rogers, unlike Mencken or his other contemporaries, attributed Al Smith's loss to Herbert Hoover in 1928 to Coolidge prosperity rather than to Smith's stand against Prohibition or his Roman Catholic religion, an appraisal sustained eventually by historians.[25] Yet like Mencken and Ring Lardner, Rogers derided Prohibition as a travesty of law and social order. "The South is dry and will vote dry," Rogers predicted in 1926. "That is, everybody sober enough to stagger to the polls will."[26]

The major political parties afforded Rogers his bread and butter. He once ventured that, "You take a Democrat and a Republican and you keep them both out of office, and I bet you they will turn out to be good friends and maybe make useful citizens."[27] In 1924, Rogers sought to justify the extraordinary length of the Democratic Party's platform, due to its convention's deadlocks over the Ku Klux Klan and Prohibition issues. "When you straddle a thing, it takes a long time to explain it," he pronounced.[28] After the Wall Street crash in 1929, Rogers volunteered his services for the campaign to restore confidence, "But you will have to give me some idea where 'Confidence' is," he insisted, "and just who you want it restored to."[29] Of President Hoover's stiff appeal to revive the spirit of Valley Forge, Rogers complained: "He found somebody that was worse off than we are, but he had to go back 150 years in history to do it."[30] In summing up the depression's tragedy in 1931, he observed: "So here we are in a country with more wheat and corn and

24. Rogers, *How We Elect Our Presidents*, 3.

25. James M. Smallwood, ed., *Will Rogers' Daily Telegrams* (Stillwater: Oklahoma State Univ. Press, 1978), I, 8, 9 Nov. 1928, 274; 1, 2 Jan. 1929, 293; 4 March 1929, 315. For Alfred E. Smith and Prohibition, see also Steven K. Gragert, ed., *Radio Broadcasts of Will Rogers* in *The Writings of Will Rogers*, Series VI (Stillwater: Oklahoma State Univ. Press, 1983), I, 4 May 1930, 21–25; and 8 June 1930, 49–53. The innovative quantitative study of the 1928 election, which measures the divisive importance of religion and other issues, is Allan J. Lichtman, *Prejudice and the Old Politics: The Presidential Election of 1928* (Chapel Hill: Univ. of North Carolina Press, 1979); and see Frank Freidel and Alan Brinkley, *America in the Twentieth Century*, 5th ed. (New York: Alfred A. Knopf, 1982), 194–96.

26. Smallwood, ed., *Will Rogers' Daily Telegrams*, I, 28 Oct. 1926, 22.

27. Will Rogers, *New York Times*, (11 Nov. 1923), Section 9, 2.

28. Will Rogers, *New York Times*, (29 June 1924), Section 1, 5.

29. Smallwood, ed., *Will Rogers' Daily Telegrams*, II (1978), 19 Nov. 1929, 98.

30. Ibid., III (1979), 31 May 1931, 36.

more money in the bank, more cotton, more everything in the world—there's not a product that you can name that we haven't got more of than any other country ever had on the face of the earth—and yet we've got people starving. We'll hold the distinction of being the only nation in the history of the world that ever went to the poor house in an automobile."[31] Will Rogers was a Democrat openly. Yet he lambasted both parties for the nation's disaster. "I don't want to lay the blame on the Republicans for the Depression," he confessed in 1932, when it was easy to blame Hoover. "They're not smart enough to think up all those things that have happened."[32]

Once, in Franklin D. Roosevelt's heyday, Rogers spelled out the distinctions between the major parties in a "bedtime story" to millions of radio listeners. The Republicans were extinct by the mid-1930s, as Rogers and his audience knew, but he recalled them as "a thrifty race," who "controlled most of the money" at one time long ago. Republicans were "never warlike," he went on. "In fact they'd step aside and egg the Democrats on till the Democrats would start a war. And then when it came time to pay 'em for it, why the Republicans would come in and say the Democrats started it you know." What could he say about the Democrats? Their greatest traits were optimism and humor, Rogers avowed. "You've got to be [an] optimist to be a Democrat, and you've got to be a humorist to stay one."[33] What would Lincoln do if he were here?

> Well, in the first place, he wouldn't chop any wood, he would trade his axe in on a Ford. Being a Republican he would vote the Democratic ticket. Being in sympathy for the underdog he would be classed as a Radical Progressive. Having a sense of humor he would be called eccentric.[34]

Like Lincoln himself, Will Rogers touched hearts as well as minds with his humor. His engaging mixture of homespun democracy, his common-sense wisdom and sly insights inspired confidence in himself and in his messages. His effortless style of acting confirmed his unpre-

31. Gragert, ed., *Radio Broadcasts of Will Rogers*, I, 18 Oct. 1931, 66, 186–88.

32. Rogers, *How We Elect Our Presidents*, 22 Dec. 1932, 139.

33. Gragert, ed., *Radio Broadcasts of Will Rogers*, I, 24 June 1934, 92.

34. Smallwood, ed., *Will Rogers' Daily Telegrams*, IV (1979), 12 Feb. 1934, 138. See Brant House, ed., *Lincoln's Wit* (New York: Ace, 1958).

tentious demeanor. Rogers built upon the major traditions of American political humor while cheerfully conquering the mass audiences of the motion pictures and radio airwaves. More than anyone else before his time or since, he bridged the past and the present to make millions and millions of people laugh at their dilemmas—and the nation's. His sudden death in 1935 grows ever more grievous in retrospect.

In Rogers's wake a different order came to prevail, in time to challenge political humor's function and place in American culture. The unbroken sequence of catastrophes and historic transformations of everyday circumstances, beginning with the Great Depression, the Second World War, and the Cold War, diverted American political humor's characteristic manifestations away from solo performances by solitary talents toward spasmodic yet synchronous outbursts by comedians of all sorts against government's proclivity for corruption, errors of judgment, bankruptcy, inhumanity, or warfare. Issues of race relations and racism, sexuality and sexism, arising from civil rights and liberation movements, supplemented traditional topics with new targets for political humor's aim. The new political humor exceeded previous levels of antidemocratic mockery by its universally derisive tone, even when its aim was intended to improve the society's downtrodden elements, most notably women and blacks. Unwittingly Ambrose Bierce and Henry L. Mencken were the harbingers of this new order. Bierce's savage scorn and Mencken's antidemocratic derision defined the iconoclastic social style of American political humor that now dominates the closing decades of the twentieth century.[35]

Bierce and Mencken, each in his own way, ridiculed the bloated pride in the nation's achievements and the blind faith in the progress of democracy. Their efforts have been imitated ever since Bierce devilishly defined his convictions: "*Aristocracy:* Government by the best men. (In this sense the word is obsolete, so is that kind of government.)" He dismissed the populists' pretensions to be democracy's saviors by ridiculing them as fossilized patriots of the early agricultural period.[36] Mencken, likewise a caustic lexicographer, refused to lodge his hopes for the future with the collective wisdom of the ordinary citizenry, yet he proved easier to take than Bierce because he professed to be enter-

35. Bryan B. Sterling, comp., "Biography," *The Best of Will Rogers* (New York: Crown, 1979), 3–4, 28; Dudden, *Pardon Us, Mr. President!*, 36–39.

36. Bierce, *The Devil's Dictionary* in *The Collected Writings*, 197, 329.

tained rather than revolted by the nation's follies. Mencken's favorite targets were democracy and puritanism. He defined puritanism indelibly as "the haunting fear that someone, somewhere, may be happy."[37]

For Mencken, democracy itself was the fundamental trouble. The facts dispute Jefferson's faith that wisdom and a decent respect for the opinions of mankind could grow out of a popular majority. "If X is the population of the United States and Y is the degree of imbecility of the average American," he reasoned, "then democracy is the theory that X x Y is less than Y." Democracy led directly to demagoguery. Politics consisted of sniffing and snooping, with the witch-hunting mob and its leaders ceaselessly chanting "Fe! Fi! Fo! Fum!" Public opinion was no more than mob fear sloganized into hysterical outcries. America's popular heroes were frauds and pretenders. William Jennings Bryan was the "fundamentalist Pope," Theodore Roosevelt the "national Barbarossa," and Woodrow Wilson the "perfect model of the Christian cad." A typical congressman was "a knavish and preposterous nonentity, half way between a Kleagle of the Ku Klux Klan and a Grand Worthy of the Knights of Zoroaster." Was there any hope for better men? Emphatically not. Urging gentlemen to go into democratic politics made no more sense than trying to end prostitution by filling bawdy houses with virgins. "Either the virgins would leap out of the windows," Mencken predicted, "or they would cease to be virgins."[38] In debunking democracy and its "bitch goddess" of worldly success, Mencken paraded his lineup of American's dubs, oafs, yahoos, galoots, wowsers, trimmers, stoneheads, and of course the storied boobs, to say nothing of the boob-bumpers and boob-squeezers and other feeders at the public trough, to support his contentions. No sanctuary was safe from the dead cats Mencken flung, whether political, social, religious, or educational. Except for Mencken's own iconoclasm, nothing was left. "He had no credences at all finally," it has been judged, not unkindly, "and in this

37. Henry L. Mencken, "On Being an American," and "Das Kapital," *Prejudices: Third Series* (New York: Alfred A. Knopf, 1922), 9–64; 105–10ff; Mencken, "Ambrose Bierce," *Prejudices: Sixth Series*, (New York: Alfred A. Knopf, 1927), 264–65; Mencken, *Notes on Democracy* (New York: Alfred A. Knopf, 1926), 24–25 and passim; Mencken, *A Mencken Chrestomathy* (New York: Alfred A. Knopf, 1949), 621, 624.

38. Mencken, *Notes on Democracy*, 4–9, 22, 106–7, 126, 137, 176, 192; Mencken, *A Mencken Chrestomathy*, 621; Mencken, *Prejudices: Second Series* (New York: Alfred A. Knopf, 1920), 102, 117; Mencken, *Prejudices: Fifth Series* (New York: Alfred A. Knopf, 1926), 64–74.

sense his mockeries and disengagements are more unsettling than the worst of Poe, Twain and Bierce put together."[39]

Serious times lay at hand however. Rogers and Mencken's day was ending, not beginning. Their leading contemporaries were either dead or nearly finished. The herd-like patriotic unities demanded by the Second World War and the Cold War aftermath effectively suppressed the traditional toleration for jesting at the nation's leaders. By the early 1950s political humor wallowed dead in the water, becalmed like a vessel without a breeze. Even presidential nominee Adlai E. Stevenson, Jr., was criticized for his habit of joking at serious public concerns.[40]

Malcolm Muggeridge and James Thurber blamed the frightful hazards of the atomic age. "The enemy of humor is fear," Muggeridge wrote.

> Fear requires conformism. It draws people together into a herd, whereas laughter separates them as individuals. When people are fearful, they

39. For a spectrum of Mencken's critical judgments, see his *Prejudices*, Series 1–6 (1919–27; rpt. New York: Octagon, 1977). Biographical treatment is comprehensive in Carl Bode, *Mencken* (Carbondale and Edwardsville: Southern Illinois Univ. Press, 1969). See also Mencken, *A Carnival of Buncombe* for his Monday columns from the *Baltimore Sun;* and Bier, *The Rise and Fall of American Humor*, 210–11, for a pungent appraisal.

40. Though they were not primarily political humorists, Ring Lardner, James Thurber, Robert Benchley, and Langston Hughes all carried on from Mencken's example. Lardner limned the new folk heroes pitilessly—the *boobs* in Menckenese—the class-conscious snobs, egomaniacs, and arrivistes who were worshipped by hordes of inferior and unluckier boobs. See Ring W. Lardner, *You Know Me Al: A Busher's Letters* (New York: Charles Scribner's Sons, 1925); Lardner, *Round Up: The Stories of Ring Lardner* (New York: The Literary Guild, 1929); Lardner, *First and Last* (New York: Charles Scribner's Sons, 1934). Thurber built his fame on reporting the battle between the sexes, but he also exposed democracy's feet of clay. He attacked the people's proclivity for idolatry. He satirized their worship of the military hero in "If Grant Had Been Drinking at Appomattox," wherein the general, dazed after a siege of imbibing, believed the war was lost and proffered his sword in a comically reversed surrender to Robert E. Lee. He caricatured the aviator hero Charles "Lucky" Lindbergh as the repulsive Jacky Smurch in "The Greatest Man in the World." Also, in uncovering Walter Mitty's truth about American manhood, he demonstrated the hollowness of super-patriotic masculinity. See James Thurber and E. B. White, *Is Sex Necessary? or Why You Feel the Way You Do* (New York: Harper and Bros., 1929); Thurber, *Men, Women, and Dogs* (New York: Harcourt, Brace, 1943); Thurber, *My Life and Hard Times* (New York: Harper and Row, 1933); Thurber, *The Middle-Aged*

want everyone to be the same, to accept the same values, say the same things, nourish the same hopes, to wear the same clothes, look at the same television, and ride in the same motorcars. In a conformist society there is no place for the jester. He strikes a discordant note, and therefore must be put down.

Thurber explained that we live next door to total destruction, "on the Brink of Was," as he put it. He wrote at the end of 1958 that we were too near the witch-hunting era of Senator Joseph McCarthy to deal comically with politics or any of the shibboleths of "the American way of life." Indeed Mort Sahl worried at this time that he could not be certain whether the unidentified aircraft approaching would "drop a hydrogen bomb or spell out Pepsi-Cola in skywriting." "It is not expected that we will soon recover," Thurber went on, "and contribute to a new and brave world literature of comedy." Political satire, he judged a short time later, in words that brought anguished protests from the dairy industry and threats to investigate him from congressmen, had

---

Man on the Flying Trapeze (New York: Harper and Bros., 1935); Thurber, *The Thurber Carnival* (New York: Harper and Row, 1945); "The Secret Life of Walter Mitty," 47–51; "If Grant Had Been Drinking at Appomattox," 140–42; and "The Greatest Man in the World," 154–60. Robert Benchley meanwhile reduced American history from epic to comic opera by recasting Paul Revere's midnight ride as a nocturnal misadventure of "some god-dam drunk." Then he fixed the complex distinction between Republicans and Democrats on the general rule that Republicans were "more blonde" than Democrats. See Robert Benchley, "Paul Revere's Ride," in *The Benchley Roundup*, selected by Nathaniel Benchley (New York: Dell, 1962), 101; Benchley, "Political Parties and Their Growth," in *20,000 Leagues Under the Sea or David Copperfield* (New York: Henry Holt, 1928), 4. Other Benchley successes include: *My Ten Years in a Quandary and How They Grew* (New York: Harper and Bros., 1936); *Inside Benchley* (New York: Grosset and Dunlap, 1942); *Benchley Beside Himself* (New York: Harper and Bros., 1947); and *Chips Off the Old Benchley* (Harper and Bros., 1949). Movie fans can cherish *The 'Reel' Benchley* (New York: A.A. Wyn, 1950). Similarly, Langston Hughes ennobled the Afro-American people to measure democracy's working limits. Hughes created the character of Jess B. Simple who, like Mr. Dooley, was a hard-working philosopher with enough racial scar tissue to protect himself against sentimental fantasies. Mr. Simple decided that his own enslaved and caste-repressed people could never be annihilated, even by an atomic bomb. "If Negroes can survive white folks in Mississippi," Simple reasoned, "we can survive anything." See Langston Hughes, "Radioactive Red Caps," in *The Best of Simple* (New York: Hill and Wang, 1961), 210–13.

declined to the point where it reminded him of a drink of milk. "It won't hurt anybody, but who likes it?"[41]

Eventually the civil rights struggles of the 1960s reconstituted political humor's vitality by escalating the intensity of confrontation. Skepticism about segregation's prolonged absurdities bubbled up comically from deep, underlying veins of doubt, disillusionment, pessimism, cynicism, and moral indignation, though not simply from any superficial or temporary indisposition. Laughter began to succeed once again where other weapons were failing. Performing comedians assailed the hollow rhetoric, the principles betrayed, the meanness, the ignobility, and all the crass pieties of usefulness. Mockery, nonsense, parody, and the antiproverb armed their comic style to fortify the democratic tendencies of their audiences. Ethnic comedians charged across the battlefields, where their own peoples, immigrant Jews, blacks, Italians, and Poles especially, had served earlier as the victims of humorists. Mort Sahl hoped that there were no groups of people he had not yet offended, and plowed ahead trampling them all "anyway onward." Cleverly, Dick Gregory aided the civil rights cause by ridiculing American society from the back seat of his segregated bus. Taken together, they were following the examples of Twain, Bierce, Mencken, Lardner, Thurber, Benchley, and Hughes, knowingly or unknowingly. They pushed their points to profane or even obscene ends against the barriers waspish, prudish, one-hundred-percent, stand-pat Americanism erected in their paths.[42]

Lenny Bruce, the heroic antihero of the revival, flailed away at everybody and everything. Bruce urbanized and ethnicized Mencken's boobs and Lardner's rubes to define his fellow Americans in Jewish

41. Malcolm Muggeridge, "America Needs a PUNCH," *Esquire* (April 1958), 59–61; James Thurber in "State of the Nation's Humor," *New York Times Magazine* (7 Dec. 1958), 26, and Thurber's comments broadcast on a television program as cited in an editorial in the *Philadelphia Inquirer* (25 March 1959), 22; also see Thurber, "The Future, If Any, of Comedy, or Where Do We Non-go from Here?" *Harper's Magazine*, 223 (Dec. 1961), 40–45. Mort Sahl's manager as quoted by Herbert Mitgang, "Anyway, Onward with Mort Sahl," *New York Times Magazine* (8 Feb. 1959), 32.

42. Mort Sahl in Mitgang, "Anyway, Onward with Mort Sahl," 32; Dick Gregory, *From the Back of the Bus*, ed. Bob Orben (New York: E. P. Dutton, 1962), passim. For a foreign look at the American "sickniks" of comedy, see Kenneth Allsop, "Gone Is The Subtle Touch—Comedians Now Wield a Dull Ax," reprinted in the *National Observer* (25 Feb. 1962), 15. See also Mel Gussow, "Political Satirists Descend on Convention City Clubs; View Leaders with Alarm," *New York Times*, (13 July 1976), 31.

metaphor as schmucks living in a land of schmucks. A schmuck, as Bruce saw him, believed in Santa Claus and Uncle Tom even while he struggled in vain to sing "The Star Spangled Banner." Unfortunately the schmuck brought up his children to do likewise. A schmuck, lest we forget, "is a guy who gets out of his shower to piss in the toilet!"[43]

With the Watergate affair, all restraints collapsed, and the clouds vanished. The attempted cover-up afforded humorists a world series opportunity. President Richard Nixon's concealment of his connection with the Watergate burglary led to charges of obstruction of justice, next to impeachment proceedings, and finally to his resignation. The shocking revelations of the conversations taped in the Oval Office convinced citizens of Nixon's guilty complicity in this sordid adventure. In spite of President Ford's pardon, Nixon's reputation will forever languish in the Watergate, because Watergate erupted uncontrollably into a laughing matter, once its dark secrets were revealed. Laughing offered almost the only way out of the well-nigh universal dismay and chagrin at the Watergate scandal.[44]

Jokes and tall tales connected with the cover-up abounded. Bumper stickers prompted drivers to "Honk If You Think He's Guilty," intensifying the din of automotive traffic. Lapel buttons carried the messages: "Behind Every Watergate Stands a Milhous," "Impeach with Honor," "Dick Nixon Before He Dicks You," "Bail to the Chief," and the unforgiving "Jail to the Chief!" Even "Nixon's the One," the triumphant slogan used to reelect him, perverted its purpose to indict the faltering hero. Watergate novelties proliferated. *The Watergate Cookbook* (1973) opened its recipes with "Puree of Scoundrel" and "Watergate Vichysoisse" (which begins with "Take a bunch of leaks. . . .") Another book, *The Watergate Follies* (1973), applied impertinent captions to pertinent pictures, one of Queen Elizabeth recalling Nixon, "Yes, he once visited me. He took a spoon." For smokers, there was the nationally advertised Watergate, "a Crooked Cigar." A Los Angeles firm sold a wristwatch with President Nixon's own deceitful plea, "I'm not a

43. Lenny Bruce, *How to Talk Dirty and Influence People: An Autobiography* (1963; rpt. Chicago: Playboy Press, 1966), passim; John Cohen, ed., *The Essential Lenny Bruce* (New York: Ballantine, 1967), passim; Kitty Bruce, comp., *The Almost Unpublished Lenny Bruce* (Philadelphia: Running Press, 1984).

44. Dudden, *Pardon Us, Mr. President!* 23–26, 45–47, 55–113.

crook!" over his face on the dial. "Watch his eyes . . . ," the advertisement shrilled, "they shift back and forth 60 times a minute."[45]

Humorists attacked from all sides. Philip Roth leveled his sledgehammer attack, *Our Gang* (1971), point blank at "Tricky" Nixon.[46] In "The Waterbury Tales," Chicago's Chaucerian parodist, Judith Wax, sketched that merry crew of electronic buggers and clumsy burglars, including presidential assistant John Erlichman, who, she sang, looks like "he eats babys for dessert," and the FBI's chief Patrick Gray, who burned the files and sorely sinned "dizzy grow from hangyn slow, slow in the wind."[47] Art Buchwald proposed to celebrate June 17, the anniversary of the break-in, as Watergate Day: "Americans would memorialize this historic event by taping other people's doors, tapping telephones, spying on their neighbors, wearing red wigs, and making inoperative statements." In Washington the President would review the CIA and FBI marching bands escorting veterans of CREEP (the Committee to Reelect the President) down Pennsylvania Avenue, and later he would lay a wreath at the Watergate complex just under the window of the former headquarters of the Democratic National Committee.[48] The solution for the Watergate troubles put forward by Laurence J. Peter, whose hierarchical Peter Principle explained why things must inevitably go wrong when individuals are promoted above their levels of achievement to heights of incompetence, was to elevate President Nixon to Chairman of the Board, USA, an office with ritualistic duties only.[49] Standup commentator Mark Russell reportedly said: "I hope that Watergate never ends. If it does, I'll have to go back to writing my own

45. Ibid., 23–24, 45–47; Tom Donnelley in N.Y. Alplaus (pseud.), *The Watergate Cookbook* (Charlestown, Mass.: Emporium, 1973), 2; Gerald Gardner, *The Watergate Follies* (New York: Bantam, 1973), n.p. See also Hank Bradford and Tom Moore, *The National Watergate Test* (Los Angeles: Price, Stern, Sloan, 1973); and Jack S. Margolis, *The Poetry of Richard Milhous Nixon* (Los Angeles: Cliff House, 1974).

46. Philip Roth, *Our Gang (Starring Tricky and His Friends)* (New York: Random House, 1971), and the Watergate edition (New York: Bantam, 1973). See also Philip Roth, "The President Addresses the Nation," *New York Review of Books* (14 June 1973), 11.

47. Judith Wax, "The Waterbury Tales," *New Republic* (15 Sept. 1973), 24–25.

48. Art Buchwald, "The Anniversary of Watergate," *Philadelphia Evening Bulletin* (5 June 1973), 21, syndicated by the *Washington Post*.

49. Lawrence J. Peter, "Up from Watergate," *Psychology Today* (Oct. 1973), 91–93.

material. Now I just tear it off the news service wires."[50] All agreed that the Watergate complex was the perfect setting for the scandal. "I mean," asked Don Kaul of the *Des Moines Register and Tribune*, "what other building have you even seen where the balconies look like teeth?"[51] John Kenneth Galbraith determined that "We've passed from the age of the common man to the age of the common crook."[52] Even the *National Lampoon* headlined Nixon's resignation: "They've Fired The Shit Heard Round the World."[53]

The laughter surrounding the Watergate affair was violent and destructive, a deeply skeptical ridicule without quarter. It was cynical, yet certain of its target, deadly in its accuracy. It declared unequivocally, as events proved, that a president of the United States for the first time in history was both a knave and a fool. It distrusted all the president's men who were his closest advisors and spokesmen on public matters. It knew that Richard Milhous Nixon himself and his bribe-taking first Vice President Spiro T. Agnew had cruelly breached the faith between the governors and the governed.[54] The people's laughter expressed their defense against the national shame. Not since Franklin D. Roosevelt's New Deal had so much malicious humor directed itself at the White House. Mark Twain and H.L. Mencken would have been astounded by the Watergate affair. With honor gone, only humor was left, to supply what John Crosby once called "fresh slants on the human race and the painfully funny business of being alive."[55]

Eventually, the currents of political humor slipped back into familiar channels, when President Nixon resigned in August, 1974, to forestall his almost certain impeachment. Just one month later his successor,

50. Mark Russell, *Wild, Wierd, Wired World of Watergate*, recorded live at the Shoreham Hotel, Washington, D.C., Deep-Six Records, 1973.

51. Don Kaul on Watergate in "Over the Coffee," *Des Moines* (Iowa) *Register and Tribune* (16 April 1973), 24.

52. "I certainly wrote or said it—that I remember—but, alas, I've no idea where." John Kenneth Galbraith to author, 5 Nov. 1984.

53. *National Lampoon* (Oct. 1974), 7. The magazine's preceding issue prepared its readers for Nixon's dénouement by describing the resignation of presidential assistant Charles Colson colorfully, as, "Rat Deserts Sinking Shit." See ibid. (Sept. 1974), 7.

54. *New York Times* (11 Oct. 1973), 1; (9 Aug. 1974), 1.

55. John Crosby, "Around the Dials," *New York Herald Tribune* (6 July 1959), Section 2, 1.

President Gerald R. Ford, stunned the nation by granting Nixon "a full, free and absolute pardon" for his crimes committed in the presidential office against the United States.[56] Humorists were thrown back onto mundane events and their own devices with no fresh break-ins or cover-ups to inspire them. Political cartoonists, columnists, and comedians reverted to routine comments on the news from day to day. A singular exception was Trudeau's comic strip, "Doonesbury," which led its millions of daily readers into lengthy and skeptical examinations of the Great Society, the Indochina War, and the New Federalism, together with the mores, customs, and public celebrities of those rapidly changing times.[57] Judith Wax's "The Pardoner's Tale" about Nixon and Ford ("Til one Lord pilgrymage to San Clemente/and folk do get a new Presydente.") failed to delight readers as widely as her "Waterbury Tales" had done.[58] The reason was not that her sequel was underdeveloped (though it was), but because the Watergate scandal was ending as startlingly as it had begun. The unfortunate Gerald Ford was fastened onto as a slow-witted and clumsy president. "I'm a Ford, not a Lincoln," he himself conceded. His library was robbed, according to one office joke, and all of his books stolen—both of them! There followed the allegation that Ford hated New York City, because a city-wide blackout of electrical power had stranded him for over six hours on an escalator! This was insipid stuff, however, compared to the comic outrage against Nixon over Watergate.[59]

56. *New York Times* (9 Sept. 1974), 1.

57. One series, for example—the campaign for Congress of his character Virginia Slade—served as Trudeau's platform for political humor. See the advertisement for Slade's campaign collectibles in the *Washington Post* (30 Sept. 1976), C11. G. B. Trudeau's collected works at this time were *Guilty, Guilty, Guilty* (1974), *Dare to be Great, Ms. Caucus* (1975), *The Doonesbury Chronicles* (1975), *What Do We Have for the Witnesses, Johnnie?* (1975), all published in New York City by Holt, Rinehart and Winston.

58. Judith Wax, "The Pardoner's Tale," *New York Times* (11 Sept. 1974), 45; and Wax, "The Waterbury Tales," *New Republic* (15 Sept. 1973), 24–25.

59. For Gerald Ford's modest confession of his own limitations, see his address to Congress after being sworn in as vice-president on 6 Dec. 1973, reprinted in the *New York Times* (7 Dec. 1973), 27. The origins of office jokes are difficult, if not impossible, to determine. The joke about Ford's books being stolen, for example, was a refurbished version of an older thrust at George Wallace. See also P.J. O'Rourke, "More Jerry Ford Jokes," *National Lampoon* (Nov. 1974), 98; Richard Reeves, "The High Art and Low Estate of Political Humor," *Washington Post Potomac* (16 Feb. 1975), 10–17, 22; Sandy Grady, "Anti-Ford Gags Rile His Staff," *Philadelphia Sunday Bulletin* (4 Jan. 1976), B-1.

During the Jimmy Carter era, political humor turned out to be even more old-fashioned, manifesting itself in Deep South accents. Tales and anecdotes of southern country folk and small-town denizens spread across the nation, conveying their own dialects, customs, beliefs, happenings, and settings from back-country, pineywoods, rural Georgia, and elsewhere. Slow pace and exquisite timing were more important than one-liner smart cracks. When Mark Russell saluted Carter's hometown of Plains, Georgia, as the new capital of the United States. Americans at large felt bemused by this belated southern conquest of the union. The problem for nonsoutherners in dealing with the White House, it soon developed, was that a communications barrier existed. Lexicons and guides to southern speech and its meanings quickly appeared in print. The *Jimmy Carter Dictionary* by William E. Maloney was subtitled *How to Understand Your President and Speak Southern* and dedicated "to all Yankees in the hope that it will teach them to talk right." Jake Moon's *The Dixie Doodle Dictionary* concentrated on southern speaking terms, such as "lil" and "prolly" in the sentence, "Ah'll prolly go to lil ol' Etlanna this weekend." To make matters worse, the religious sectarianism of the South's politics proved far more mystifying to outsiders than the region's racial distinctions, which were self-explanatory whether one liked them or not.[60]

In time an uneasiness over Jimmy Carter and his Georgia following spread across the country. People were wondering who on earth Carter represented, what he signified, and what it was he intended to do. Some northerners were so disturbed by the southern folks surrounding him that they acted as though the nation had been seized by unknown beings from outer space.

The Carters were an odd lot even for American politics. Billy Carter, the President's filling-station operator brother, was funny for a while, until he transformed himself by his words and deeds into a political liability. Billy proved to be the archetypical redneck backcountryman in a world of city slickers; his favorite seven-course dinner was said to be a six-pack of beer and a racoon. Truth to tell, Billy Carter was *Red,*

60. William E. Maloney, *The Jimmy Carter Dictionary: How to Understand Your President and Learn to Speak Southern* (Chicago: Playboy Press, 1977); Jake Moon, *The Dixie-Doodle Dictionary: How to Understand a Southerner* (New York: Piasa Publications, n.d.); Steve Mitchell, *How to Speak Southern* (New York: Bantam, 1976); Leon Hill, *O' For the Life of a Preacher!* (Amarillo, Tex.: Baxter Lane, 1975).

White and *Blue* himself, in that he was a redneck, he wore white socks, and he drank large quantities of Pabst Blue Ribbon Beer.[61] Someone in the television industry who put together situation comedies once told Robert Orben, according to Marjorie Hunter, that President Carter's family was altogether like a situation comedy. Besides his brother Billy, the president had a mother, Miss Lillian, who served in the Peace Corps in India in her seventies, a sister who rode motorcycles, another sister who was an evangelist, and last but not least, a young daughter named Amy, the family's "nuclear expert" in her father's unguarded view. "You put all that together," Orben's friend asserted, "and you could sell it to any network in the country."[62] Indubitably the unvarnished, everyday truth from Washington or Georgia was funnier than any attempts at political comedy, as two popular songs made evident. One ballad about Billy Carter was "I'll Pump the Gas, Jimmy. (You Run the World!)" while the other was a movingly inspirational hymn popular in Georgia, cast in athletic metaphor, "Drop Kick Me, Jesus, Through the Goal Posts of Life!"[63]

Unfortunately, like Nixon, Jimmy Carter never appeared to be comfortable with humor, in spite of his big, open, friendly grin. Jerry Ford and Ronald Reagan have managed in contrast to project their own outwardly easygoing, self-deprecating styles to smooth things over, to heal, to build, and to move onward.

Nevertheless, bureaucratic attitudes were consistently stern-faced over the past three or four decades. Super-patriots demanded unquestioning likemindedness or loyalty. Their slogan, "America: Love It or Leave It!," left little room for equivocation. Their formulaic postulate that one is "Better Dead than Red," transferred the issue to metaphysics. Nationalistic piety was invoked in the prayer to "Keep God in America!," though His or Her exact whereabouts in the country have yet to be specified. The bumper sticker proclaiming "Abortion is First-Degree Murder of God" constituted a prima facie attempt to banish the political issue from political controversy and henceforth from the customary arena for political humor. The countermeasures devised to halt

61. Jeremy Rifkin and Ted Howard, comps. and eds., *Redneck Power: The Wit and Wisdom of Billy Carter* (New York: Bantam, 1977).

62. Hunter, "Q. and A.: Bob Orben," A20.

63. George Daugherty, "I'll Pump the Gas, Jimmy (You Run the World)," with Ernie Dunlap, CIN KAY Records, 1977; Paul Craft, "Drop Kick Me, Jesus, Through the Goal Posts of Life!" with Bobby Bare, on *The Winner and Other Losers*, RCA, 1976.

the skyjacking of airplanes went so far as to impose curfews on humor, as the signs attest at check-in counters in airport terminals throughout the land: "NO JOKING MATTER." Anyone overheard making a joke about guns, bombs, or highjacking an aircraft can be arrested and prosecuted under Federal Law. The problem is that passengers are further victimized beyond the terrible acts of terrorism to the extent that they cannot legally even try to be funny about their unhappy circumstances. Democracy's men and women are wobbling uneasily, it seems. The dangers of the times and the rising distrust of government have deepened the antithetical relationship that ordinarily operates in the United States between the pole of humor and the pole of fear.[64]

Perhaps this popular insecurity explains the apparent immunity of diplomacy and international relations to political humor. Even Jimmy's brother Billy Carter's greedy, headstrong, and naïve dealings with Libya's leaders were taken seriously instead of humorously by many commentators. Only the dozen or so top political cartoonists of the newspapers' editorial pages, the witty purveyors of the "one-note message" (as Richard Samuel West, publisher of *Target: The Political Cartoon Quarterly*, calls them), regularly crystallize public opinion humorously about foreign affairs.[65]

Art Buchwald has tried, it has to be conceded. Buchwald, who in 1974 won the first Noble Award from the Association for the Promotion of Humor in International Affairs and later, in 1982, the Pulitzer Prize for outstanding commentary, has insisted that, on the issue of human rights in Central America, "we'll defend to their death the rights of our

---

64. The myriad legends of the nation's bumper stickers have to be cited and accepted on faith, as almost anything has become possible to display in recent years.

The basic law against highjacking is the Federal Aviation Act of 1958, amended in 1974. The Federal Bureau of Investigation will investigate, and prosecute, jesters, if deemed necessary, under Title 49 of the United States Code, Section 1472(M)(1)(2) and Title 18, Section 35(B). See Interpretive Notes and Decisions I, 1–3, and II, 4, in Lawyers Edition, *United States Code Service* (Rocherster, N.Y.: Lawyers Co-operative, 1979), 126.

65. The foremost political cartoonists include Tony Auth, Herblock, Paul Conrad, Jeff McNelly, Pat Oliphant, Jules Feiffer, and Don Wright. For a feature story on Richard Samuel West and *Target*, his political cartoon quarterly, see the *Philadelphia Inquirer* (3 July, 1983), 3W. For a thematic concentration, see *A Cartoon History of United States Foreign Policy, 1776–1976*), compiled by the editors of the Foreign Policy Association (New York: William Morrow, 1975). See also John Twohey, "The Acid Art of Political Cartooning," *Washington Post Potomac* (20 April 1975), 8–11, 27–33.

Latin friends." In one column Buchwald fingered the Garcia family of Miami for allegedly financing Miguel Tortilla's Liberal Peasant Assassination Party in the archetypical Central American Republic of Enchilada. Although as Buchwald disclosed, Tortilla was known as "The Hammer" in Enchilada, because his deputies like to belt their opponents with hammers, the United States was nevertheless able to certify his regime as upholding human rights for military assistance. "That's no problem," announced Buchwald's Department of State spokesman. "I spoke to Tortilla on the phone this morning, and he assured me that anyone who opposed the new government's policy will be shot in the knees." Buchwald fears that World War III will not be started by any two parties to a dispute, such as Enchilada and the United States, but because some television evening news anchorman has pushed the quarreling parties into a corner from which neither will be able to escape without violence. Buchwald's nightmare that World War III is brewing on the six o'clock news should keep us all awake for a long time to come.[66]

It should be clear by now that antithesis or nay-saying underscores American humor on politics. Antagonism and contempt are its characteristics. The nation's comparative freedom of utterance explains its public displays. America's humorists consume each other and their countrymen over political issues. Yet the humorists, with the occasional exception, have never operated more than an eyelash away from affectionate sentimentalism. The reason is that Americans inhabit a much less integrated nation than other peoples. As Jesse Bier sees it,

> Without the comfort of homogeneousness, they are without the security of national identity, on which concept therefore they are always fixated. They cannot take for granted what other people can, therefore, as a social body, they more willingly impose shibboleths and ideals; at the same time, they need the rectifications humorists vengefully supply. The necessary impositions and the grateful exceptions taken are two sides of

66. Art Buchwald, *Philadelphia Inquirer* (6 April 1982) and *New York Post* (13 April 1982), The Eighth Noble Award went to Lawrence J. Peter, 23 May 1984, who was honored for his "principles." The Association for the Promotion of Humor in International Affairs (APHIA) has its headquarters in Paris, France. Art Buchwald and Mark Russell were acclaimed for the global outreach of their comic punditry as "The Secretaries of Humor," on the cover of the *Washington Dossier* (June 1983).

the same thing; tyranny and freedom are uniquely wedded. And so fury is bound with regard.[67]

On July 1, 1982, a seventeen-foot, two-ton "World's Record Apple Pie" was placed on the grounds of the Washington Monument in the Capital City, where it was to be sliced symbolically and distributed to the first 3,000 people in line. Billed in news releases as a "Titanic Tart," a "Special Tax Pie," it would celebrate that date as the starting day of President Reagan's ten-percent tax cut. Senator William V. Roth, sponsor of the tax cut legislation boomed out to begin the festivities, "It's about time for the doubters to eat humble pie." As the senator spoke four men dressed in pillow stuffed suits displaying signs to identify themselves as "Reagan's Millionaire Friends" pushed their way through the crowd. Before anyone could stop them they leaped into the pie, stomping and squishing the filling, smashing the pastry, and shouting "It's all mine! It's all mine!" Said Senator Roth, after the offenders were dragged away, "Well, obviously there are still a few doubters."[68] If there were no doubters, there would be no political humor. Yet doubts and doubters there always were. Political humor has always erupted as the result, so political humor there very likely always will be.[69]

As it turned out, Robert Orben capsulized the history of 1984 more effectively than even George Orwell had done. "Nineteen eighty-four," Orben observed, "was the year they said Ronald Reagan could beat Walter Mondale with his eyes closed—and did."[70]

67. Bier, *The Rise and Fall of American Humor*, 457.

68. *New York Times* (2 July 1982), A11.

69. See Bill Adler, *Reagan Wit* (Naperville, Ill.: Caroline House, 1981); L. William Troxler, *Along Wit's Trail: The Humor and Wisdom of Ronald Reagan* (New York: Holt, Rinehart and Winston, 1983); Art Buchwald, *While Reagan Slept* (New York: G.P. Putnam's Sons, 1983); USCO Parody, Inc., *The Reagan Report* (New York: Doubleday, 1984); Tom Tierney, *Ronald Reagan Paper Dolls in Full Color* (Mineola, New York: Dover, 1984); and the feature story by Michael S. Malone on comedy entrepreneur Malcolm L. Kushner of San Francisco, "It's No Joke to Be a Humor Consultant to Industry," *New York Times* (26 Nov. 1984), B12.

70. Quoted by William E. Farrell and Warren Weaver, Jr., in "Washington Talk," *New York Times* (19 Dec. 1984), B10.

What's So Funny About
the Comics?

M. THOMAS INGE

Historians of the comic strip have traced its origin back to a number of sources in Western art and culture—the pictorial narrative of the medieval Bayeux tapestry, the eighteenth-century print series of such artists as William Hogarth and Thomas Rowlandson, the illustrated European broadsheet, the illustrated novels and children's books, and European and American humorous periodicals.[1] Usually the interest in such cultural genealogical research is to dignify and make respectable what is considered a low-brow form of entertainment, and while it may reflect the influence of all of these antecedents, the comic strip as we know it is a distinct form of artistic expression primarily American in its origin and development.

Any effort at definition must take into account a number of characteristics, such as its use of an open-ended dramatic narrative essentially

1. See, for example, Stephen Becker, *Comic Art in America* (New York: Simon and Schuster, 1959), 1–4; Pierre Couperie et al., *A History of the Comic Strip* (New York: Crown Publishers, 1968), 7–19; David Kunzle, *The Early Comic Strip* (Berkeley: Univ. of California Press, 1973); and Maurice Horn, ed., *The World Encyclopedia of Comics* (New York: Chelsea House, 1976), 9–10, 37–38. For a survey of the scholarship on the comics, see "Comic Art," in M. Thomas Inge, ed., *Handbook of American Popular Culture* (Westport, Ct.: Greenwood Press, 1978), 77–102.

76

without beginning or end about a recurring set of characters on whom the reader is always dropping in *in medias res*. Relationships have been established before we arrive and they continue with or without our attention, even beyond the life of the comic strip in a world seldom bound by or conscious of time, except in such stories in which characters age as in *Gasoline Alley* or in such an intentionally anachronistic strip as *B.C.* The story is told or the daily joke made through a balance of narrative text and visual action, although the proper aesthetic balance remains to be determined, with allowances to be made for the totally visual story like *Henry* and the heavily textual Sunday page *Prince Valiant*. Dialogue is contained in seeming puffs of smoke called balloons, a feature which goes back to medieval art and early political cartoons, and the strips are published serially in daily newspapers, to be followed by readers in much the same way as the public followed the novels serialized in nineteenth-century periodicals.

The comic strip draws on many conventions associated with the theatre, such as dialogue, dramatic gesture, background or scene, compressed time, a view of the action framed by a rectangular structure, and a reliance on props and various stage devices. It also anticipated most of the techniques associated with the film, such as montage (before Eisenstein), angle shots, panning, cutting, framing, and the close-up.[2] Beginning photographers and film makers are often referred to such well-designed and highly visual strips as *Buzz Sawyer* and *Steve Canyon* for rudimentary lessons in effective framing and angle shots. Yet the comic strip remains quite unlike the play or the film in that it is usually the product of one artist (or a writer and artist team) who must fulfill simultaneously the roles of scriptwriter, scene designer, director, and producer. The actors must be brought to life in the flat space of a printed page, engage our interest such that we want to return to them on a daily basis, and take less than a minute of our reading time. Working in the context of these characteristics establishes the challenge to the comic artist and contributes to the particular features of an art form very unlike any of its related forms in literature and the fine arts.

While any effort to identify the first comic strip is open to challenge, the artist who helped establish many of its basic features was Richard Outcault in *The Yellow Kid*, his depiction of the adventures of a street

2. John L. Fell, *Film and the Narrative Tradition* (Norman: Univ. of Oklahoma Press, 1974), 89–121.

urchin in the low-class immigrant section of the city. First produced for the New York *World* in 1895 as a single panel cartoon, Outcault's focus on a central character (clad in a yellow shift with dialogue printed across it) and his move to a progressive series of panels with balloon dialogue essentially defined the art form.[3] Despite the enormous popularity of *The Yellow Kid*, its use of the coarse reality of urban life would not prove to be staple fare for American comic strips, even though such writers as Stephen Crane, Frank Norris, and Theodore Dreiser were bringing naturalistic views of city life into the mainstream of American literature. It would be two decades before the tensions of urban existence fully entered the comics, and even then it was in the safe Midwestern worlds of Sidney Smith's *The Gumps* in 1917 and Frank King's *Gasoline Alley* in 1918, both of which emphasized the pathos of lower middle-class life and the impact of industrialism and technology on the ordinary family. By and large, however, critical realism was never to be a common attitude among comic artists.

What would prove to be an abiding presence in the comic strip was the American sense of humor. Most of the popular titles that came in the wake of the Kid for three decades were primarily characterized by humor and fantasy. These included Rudolph Dirks's *The Katzenjammer Kids* whose hijinks on an island which was an absurd world unto itself would continue for over eighty years under other hands and titles; Frederick Burr Opper's wonderfully wacky creations *Happy Hooligan*, *Maude the Mule*, and the eternally polite *Alphonse and Gaston*; Outcault's *Buster Brown*, a naughty Lord Fauntleroy whose continual "Resolutions" provided a kind of penance for Outcault's illiterate, dirty Yellow Kid; Winsor McCay's dream fantasy *Little Nemo in Slumberland*, the most beautifully drawn and aesthetically pleasing Sunday page ever to grace the weekly color supplements; Bud Fisher's *Mutt and Jeff*, the first daily comic strip featuring the first successful comic team outside vaudeville with a breezy style all their own; George Herriman's *Krazy Kat*, a classic in abstract absurdist fantasy and a uniquely lyrical love poem; Cliff Sterret's *Polly and Her Pals*, a family situation comedy drawn in an oddly out of kilter style reflecting elements of cubism and surrealism; George McManus's *Bringing Up Father* whose featured players Maggie and Jiggs became a part of marital comic folklore; Billy DeBeck's inspired portrayals of the sporting life and the Appalachian

3. Horn, 711–12.

mountaineer in *Barney Google and Snuffy Smith*; Elzie Segar's *Thimble Theatre* which, after a ten-year run, introduced Popeye, our first and still most popular comic superhero; and Frank Willard's *Moon Mullins*, a farce about boarding house life which has long outlasted the existence of the boarding house.

These were the years in which the terms *comics* and *funnies* naturally, suitably, and inseparably became identified with this new form of entertainment so outrageously popular that the world sometimes seemed to wait on developments in certain titles (the stock market once suspended operations to see if Uncle Bim got married in *The Gumps*), and many a newspaper would owe its very survival to the popularity of these attractive features. Then after three decades of fun and frolic, several new elements entered the funnies with the introduction of adventure and dramatic suspense. These had appeared to a certain degree as early as 1906 in *Hairbreadth Harry*, an inventive burlesque of melodrama by C. W. Kahles. The adventure comic strip was established, however, in 1924 by Roy Crane in his vividly rendered *Wash Tubbs* and by Harold Gray whose *Little Orphan Annie* was a successful combination of gothic characterization, exotic suspense, and homespun right-wing philosophy, which gave us our favorite picaro aside from Huckleberry Finn (Annie has now achieved an independent stage and screen life).

The adventure strip would not become a dominant genre, however, until 1929 when Richard W. Calkins and Phil Nowlan introduced *Buck Rogers*, the first science fiction strip, and Edgar Rice Burroughs's classic primitive hero *Tarzan* was given his first translation into comic strip form (most admirably drawn in the early days by Harold Foster and later by Burne Hogarth). Directly on their heels the 1930s and 1940s would witness a great expansion in this category: Chester Gould's gothic morality play in the police detective mode *Dick Tracy*, Vincent Hamlin's combination of advanced technology and prehistory in *Alley Oop*, Milton Caniff's realistically drawn and effectively plotted tales in *Terry and the Pirates* and his postwar *Steve Canyon*, Alex Raymond's futuristic visions and space fiction in *Flash Gordon*, Lee Falk's men of magic and mystery *Mandrake the Magician* (drawn by Phil Davis) and *The Phantom* (drawn by Ray Moore), Fred Harman's nicely stylized western story *Red Ryder*, Fran Striker's masked cowboy *The Lone Ranger* (drawn by Charles Flanders), Harold Foster's grand contribution to the Arthurian romance *Prince Valiant*, Alfred Andriola's well-crafted detective stories in *Charlie Chan* and *Kerry Drake*, Roy Crane's second contribution to the tradition with a World War II setting *Buzz Sawyer*, and Will Eisner's gently satiric and impressively rendered masterpiece of crime fiction *The Spirit*. Because of their use of mystery and suspense, the soap opera strips also belong in the adventure category. The best know of these are Allen Saunders and Dale Connor's *Mary Worth*, the matronly Miss Lonelyhearts of the Geritol set; writer Nicholas Dallis's several professionally oriented melodramas *Rex Morgan, M.D.*, *Judge Parker*, and *Apartment 3-G*; and Stanley Drake's fashionplate love story *The Heart of Juliet Jones*.

During the 1950s and 1960s satire flourished and dominated the comic strips, although it was consistently present at least from 1930 when Chic Young's *Blondie* satirized at first the flappers and playboys of the jazz age and subsequently the institution of marriage in what has proven to be the most popular comic strip in the world.[4] Al Capp's hillbilly comedy of 1934, *Li'l Abner* (with little of the authentic southern humor Billy DeBeck had used in *Snuffy Smith*)[5], evolved into an influential forum for ridiculing the hypocrisies and absurdities of the larger social and political trends of the nation. Just as Capp used the denizens of Dogpatch as vehicles for his satire, other artists of post-war America would follow his example and use even more imaginative vehicles, such as the fantasy world of children in *Peanuts* by Charles Schulz, the ancient form of the animal fable by the master of comic mimicry Walt Kelly in *Pogo*, an anachronistic military life in *Beetle Bailey* by Mort Walker, a fantasy world of prehistoric man by Johnny Hart in *B.C.*, and the absurd world of a medieval kingdom in *The Wizard of Id* by Hart and Brant Parker. During the 1970s, this trend would continue in such strips as Dik Browne's *Hagar the Horrible*, which relied on a farcical recreation of life among Viking plunderers, but it would also move in interesting new directions. Russell Myers's *Broom Hilda*, a wacky ancient witch, lives in a totally abstract world in the imaginative tradition of George Herriman's *Krazy Kat*, while Garry Trudeau's *Doonesbury* moved into the realistic world of the radical student generation of the preceding decade. Jeff MacNelly's *Shoe* and

4. Horn, 118–19.

5. M. Thomas Inge, "The Appalachian Backgrounds of Billy DeBeck's Snuffy Smith," *Appalachian Journal*, 4 (Winter 1977), 120–32.

Jim Davis's *Garfield* both return to animals as effective ways of reflecting on the eccentricities of human behavior.

Because of the strong development of strips of a serious caste devoted to adventure and melodrama, and the efforts of artists to render these stories in a more life-like style, critics and historians of comic art have never been satisfied with the use of the word *comics*, and have found even more objectionable the word *funnies*. It is true, they say, that in the beginning comic strips were devoted to humorous stories, activities, and situations, but the development of realistic adventure strips calls for another less narrow term. In answer to this concern, commentators have suggested alternative terms such as visual narratives or pictorial fiction, none of which have gained widespread acceptance. Equally unsuccessful have been efforts to coin names for the field of study of the comics—such as Jerry Bails's *panelology* or Fred Stewart's *bildegra-phics*.[6]

The use of the word *comic*, as in the plural noun *comics* or as an adjective in *comic art*, is perfectly appropriate and suitable, however, for this popular form of creative expression, in spite of the great range of topical categories which have developed including domestic drama, science fiction, western and detective stories, medieval romance, war and crime stories, adventure in exotic places, fantasy, satire, situation comedy, and slapstick humor. Not all things "comic" are necessarily funny or laughable. Comedy implies an attitude towards life, an attitude that trusts in man's potential for redemption and salvation, as in Dante's *Divine Comedy* or Shakespeare's *Hamlet*. Since comic strips always conclude with resolutions in favor of morality and a trust in the larger scheme of truth and justice, they too affirm a comic view of the social and universal order. While *Krazy Kat* and *Smokey Stover* may appear absurd, they do not reflect on the world around them as being irrational or devoid of meaning, as in the drama of the absurd. Comic art is supportive, affirmative, and rejects notions of situational ethics or existential despair. For this reason, modern social concerns such as homosexuality, premarital sex, and abortion seldom enter the funnies, and when they do, as in recent episodes of *Doonesbury* and *Mary*

6. See Jerry G. Bails, *Collector's Guide: The First Heroic Age* (Detroit: Panelologist Publications, 1969), 8, and the subtitle of the journal begun by Fred Stewart in 1978 *Cartonaggio: A Journal of Bildegraphics*.

Worth, they rest uncomfortably and cannot be treated with the full complexity these ambiguous issues require.

Most of the popular adventure and suspense titles also reflect a satiric stance on the part of the author/artist—this includes the grotesque villains of Chester Gould's *Dick Tracy*; the stumbling, romantic, and often adolescent adventures of the characters in Milton Caniff's stories, *Terry and the Pirates* and *Steve Canyon*; the exotic and exaggerated antics of such supporting characters as Wash Tubbs, Roscoe Sweeney, and Pepper Sawyer in the works of Roy Crane; the smug cynicism of Dr. Keith Cavell and the exaggerated villains in *Rex Morgan, M.D.*; the arrested adolescent love play of Sam Driver and Abbey Spencer in *Judge Parker*; or the inherent sense of literary and visual parody that invests the world of Will Eisner's *The Spirit*. Such strips as *Li'l Abner*, *Pogo*, *Peanuts*, and *Doonesbury* have never been alone in their overt satire and witty criticisms of the status quo.

To satirize life and institutions is to believe in a better mode of conduct which people fail to live up to, and humor may serve as a gentle but sometimes bitter or angry corrective. From the self-conscious parody of the super-hero in C.C. Beck's Captain Marvel to Stan Lee's neurotic and insecure Peter Parker, Spider-Man's alter ego, comic books also partake of the pervasive spirit of satire. The underground comic books such as *Zap*, *Fritz the Cat*, the *Fabulous Furry Freak Brothers*, and *Wonder Wart-Hog* were almost exclusively devoted to debunking not only society but the very forms of comic art itself. When a contemporary comic artist like Art Spiegelman wants to treat the Holocaust, he resorts to the satiric tradition of animal fable and the imagery of funny animal comic books and animated cartoons in his work-in-progress *Maus*, the effect of which is to make the subject all the more terrifying because of the incongruity between theme and visual imagery.

In its depictions of characters, physical objects, and landscape, all comic art draws upon and clearly belongs to the tradition of caricature and comic exaggeration. There is no such thing as realism to be found in the comics, either in the photographic sense or the sentimental sense of a Norman Rockwell. Even comic strips which have been praised for their authentic detail and meticulous draftsmanship, such as *Terry and the Pirates*, *Buzz Sawyer*, *Prince Valiant*, or *Scorchy Smith* as drawn by Noel Sickles, do not for all their obvious qualities succeed in bringing to the flat printed page any sense of dimensional reality or visual depth.

Early efforts at 3-D comic books went the way of similar efforts in film the first time around. Realism is incompatible with comic art, whose virtues reside in the distinctive and inimitable drawing styles and points of view of the individual comic artists. *Steve Canyon* and *Buzz Sawyer* are not better than *Smilin' Jack* because they are more realistic but because Caniff and Crane are better artists and stylists than Zack Mosely. *Dick Tracy* does not continue to hold our attention and interest because of its use of authentic police methods, a point in which Chester Gould took pride, but because of its grotesque villains (with ugly exteriors to match their warped souls), stylized violence (long before Arthur Penn's film *Bonnie and Clyde*), and an uncompromising belief in evil and incorrigibility. It is interesting to note that some of the most popular and enduring strips—*Krazy Kat, Peanuts, Pogo, Li'l Abner*, or *Nancy*—have intentionally opted for the abstract, the non-representational, and the art of caricature through either exaggeration or over-simplification.

The comics also belong in the major divisions or patterns of American mainstream humor. The three major comic strips set in the South—*Li'l Abner, Snuffy Smith* (without Barney Google), and *Pogo*—all owe allegiance to the lively school of southern frontier humor in the nineteenth century whose authors used regional dialects, folk humor, and outrageous actions to puncture the pretensions and hypocrisies of polite society. Some of Snuffy Smith's antics, in fact, were directly inspired by Billy DeBeck's readings in the Sut Lovingood yarns of George Washington Harris,[7] and surely in his study of Georgia dialects before creating Pogo, Walt Kelly must have encountered the Uncle Remus stories of Joel Chandler Harris.[8]

The wise fool who speaks more truth than he knows, from Benjamin Franklin's Poor Richard to Will Rogers and Archie Bunker, has his counterparts in Li'l Abner, Pogo, and Popeye. The timid soul or the little man trapped in the complexities of modern existence, as represented by Thurber's Walter Mitty, Charlie Chaplin's tramp, or Woody Allen's on-screen character, has his comic strip existence in a multitude of characters, including Andy Gump, Krazy Kat, Casper Milquetoast, Skeezix Wallet, Dagwood Bumstead, Mickey Mouse, Charlie Brown, Jiggs, Beetle Bailey, Ziggy, and the Perfessor in *Shoe*. The school of

7. Inge, "The Appalachian Backgrounds of Billy DeBeck's Snuffy Smith," 120–32.
8. Murray Robinson, "Pogo's Papa," *Collier's*, 129 (8 March 1952).

zany anarchy and irreverent ridicule to which S.J. Perelman, the Marx Brothers, and Robert Benchley belonged finds its practitioners in the comic strip work of George Herriman, Bill Holman (*Smokey Stover*), Rube Goldberg, and Milt Gross, the last in fact bridging the two worlds of literature and the comics with his columns and books using Yiddish-dialect humor and his screwball comic strips such as *Nize Baby*, *Count Screwloose*, and *That's My Pop*!

What's so funny about the comics? Everything. They clearly belong to the great body of humor which Americans cherish in their oral traditions, literature, stage entertainments, film, radio, and television. They soften the impact of reality by providing a comic distance on life's dangers, disasters, and tragedies, and enable us to laugh at ourselves as the pretentious creatures we happen to be. The comics are a unique form of cultural expression which we have come neither to understand nor appreciate. When we do, the comics will be found to be one of those humanistic forces which add quality to life and enable us to believe in man's potential through the saving grace of comedy.

Standup Comedy as Social and Cultural Mediation

Lawrence E. Mintz

Standup comedy is arguably the oldest, most universal, basic, and deeply significant form of humorous expression (excluding perhaps truly spontaneous, informal social joking and teasing). It is the purest public comic communication, performing essentially the same social and cultural roles in practically every known society, past and present. Studies dealing with humor often begin with defensive, half-hearted apologies for taking so light a subject seriously or for failing to reproduce the spirit and tone of the entertainment examined; this one will argue that humor is a vitally important social and cultural phenomenon, that the student of a culture and society cannot find a more revealing index to its values, attitudes, dispositions, and concerns, and that the relatively undervalued genre of standup comedy (compared with film comedy or humorous literature, for example) is the most interesting of all the manifestations of humor in the popular culture. In this essay, at least, Rodney Dangerfield and his colleagues will finally get some respect.

A strict, limiting definition of standup comedy would describe an encounter between a single, standing performer behaving comically and/or saying funny things directly to an audience, unsupported by very much in the way of costume, prop, setting, or dramatic vehicle. Yet standup comedy's roots are, as I shall discuss below, entwined with rites, rituals, and dramatic experiences that are richer, more complex than this simple definition can embrace. We must therefore broaden our scope at least to include seated storytellers, comic characterizations that employ costume and prop, team acts (particularly the staple two-person comedy teams), manifestations of standup comedy routines and motifs within dramatic vehicles such as skits, improvisational situations, and films (for example, Bob Hope in his "Road" pictures, the Marx Brothers movies), and television sitcoms (Jack Benny's television show, Robin Williams in *Mork and Mindy*). To avoid also having to include all theatrical comedy and its media spinoffs, however, our definition should stress relative directness of artist/audience communication and the proportional importance of comic behavior and comic dialogue versus the development of plot and situation. Such a definition is hardly pure, but it is workable.

Standup comedy has been an important feature of American popular culture since its earliest days.[1] Popular theater incorporated variety comedy as complement to the main plot. Circus clowns provided verbal standup comedy in the early years of these productions, as well as physical and prop comedy, in the tradition of fools, jesters, clowns, and comics, which can be traced back at least as far as the Middle Ages. The enormously popular minstrel theater featured the comic interaction of the two end-men, Tambo and Bones, and the Interlocutor, a straight-man, as well as various comedy routines within the show itself. The lecture circuit in the nineteenth century supported dozens of successful humorists, the most famous of whom were Mark Twain and Artemus Ward. Medicine shows, tent shows, and other traveling variety entertainments all boasted standup comedy as a central element.

In the twentieth century, standup comedy has been the backbone of vaudeville and burlesque and the variety theater (for example, Earl Carroll's *Vanities*, the *Ziegfeld Follies*), as well as night-club and resort

---

1. There is no comprehensive, definitive history of standup comedy in America. Phil Berger calls his book, *The Last Laugh* (New York: Morrow, 1975 Limelight edition, 1985), a history of the genre, but it is impressionistic, more "new journalism" than anything else. Joe Franklin's *Encyclopedia of Comedians* (Secaucus, N.J.: Citadel Press, 1972) is helpful, as are Steve Allen's *Funny Men* (New York: Simon and Schuster, 1956); *Funny People* (New York: Stein and Day, 1981); and *More Funny People* (New York: Stein and Day, 1982).

entertainment. More recently, standup comedy has spawned a popular entertainment movement of its own, the comedy clubs, where a rather lengthy bill of comics have exclusive possession of the stage and audience for a long evening of laughter. Standup comedy has also contributed to all of the mass media in America, from the silent films through radio, to the record industry and, of course, to television. Clearly it is a popular art that is central to American entertainment, but in the universal tradition of public joking rituals it is more than that as well; it is an important part of the nation's cultural life.

The motives and functions of standup comedy are complex, ambiguous, and to some extent paradoxical. Anthropologists and sociologists have paid some attention to teasing relationships and the roles of social joking. Students of theater and humor have recognized comedy's more profound aspects, but there is no developed study of the social and cultural functions of standup comedy as such. In his book, *Heroes, Villains, and Fools*, Orrin Klapp does, however, briefly mention a few of the functions of standup comedy in his discussion of fools. He observes that

> Every kind of society seems to find fool types useful in: sublimation of aggression, relief from routine and discipline, control by ridicule (less severe and disruptive than vilification), affirming standards of propriety (paradoxically by flouting followed by comic punishment), and unification through what Henri Bergson and Kenneth Burke have called the communion of laughter.[2]

In her vitally important work on public joking, the anthropologist Mary Douglas emphasizes properly that the contents and processes of joke telling are at least as important as the texts of the jokes themselves to any understanding of the meaning of humor. This is obviously the case with standup comedy performance as well. As Douglas observes, "the joke form rarely lies in the utterance alone, but . . . can be identified in the total social situation." Douglas further concerns herself with the joking activity as *rite* and *anti-rite*, or as public affirmation of shared cultural beliefs and as a reexamination of these beliefs. She notes that the structure of jokes tends to be subversive; in other words, jokes tear down, distort, misrepresent, and reorder usual patterns of

---

2. Orrin E. Klapp, *Heroes, Villains, and Fools: The Changing American Character* (Englewood Cliffs, N.J.: Prentice-Hall, 1962), 60.

expression and perception. Yet she also agrees with Victor Turner that the *experience* of public joking, shared laughter, and celebration of agreement on what deserves ridicule and affirmation fosters community and furthers a sense of mutual support for common belief and behavior (hence *rite*).[3]

Turner's work is also helpful when thinking about standup comedy. His concept of "plural reflexivity," or "the ways in which a group or community seeks to portray, understand, and then act on itself" has important implications for our understanding of art, popular culture, and humor. In addition, his discussion of *liminal* or *liminoid* activity in the rituals of performance and of artistic expression is potentially adaptable to a theory of public comedy. Turner sees rituals as an opportunity for society to explore, affirm, deny, and ultimately to change its structure and its values:

> Public liminality can never be tranquilly regarded as a safety valve, mere catharsis, "letting off steam," rather it is communitas weighing structure, sometimes finding it wanting, and proposing in however extravagant a form, new paradigms and models which invert or subvert the old.[4]

Other writers whose work contributes to this view of the social functions of comedy include Hugh Dalziel Duncan in his book *Communication and the Social Order* (1970), and William Martineau in his article outlining the various social motives of humor.[5]

The key to understanding the role of standup comedy in the process of cultural affirmation and subversion is a recognition of the comedian's traditional *license* for deviate behavior and expression. Probably originating in the cruel but natural practice of ridiculing physical and

---

3. Mary Douglas, "Jokes," *Implicit Meanings: Essays in Anthropology* (Boston, 1978), 93.

4. Victor Turner, "Frame Flow, and Reflection: Ritual and Drama as Public Liminality," in Michael Benamou and Charles Caramello, eds., *Performance in Postmodern Culture* (Madison: Univ. of Wisconsin Press, 1977), 33. See also Turner's books, *The Ritual Process: Structure and Anti-Structure* (1966; rpt. Ithaca: Cornell Univ. Press, 1977); and *Dramas, Fields, and Metaphors: Symbolic Action in Human Society* (Ithaca: Cornell Univ. Press, 1974).

5. Hugh Dalziel Duncan, *Communication and Social Order* (New York: Oxford Univ. Press, 1970), 373–424; William H. Martineau, "A Model of the Social Functions of Humor," in Jeffrey Goldstein and Paul McGhee, eds., *The Psychology of Humor* (New York: Academic Press, 1972), 101–24.

mental defectives, this license presents a paradox crucial to the development of the standup comedy tradition. Traditionally, the comedian is defective in some way, but his natural weaknesses generate pity, and more important, exemption from the expectation of normal behavior. He is thus presented to his audience as marginal. Because he is physically and mentally incapable of proper action, we forgive and even bless his "mistakes." This marginality, however, also allows for a fascinating ambiguity and ambivalence. In his role as a *negative exemplar*, we laugh *at* him. He represents conduct to be ridiculed and rejected, and our laughter reflects our superiority, our relief that his weaknesses are greater than our own and that he survives them with only the mild punishment of verbal scorn. Yet to the extent that we may identify with his expression or behavior, secretly recognize it as reflecting natural tendencies in human activity if not socially approved ones, or publicly affirm it under the guise of "mere comedy," or "just kidding," he can become our *comic spokesman*.[6] In this sense, as a part of the public ritual of standup comedy, he serves as a *shaman*,[7] leading us in a celebration of a community of shared culture, of homogenous understanding and expectation.

The oldest, most basic role of the comedian is precisely this role of *negative exemplar*. The grotesque, the buffoon, the fool, the simpleton, the scoundrel, the drunkard, the liar, the coward, the effete, the tightwad, the boor, the egoist, the cuckold, the shrew, the weakling, the neurotic, and other such reifications of socially unacceptable traits are

6. Recent studies dealing with the personality of standup comedians suggest that they tend to accept this role more or less consciously, viewing their art as a protection of society. Most comedians have had troubled pasts, view themselves as outcasts to some extent, and express a need for the approval of the audience. See Susan Witty's review of this research, "The Laugh Makers," *Psychology Today* (Aug. 1983), for the views of Samuel Janus, Waleed Salameh, and others. Seymour Fisher and Rhonda Fisher, *Pretend the World Is Funny and Forever: A Psychological Analysis of Comedians, Clowns, and Actors* (Hillsdale, N.J.: Erlbaum, 1981) is the essential book-length study. See also collections of interviews with performers, notably Larry Wilde's *The Greatest Comedians* (Secaucus, N.J.: Citadel Press, 1973); and Wilde, *How the Great Comedy Writers Create Laughter* (Chicago: Nelson-Hall, 1976); and William Fry and Melanie Allen, *Make 'Em Laugh: Life Studies of Comedy Writers* (Palo Alto: Science and Behavior Books, 1975).

7. Albert Goldman uses the term in his discussion of comedians such as Lenny Bruce in *Freakshow* (New York: Atheneum, 1971). See also E. T. Kirby, "The Shamanistic Origins of Popular Entertainments," *Drama Review*, 18 (March 1974), 5-15.

enacted by the comedian to be ridiculed, laughed at, repudiated, and, finally, symbolically "punished." Modern American standup comedy reflects the universal range of this phenomenon, from Jerry Lewis's grotesques, to the many fools and simpletons of the genre: Jackie Gleason's Poor Soul, Irwin Corey's mindless professor, Dean Martin's drunkard, the legion of "transvestites," and the "little men" or weaklings portrayed by such comics as Woody Allen and Rodney Dangerfield, among others. We laugh at the egotism of Bob Hope and Jack Benny, at the frustration of Alan King, the sex-role inadequacy of Joan Rivers and Phyllis Diller, the promiscuity of Redd Foxx and Richard Pryor, the boorishness of Steve Martin and Martin Mull, and at a host of other follies and frustrations reflected by the army of self-deprecating comedians whose domestic life is a disaster, whose battles with everyday life become overwhelming routs, and whose flaws are immense exaggerations of all we fear and reject in our own self-definitions.

Though the time-honored function of the standup comedian has been to provide a butt for our humor, this function is perhaps less interesting, even less important, than his role as our comic *spokesperson*, as a mediator, an "articulator" of our culture, and as our contemporary *anthropologist*.[8] To be sure, the separation of the two roles is rarely absolute or even entirely clear. For instance, Joan Rivers's comic persona is established as essentially negative. We laugh at her characterization of herself as a failed or flawed woman, because she is unattractive, lacks the proper female attributes, is unpopular, rejected by parents and friends, and inept in domestic skills such as cooking and housekeeping. Yet over the years her act has begun to emphasize an expression of pride in these very "failings." Rivers in fact often seems aggressively to repudiate these traditional cultural values, and to attack more "perfect" cultural role models, such as Elizabeth Taylor and Cheryl Tiegs. She seems to engage in a conspiracy with women in the audience to reject male demands that women fulfill their romantic and domestic fantasies. Indeed she shares this perspective with Phyllis Diller, another standup comedienne, and with Erma Bombeck, the columnist and comic-lecturer. It seems likely, therefore, that these female comics are voicing

8. See Stephanie Koziski, "The Standup Comedian as Anthropologist," *Journal of Popular Culture*, 18 (Fall 1984), 57–76. Her dissertation on standup comedy is in process. The term "articulator" is used by Chauncy Ridley in an unpublished ms., "Insight and Regeneration in Richard Pryor's Stand Up Comedy."

changing attitudes about gender roles that have begun to take hold in American society as a result of the most recent wave of feminist agitation.

Similarly, Alan King serves as a comic spokesman for contemporary Americans by outlining his frustrations with the bureaucracy, with doctors, with all of the pitfalls of modern American life. His persona, however, is also clearly negative; he is a bully, a boor, a malcontent, a loudmouth, and a loser.

The ambiguity, then, is an essential feature of an audience's reaction to standup comedy.

Redd Foxx's Las Vegas routine, like so many other comic acts, is based on a persona that is sexually libertine. He is a constant violator of both verbal and behavioral taboos. I witnessed one of his sets, for instance, in which virtually all of his jokes dealt with the topic of oral sex. Foxx presented himself as a successful practitioner of these taboo arts and repeatedly claimed that all successful lovers indulge in the techniques whether or not they admit it. The audience laughed loudly and enthusiastically, but a close look at the physical responses in the room revealed two different types of laughing behavior. The older people in the audience gasped, flinched, physically backed away while laughing at the punch-lines, and frequently looked at each other nervously, perhaps for confirmation that the license of comedy was still in effect. They seemed to be saying to themselves and each other, "Can you believe that he is as daring to say these things in public? Isn't this exciting, dangerous stuff?" The younger people in the audience were laughing in a manner that I term "anthemic." They leaned *toward* Foxx, often applauded, raised their hands or fists as though cheering a political speaker with whom they were in agreement, while occasionally yelling, "yeah," or "right-on," or "all right," or just yelping with delight. For them Foxx was the counter-culture spokesman with the courage (and the comically protected situation) to state publicly and openly that the sexual taboo against oral sex was, in their view at least, no longer valid or operative. Foxx led them in an expression of their cultural truths.

This role of the comedian as social commentator is surely not a new one. Shakespeare made extensive use of the fool's traditional license to have the innocent but sharp, shrewd observer speak the "truth" which was universally recognized but politically taboo. If nineteenth-century Americans laughed *at* the racist images of Tambo and Bones for their licentiousness, they probably also laughed *with* their Dionysian freedom to enjoy life and their common-sense victories over the stuffy, pompous, dull Interlocutor. No doubt, they identified also with their topical commentaries expressing the democratic, popular, if often cynical, opposition to "official" social attitudes and public positions.[9] Twain, Ward, and the other platform lecturers similarly offered down-to-earth, comically acceptable, but "opposition line" to the views of polite society. Ethnic and blue-collar comics of vaudeville and the variety theater were vulnerable fools, frequently, but they also won ironic victories and expressed many of the social proclivities of their audiences, as well as a more realistic if not more admirable view of their worlds.

It might be said, then, that the trickster, con-man, and likeable rogue all turn dishonesty, selfishness, disruptive and aggressive behavior, and licentiousness into virtues, or at least into activity that the audience can applaud, laugh with, and celebrate. The pleasure the audience derives from this sanctioned deviance may be related to the ritual violation of taboos, inversion of ritual, and public iconoclasm frequently encountered in cultural traditions. If, as Freud posited, there is a battle going on between our instincts and our socially developed rules of behavior, comedy provides an opportunity for a staged antagonism.[10] Another way of expressing the same process would be as a dialectic in which a thesis—basis human traits and characteristics—is confronted with an antithesis—polite manners and social restraints—with a synthesis perhaps being tolerance or at least a relaxation of hostility and anxiety.[11]

Given this analysis, it is possible to see that our modern American

9. See Robert Toll, *Blacking Up: the Minstrel Show in Nineteenth Century America* (New York: Oxford Univ. Press, 1977), which emphasizes the racism of the characterizations; and William Stowe and David Grimsted's review which corrects Toll by calling attention to the more positive functions of the portrayal, "Review Essay: White-Black Humor," *Journal of Ethnic History*, 3 (1975).

10. Sigmund Freud, *Jokes and Their Relation to the Unconscious*, ed. James Strachey (New York: Norton, 1960).

11. An important essay by Louis D. Rubin, Jr., "The Great American Joke," reprinted in Enid Veron, ed., *Humor in America* (New York: Harcourt Brace Jovanovich, 1976), 225–65, maintains that the consistent feature of American humor is its examination of our ideals in the light of the reality of our lives.

standup comedians provide us with some of our most valuable social commentary. While some critics of popular entertainment try to distinguish between a traditional standup comedy characterized by an irrelevant quest for laughs, and a so-called "new wave" comedy which is more socially and politically satiric or insightful, such categorization belies the consistent role of standup comedy as social and cultural analysis. Traditional comics like Bob Hope, Johnny Carson, and Alan King are less openly "counter-culture," certainly, but their complaints contain a critique of the gap between what is and what we believe should be. Moreover, the "new wave" comics were not always exclusively, openly political or even satiric. Mort Sahl, Lenny Bruce, Dick Gregory, and others were controversial because many of the issues they addressed were causing social divisions. Yet other "new wave" comedians—Jonathan Winters, Shelley Berman, Mike Nichols and Elaine May, Bill Cosby, and Joan Rivers chose less openly divisive material. Even the informal "new wave" style, casual dress, the use of longer "bits," fewer "punch-lines," and more spontaneous improvisation—recalls the nineteenth-century platform lecturers as much as it heralds a break with tradition.[12] The young comedians currently performing on the club circuit[13] reflect the entire range of standup comedy performance, from one-liners, verbal games involving puns, malapropisms, double-entendres, and the violation of socially acceptable language taboos to physical and prop comedy, insult comedy, parodies and put-

12. The March 1961 issue of *Playboy* magazine features an interesting symposium on the "new wave" standup comedy, involving Lenny Bruce, Mort Sahl, Jonathan Winters, and Jules Feiffer among others.

13. Several articles in the popular press and entertainment industry newspapers have chronicled the growth of comedy clubs throughout America in recent years. Night clubs such as San Francisco's *The Hungry I* and New York's *The Bitter End* promoted the genre in the 1960s and Budd Friedman's *The Improvisation* led to the establishment of several clubs in New York and Los Angeles. Today almost every American city has a small comedy club or two, offering young comedians a chance to learn their craft through frequent appearances. These comedy clubs generally feature one or two "name performers" who travel the circuit and whose reputations are fostered by television exposure (Jay Leno, Byron Allen, and David Brenner, among others), local professionals, and amateur, would-be standup comedians. The success of the urban comedy clubs alone would suggest that standup comedy in contemporary America is experiencing its finest hours, certainly since the days of vaudeville.

downs of current popular culture, and of course social and political criticism.[14]

Perhaps the best, if not the only, place to witness standup comedy as true social and cultural mediation is in live performance, preferably at one of the small comedy clubs or intimate night-club rooms where the interaction between the comedian and the audience is more prominent. The comedian begins by performing two important functions. He or she establishes the nature of the audience by asking questions of a few people close by or by making statements about the audience followed by a call for agreement or acknowledgement (if the audience is too large for the question-and-answer session). This function is often performed by an MC or a warm-up comic, but it is not merely a matter of gathering information. The comedian must establish *for the audience* that the group is homogeneous, a community, if the laughter is to come easily.[15] "Working the room," as comedians term it, loosens the audience and allows for laughter as an expression of shared values rather than as a personal predilection (since people are justifiably nervous about laughing alone and what that might reveal). This interaction with the audience often, but not always, includes ritual insults directed at audience members, and sometimes heckling and the putting down of

14. James Walcott argues that today's club comics are not worthy successors of the "new wave" tradition. Rather, he sees them as heirs of the traditional professional standup comedy with its emphasis on commercial success, mass-media exposure, shorter routines, more concern with laughter and entertainment than message, and slick, polished style. Moreover, Walcott laments that the young professionals today are less interesting, less socially relevant: "most comedians are ignoring the shifts in American Society, mostly ignoring politics . . . ignoring quirks in the quest for status and power in a society that demands success, overlooking even the anomalous state of affairs between men and women, a great subject in these confusing post-liberation days." "The Young Comedians: But Seriously Folks," *Village Voice* (30 Dec. 1974), 8. While it is easy for comedy aficionados to share Walcott's nostalgia for the more pointed satire of some of the "new wave" comedians, his charges simply do not stand up after even an introductory tour of the clubs today. The standup comedians of the past decade compare favorably in style and substance with those of any previous era.

15. See studies by Howard Pollio and various associates: Pollio and John Edgerly, "Comedians and Comic Style," in Antony Chapman and Hugh Foot, eds., *Humour and Laughter: Theory, Research, and Applications* (London: Wiley, 1976); Howard R. Pollio, John Edgerly, and Robert Jordan, "The Comedian's World: Some Tentative Mappings," *Psychological Reports*, 30 (1972), 387–91; and "Predictability and the Appreciation of Comedy," *Bulletin of the Psychonomic Society*, 4 (1974), 229–32.

the heckler (also relaxing the audience, making them feel less vulnerable (it doesn't *really* hurt . . . much . . . even if you are the target). So-called "kamikaze" comedians such as Don Rickles make the insult banter a feature of their act, but that is a special brand of standup comedy not necessarily connected with the process of establishing a community.

The comedian then establishes his or her comic persona, discussing personal background, life-style, and some attitudes and beliefs. This allows the audience to accept the comedian's marginal status and to establish that the mood of comic license is operative. This mood is accentuated by encouraging applause and laughter, thereby establishing a tone of gaiety and fun. Then the comedy routine itself can begin.

The styles of standup comedy differ almost as much as the content of jokes and joke routines themselves, but the essence of the art is creative distortion. Such distortion is achieved through exaggeration, stylization, incongruous context, and burlesque. (Treating that which is usually respected disrespectfully and vice versa). These and other techniques all disrupt expectation and reorder it plausibly but differently from its original state. There are dozens of theories explaining why this is humorous, ranging from formal analyses that stress incongruity reconciled or the simultaneous consideration of opposites to theories that stress socially functional factors such as superiority, hostility, aggression, taboo violation, and so forth.[16] Comedians themselves, like most popular artists, tend to eschew theory in favor of trial-and-error practice ("I don't know why it works and I don't care," "I learn from others and try things out, keeping what works for me," "I express what *I* think is funny and let the audience decide," are the frequently voiced opinions).

The observer has to agree that it does work, most of the time. Audiences laugh and enjoy themselves, but they also express themselves, nodding concurrence, applauding, and offering verbal encouragement. When members of the audience are asked to discuss what they liked about comedy performance and why they liked it, they are usually

16. Humor theory is an indispensable if unpleasant part of any study of the social and cultural meaning of comedy. Recent books such as Antony Chapman and Hugh Foot, *It's a Funny Thing, Humour* (London: Wiley, 1977); and the two-volume *Handbook of Humor Research*, ed. Paul McGhee and Jeffrey Goldstein (New York: Springer-Verlag, 1984) survey the entire field of contemporary humor research and introduce the appropriate, more specific studies.

not much more helpful than the performers. "It was funny," "He was cool, great," "I could really identify with that," "That's just like my life," "He's crazy, really nuts," "He was wild, far out." When pressed they will often assert agreement with the content of the comedy or sympathy with the comedian's persona, but perhaps here they are pushed into such overt self-perception by their knowledge of what the questioner wants to hear.

There is much more work to be done if we are to appreciate properly the role of standup comedy in America. An authoritative, comprehensive history of the genre is necessary so that we can appreciate what has changed as well as what has remained constant. Thorough studies of joke texts and comedy routines are needed as well as more careful analyses of forms and techniques. We need ethnographic and demographic research to clarify, to substantiate, and no doubt to correct the theoretical assumptions about the performer-audience relationship and the motives and functions of the ritual. Until standup comedy is studied as a social phenomenon, we can only speculate concerning its real meaning. It is safe to say, however, that standup comedy in America operates within a universal tradition, both historically and across cultures, that it confronts just about all of the profoundly important aspects of our culture and our society, and that it seems to have an important role allowing for expression of shared beliefs and behavior, changing social roles and expectations.

Ethnic Humor:
Subversion and Survival

JOSEPH BOSKIN AND JOSEPH DORINSON

People have undoubtedly always laughed at others who seemed "distinct," to reassure themselves and to blunt the threats implicit in differences. Ethnic slurs in joking form have reflected the tensions of social difference in America, and they continue to serve important, though sometimes distasteful, functions in American life. Active and resurgent, intentionally cruel and demeaning, ethnic humor has a lengthy past characterized by resiliency and adaptability. Ethnic humor against supposedly "inferior" social groups initially conveyed the thrusts of the well-entrenched members of society, the white, mostly Protestant "haves," against the newly arriving immigrants or their imperfectly assimilated offspring, or against black slaves, freedmen, their children, and children's children. Ethnic humor in the United States originated as a function of social class feelings of superiority and white racial antagonisms, and expresses the continuing resistance of advantaged groups to unrestrained immigration and to emancipation's black subcitizens barred from opportunities for participation and productivity. In time, ironically, the resulting derisive stereotypes were adopted by their targets in mocking self-description, and then, triumphantly, adapted by

97

the victims of stereotyping themselves as a means of revenge against their more powerful detractors.

Such humor is one of the most effective and vicious weapons in the repertory of the human mind. For this reason, Thomas Hobbes related laughter to power and traced the origins and purposes of laughter to social rivalry. The passion of laughter, he sensed, was nothing more than the proclaiming of "some eminency in ourselves by comparison with the infirmity of others" or with our own one-time lowly position.[1] In the Hobbesian jungle of our contemporary world, ethnic humor's primary form revolves around the stereotype. Highly developed images today, stereotypes may once have originated in the stuff of social reality, but they have long since been embellished and taken on a life of their own. As Gordon W. Allport has aptly noted, "Some stereotypes are totally unsupported by facts; others develop from a sharpening and over-generalization of facts."[2] Yet, once formed, they assume certain features of a circular structure within which all behavior conforms to the internal directives of the stereotypical image.

Although ethnic humor demonstrates aggressive intentions, empirical studies suggest that it possesses a salutary side as well. Lawrence LaFave and Roger Mannell, for example, argue that some jokes of this genre actually compliment the maligned group.[3] The disparaged group absorbs the barbs and, in fact, defuses them by passing them along as of their own manufacture. Thus, the humor of ridicule may serve to support the ladder for upward social mobility. In Buffalo, for instance, Polish Americans were reported to relate the following quips upon the elevation of Polish-born Pope John Paul II to the Holy See:

Why doesn't the Pope let any dogs into the Vatican?
Because they pee on poles.

1. Thomas Hobbes, "Human Nature, or the Fundamental Elements of Policy," in Sir William Molesworth, ed., *The English Works of Thomas Hobbes* (London: John Bohn, 1840), IV, 46. For examples of *blason populaire*, see Alan Dundes and Carl R. Pagler, eds., *Urban Folklore from the Paperwork Empire* (Austin: Publications of the American Folklore Society, 1975), 174–79; and Sterling Eisiminger, "Ethnic and National Stereotypes and Slurs," *American Humor: An Interdisciplinary Newsletter*, 7 (Fall 1980), 9–13.

2. Gordon W. Allport, *The Nature of Prejudice* (Garden City, N.Y.: Doubleday/Anchor, 1958), 186.

3. Lawrence LaFave and Roger Mannell, "Does Ethnic Humor Serve Prejudice?" *Journal of Communication*, 26 (1976), 116–17, 122.

When asked what he thought of the abortion bill, the Pope replied, "Pay it."[4]

Alan Dundes suggests that such Polish jokes are demeaning, but Lydia Fish disagrees. She argues that they actually affirm ethnic pride.[5] Is either position correct? A Yiddish joke, in which a rabbinical sage listened to a dispute, adds perspective. The rabbi found merit in each position. When the *rebbitzen*, his wife, complained that both parties could not be right, the rabbi impartially conceded: "You're right too!" Ethnic jokes have occasionally appeared as light-bulb riddles:

How many WASPs does it take to change a light bulb?
Two. One to call the electrician and one to mix the martinis.

How many Jewish children does it take to change a light bulb?
None. "I'll sit in the dark!" the mother *kvetches* (whines)[6]

Clearly, jokes of this kind reflect, or can be fused with, contemporary circumstance. The Polish joke cycle, as Dundes observed, transfers heat from other ethnic groups including Jews and blacks to the lower socio-economic classes in general.[7] It could be argued, however, that Polish jokes also manifest revenge by blacks and Jews against whites, Christians or *goyim*, presumably for centuries of indignities.[8]

Concealed by a "smile through one's teeth," aggressive humor or wit serves two salient functions: conflict and control. Conflict, which is implicit in a variety of forms—satire, irony, sarcasm, parody, and burlesque—reinforces the in-group and weakens the out-group. Stereo-

4. Lydia Fish, "Is the Pope Polish? Some Notes on the Polack Joke in Transition," *Journal of American Folklore* (hereafter *JAF*), 93 (1980), 450–54.

5. Ibid.

6. The "power" jokes are found in Judith B. Kerman, "The Light Bulb Jokes: Americans Look at Social Action Processes," *JAF*, 93 (1980), 454–55, 457–58. For further illumination, see Alan Dundes, "Many Hands Make Light Work; or Caught in the Act of Screwing in Lightbulbs," *Western Folklore*, 40 (1981), 266; Joseph Boskin, "Obscure Humor: Comments on Contemporary Laughter, Circa. 1980s," paper presented at the Third International Conference on Humor, 9–10 Aug. 1982, The Shoreham Hotel, Washington, D.C.

7. Alan Dundes, "A Study of Ethnic Slurs: The Jew and the Polack in the United States," *JAF*, 84 (1971), 186–89, 202–3.

8. Dundes, "Many Hands," 266; Boskin, "Obscure Humor," 9–10.

types figure prominently in most conflict humor. Obstinately rigid, devilishly tenacious, the stereotypes have influenced our thinking processes from early times. Because they are so deeply embedded in our individual memory and so firmly anchored in our collective folklore, stereotypes tend to be extremely difficult to dislodge. Witness, for example, the cartoons of Herblock, Jules Feiffer, and David Levine, the movies of Mel Brooks and Woody Allen, the standup comedy of Lenny Bruce, Dick Gregory, and Richard Pryor. Humor based on stereotype, the nastiest cut, can emasculate, enfeeble, and turn victims into scapegoats. *Der Sturmer* caricatures of the Jews spring painfully to mind.[9]

In origin and development, ethnic slurs are best understood in historical context. The Irish, for example, became victims of Irish jokes soon after their arrival in the United States:

Why is the wheelbarrow the greatest invention ever made?
It taught a few Irishmen to walk on their hind legs.[10]

Reputedly the Irish embodied propensities for brawling, drinking to excess, contradicting themselves unwittingly, and making incongruous statements—brutal or foolish behavior, in other words. Accident victims Pat and Mike have suffered a great fall. "Are you dead, Pat?" "I'm badly bruised, Mike, but quite alive." "I hope you are but you're such a liar, I don't know whether to believe you." Blacks sometimes employed these jokes because they conferred on themselves feelings of superiority over the Irish along with some degree of revenge against all white folk.[11] A visitor in hell saw all kinds of ethnics—Germans, English, Japanese, and Negroes—burning in torment. "Where are the Irish?" he asked. Escorting him to a room filled with Irish, the Devil said: "We are just drying them here; they are too green to burn now." At another level, an Irish orator covered a litany of ethnic achievements. "Who puts up all the fine buildings?" The audience responded on cue: "The Irish." "And

9. Joseph Boskin, *Humor and Social Change in Twentieth-Century America* (Boston: Boston Public Library, 1979), 28–31; Richard M. Stephenson, "Conflict and Control Functions of Humor," *American Journal of Sociology*, 56 (1951), 569.

10. Ray Ginger, *Ray Ginger's Jokebook about American History* (New York: Franklin Watts/New Viewpoints, 1974), 31.

11. Isaac Asimov, *Isaac Asimov's Treasury of Humor* (Boston: Houghton Mifflin, 1971), 287; Lawrence W. Levine, *Black Culture and Black Consciousness: Afro-American Folk Thought from Slavery to Freedom* (New York: Oxford Univ. Press, 1981), 302.

who puts up the court house?" "The Irish." "And who builds the state penitentiaries?" "The Irish." "And who fills them?" "The Irish."[12]

On stage, the Irish carved out a distinctive image for themselves. Vaudeville or burlesque teams including Needham and Kelly, Rooney and Rogers, the Shamrocks, and others, engaged in tongue-twisters, brawling, and blarney. They conjured up a vivid portrait described by "a figure in a derby hat and dudeen pipe, a melodic if not sentimental songster having a belligerent attitude, a love for the bottle, a penchant for politics, . . . a quizzical look." In the newspaper comics, Irish folks inhabited shanties where the chimney, a patched stovepipe, pitched crazily. One needed a ladder to get into the house filled with children and dominated by a hot-headed, washer-woman wife.[13]

This kind of cruel caricature flourished at a time when the nation was confronted by a large number of impoverished immigrants who could not easily be assimilated. Older-stock Americans aimed jokes against these newcomers and their unusual customs as one method of promoting cultural conformity. The Irish responded to such oppressive humor, however, using a counter-assertion of aggressive humor in return. If, indeed, the Irish represented unwanted alien characteristics, they readily employed their own wits to criticize American values and peculiarities, and maintained thereby a measure of self-respect. Eventually Chicago's Irish dialect commentator on public affairs turned the tide in favor of his countrymen. From his saloon on Archey Road, Mr. Dooley satirized fraud, pretense, and materialism in the American grain. He tackled Andrew Carnegie's philanthropies at the time when they were almost universally celebrated. ("Ivry time he gives a libry, he gives himself away in a speech.") He supplied the most cogent appraisal of reform politics:

Th' noise ye hear is not th' first gun iv a rivolution. It's on'y th' people iv th' United States batin' a carpet. Ye object to th' smell? That's nawthin! We use sthrong disinfectants. A Frinchman or an Englishman cleans house by sprinklin' th' walls with cologne; we chop a hole in th' flure an' pour in a kag iv chloride iv lime. Who is that yallin'? That's our ol' friend High Fi-nance bein' compelled to take his annual bath. . . .[14]

12. Ibid., 302–3.

13. Boskin, *Humor and Social Change*, 31; Douglas Gilbert, *American Vaudeville: Its Life and Times* (New York: Dover, 1940), 62.

14. Finley Peter Dunne, *The World of Mr. Dooley*, ed. Louis Filler (New York: Collier, 1962), 151.

Mr. Dooley marveled at American society with its "invintions—the steam-injine an' th' printin'-press an' th' cottin'-gin an' th' gin sour an' th' bicycle an' th' flyin' machine an' . . . crownin' wur-ruk iv our civilization—th' cash raygisther." In retrospect Dooley stands equidistant between immigrant scapegoat Teague O'Regan, Brackinridge's cunning but cowardly rogue figure in the *Modern Chivalry* series (1792–1815), and martyred hero John Fitzgerald Kennedy.[15]

Jesse Bier has suggested that Dooley's unyielding opposition to American business, militarism, politics, and customs was a displacement of his Irish and his Catholic hostilities against the English. Dooley's egalitarian needling deflated the powerful, a tendency rooted in Irish comic tradition. Indeed, Irish bards, as Vivian Mercier has argued, constantly stirred up trouble in Ireland. Dooley questioned the conventional wisdom of his day. He functioned as a critic with a paradoxical bent, in that he was "provincial and broadminded, anti-intellectual but thoughtful, pugnacious but humanitarian."[16] In time Dooley seemed to grow more peaceful. Perhaps he, likewise, had joined the "cash raygisther" crowd along with other successful Irishmen. The Irish left ethnic humor to other ethnics who followed after them, principally Jews and blacks.

Jewish ethnic humor builds on its folk sources, as these examples reveal:

> An elderly orthodox Jewish man was walking his dog. He approached a stranger with an attractive dog. "What breed is he?" "A cross between a Jew and a mongrel." "Oh!" said the elderly Jew, "then he is undoubtedly related to both of us!"

> Priest: "When will you give up those silly dietary laws?"
> Rabbi: At your wedding, excellency."

15. Jesse Bier, *The Rise and Fall of American Humor* (New York: Holt, Rinehart and Winston, 1968), 179.
16. Ibid., 181; Arthur Power Dudden, ed., *The Assault of Laughter: A Treasury of American Political Humor* (New York: Thomas Yoseloff, 1962), 285–87; Charles Fanning, "The Short Sad Career of Mr. Dooley in Chicago," *Ethnicity*, 8 (1981), 169–73, 177–83. Irish comic sensibility is canvassed in Vivian Mercier, *The Irish Comic Tradition* (Oxford: Oxford Univ. Press, 1972).

Such jokes reveal distinctive aspects of Jewish humor, the wit of retaliation and the comedy of revenge.[17]

American Jews found the origins of their comic voice in medieval
Europe. Precursors of modern stand-up comedians, *badchonim* and
marshalliks enjoined each other to "tell it like it is" well before the
advent of Jackie Mason. A seasonal event, the *Purimshpiel* (Purim
Play) sanctioned irreverent humor and granted license to a number of
fools—the *lets*, *nar*, and *payats*—to act comically. Droll characters—
shnorrers, *shlemiels*, *shlimazels*, and *luftmentshen*—originated in the
East European *shtetl* or village.[18] Some, like Motke Chabad and Hershl
Ostropolier, were real people. One night while dining, the story goes,
Hershl broke into a loud wail. "Is there anything wrong?" asked the
concerned proprietor. "Oy!" cried Hershl, "to think that for this little
morsel of meat a great big ox had to be slaughtered." Fired from a
menial job for excessive jesting, Hershl was hired by a melancholy
Hassidic rabbi to serve as his court jester. The rabbi rebuked him on
one occasion for spending so little time at prayer. Hershl protested:

> You have so much to be grateful for! Your carriage and your fine horses,
> your gold and silver, your fancy dishes. But look at me. I have a nagging
> wife, my six children and a skinny goat. And so my prayers are very
> simple: 'Wife, children, goat'—and I'm done.

As he lay dying, Hershl was visited by members of the Burial Society.
He advised: "Remember my friends, when you lift me up to lay me in
the coffin, be sure not to hold me under the armpits. I've always been
ticklish there." He died with a smile on his lips, and laughed all the way
to the grave (*keyver*). Like his fellow imps, Froyim Graydinger and
Shayke Fayfer, Hershl played the wise fool. He unmasked the rich who
pretended to be righteous and the ignorant who pretended to be

---

17. Nancy Levy Arnez and Clara B. Anthony, "Contemporary Negro Humor as
Social Satire," *Phylon*, 29 (1969), 340; the mongrel-Jew joke is related by Howard J.
Ehrlich, "Observations on Ethnic and Intergroup Humor," *Ethnicity*, 6 (1979), 394;
while the priest-rabbi repartee—one of several versions—can be found in a fascinating
study by Ed Cray, "The Rabbi Trickster," *JAF*, 77 (1964), 342.

18. Nathan Ausubel, *A Treasury of Jewish Folklore* (New York: Crown, 1948), 264–
87, 304–19. There is a wonderful evocation of the Purim Plays in Nahma Sandrow,
Vagabond Stars: A World History of Yiddish Theater (New York: Harper and Row,
1977), ch. 1.

learned. By reinterpreting his predicament, the fool triumphed in the end.[19]

Other forms of folk humor flowered in the *shtetl.* Stories from the mythical village of Chelm parodied the Jewish preoccupation with learning bereft of common sense. They poked fun at sages fixed on millennial concerns, mindless of mundane reality. Children still love these stories, because adults act foolishly in them and education leads to futility. When two wise men of Chelm went for a walk, it started to rain. "Quick, open your umbrella!" "It won't help. My umbrella is full of holes." "Why then did you bring it?" "I didn't think it would rain." In another example of inspired nonsense, the village elders of Chelm refuse to grant a raise to the underpaid Messiah-watcher because, though the salary is low, the work is steady.[20]

Some scholars contend that Jewish humor is a product of emancipation and did not blossom until the late nineteenth century, while others argue that following the Holocaust and the rise of a Jewish nation-state in Israel, this genre has expired. Jewish jokes attracted and stimulated Sigmund Freud, who, in his analysis of Jewish humor, found that it exemplified the "tendency wit" of skepticism and self-criticism.[21] Freud's supposition finds confirmation in the penchant of contemporary Jewish comedians for assailing established institutions, as in the antics of Groucho Marx, Sid Caesar, Lenny Bruce, Jackie Mason, Don Rickles, and Mel Brooks, to name only a few comic wreckers. Building on his mentor's work, Theodore Reik, like Freud, focused on Jewish wit's intimacy, its dialectical process, and its releasing of unmerry laughter at a moment of subjective truth or profound insight.

19. Ruth Wisse, *The Schlemiel as Modern Hero* (Chicago: Univ. of Chicago Press, 1971), 11–12; William Novak and Moshe Waldoks, eds., *The Big Book of Jewish Humor* (New York: Harper and Row, 1981), 26–27; Sig Altman, *The Comic Image of the Jew: Explorations of a Pop Culture Phenomenon* (Madison, N.J.: Fairleigh Dickinson Univ. Press, 1971), 131–32.

20. Ausubel, *Treasury*, 338; Israel Knox, "The Wise Men of Helm," *Judaism*, 29 (1980), 187–88; Allen Guttman, "Jewish Humor," in Louis D. Rubin, Jr., ed., *The Comic Imagination in American Literature* (New Brunswick: Rutgers Univ. Press, 1973), 331, contains the Chelm messiah-watcher anecdote.

21. The "bath" jokes are collected in Salcia Landman, *Der Jüdische Witz* (Olten: Walter-Verlag, 1960), 87, 453. Also see Sigmund Freud, *Jokes and Their Relation to the Unconscious*, trans. and ed. James Strachey (New York: W.W. Norton, 1963), 49–51, 55–56, 61–63, 111–15.

In Immanuel Olsvanger's comic treasure-trove, *Royte Pomerantsen*, we discover this gem:

> When you tell a peasant a joke he laughs three times; once when you tell it, once when you explain it, and once when he understands it.

> When you tell a land-owner a joke he laughs twice; once when you tell it and once when you explain it—he'll never understand it.

> When you tell a military officer a joke he laughs only when you tell it. Because he won't let you explain it and of course he does not understand it.

> But when you tell a Jew a joke, he tells you that he's heard it already— and, besides, you're telling it all wrong.[22]

Often some other national or ethnic representative appears in this kind of anecdote, but the Jew always get the punch in the tag line and the rabbi frequently functions as a trickster. Does Jewish humor always indicate self-hatred? Most psychiatrists who treat this subject seem to have fixed on "psychic masochism" as their descriptive explanation. However, Elliot Oring delineates a basic dichotomy in humor theory between humanists and social scientists. While humanists prefer incongruity as the primary mode of humor, as they see it, social scientists stress catharsis via "drive reduction."[23]

Unencumbered by such divergent and humorless theories, Yiddish writers Mendel Mocher Sforim and Sholem Aleichem created comic characters who snatched ironic victories from the jaws of defeat. They further improved that delicate balance between piety and complaint, the humor of marginality as epitomized earlier by Heinrich Heine and expressed in a joke cycle concerning cleanliness, sexual permissiveness, identity problems, and war.[24] To explain what happened to this humor as it crossed the Atlantic Ocean to America, Lawrence Mintz has pinpointed four stages in the process: the first featured critical humor that targeted the out-group; the second involved self-deprecatory

22. Immanuel Olsvanger, *Royte Pomerantsen* (New York: Schocken, 1965), 3; Theodore Reik, *Jewish Wit* (New York: Gamut Press, 1962), 182–240; Dan Ben-Amos, "The 'Myth' of Jewish Humor," *Western Folklore*, 32 (1973), 112–15, 118–21, 129–30.
23. Elliot Oring, *Israeli Humor: The Content and Structure of the Chizbat of the Palmach* (Albany: State Univ. of New York Press, 1981), 39–40.
24. Altman, *Comic*, 141–45, 163–68.

humor; the third stressed realism; and finally, the fourth stage reversed the first stage as the oppressed minority gained revenge by assaulting the majority culture. In stages one and four, critical hostility gained license. This helped to deflect aggression through ritualistic, as opposed to real, punishment, because, as Mintz argues, the joking relationships and resulting ritual banter serve to reduce irritants.[25]

Jews in the United States in the nineteenth century were caricatured in jokes and cartoons published in *Puck, Judge, Life,* and *Leslie's Weekly.* The jokes concerned money, bargains, and fraud (mainly arson). The graphic stereotypes reflected a mixture of "good" and "bad" traits. However maligned, Jews actually received better treatment than a number of other groups, particularly Italians, blacks, Chinese, and, surprisingly, Mormons. John Appel has charted the evolution of the Jew in caricature from the money bags of the fifteenth century to the long beards, grotesque noses, open palms, and pawnbrokers' signs prevalent in eighteenth- and nineteenth-century European cartoons. In contrast to the Irish, for example, the Jews appeared more likable in American caricatures. Harry Hirshfield helped to create a counter-image with his Abe Kabibble comic strip in 1914. With his striped trousers, saucer eyes, small bulb nose, familiar accent and peculiar syntax, Abe represented middle-class Jewish aspirations. He loved family, country, business, and pinochle.[26] As their co-religionists owned and operated many theatres, Jews flocked into vaudeville, where budding careers opened to their talent and *chutspe.*

Old Jewish jokes found renewed expression on stage:

"Have I got a girl for you!" the *shadchan* (matchmaker) insists. On cue, as rehearsed, the *shadchan's* apprentice embellishes. *Shadchan:* "A pretty girl." Apprentice: "A beauty. Queen Esther." "Intelligent." "Brilliant. She knows six languages." "She's from a good family." "The highest *yichus* (status). Her grandfather was a famous scholar." "She's

25. Lawrence E. Mintz, "Jewish Humor: A Continuum of Sources, Motives and Functions," *American Humor*, 4 (Spring 1977), 4.

26. John J. Appel, "Jews in American Caricature: 1820–1914," *American Jewish History*, 71 (1981), 103–18. For a similar thesis, namely, that the caricature of Jews was more benign in America than in Europe, see Rudolph Glanz, *The Jew in Early American Wit and Graphic Humor* (New York: Ktav, 1973), 237. The cartoons, however, on 67, 88, 113, 115, 117, appear less than benign.

rich." "Her uncle is Rothschild." "She has only one fault. She has a little hump." "A hump!" cries the apprentice. "A regular Mount Sinai!"[27]

With a gift for cultural pastiche, Jewish comedians engaged in "ethnic acts." Joe Weber and Lew Fields did Mike and Meyer, a "Double Dutch Act." Mike, a fat little man in a bizarre checkered suit, yelled at Meyer, tall, lean, and unctuous, who twisted Mike's nose. The shorter man flailed helplessly at his taller adversary. They argued over politics. Mike scored with his punch line: "Banners don't vote. Budt dey shure do show vhich vay der vindt is plowing." Mike was shoved off stage as he bellowed: "Dondt poosh me, Meyer!" When they meet again, they greet each other:

> "I'm delightfulness to meedt you."
> "Der disguzt ist all mine."[28]

Smith and Dale's classic routine of 1906 was a thinly veiled Dutch Act. Beneath Dr. Kronkhite's German accent coursed choice bits of Jewish humor.

> Patient: "What do I owe you?"
> Doctor: "You owe me $10 for my advice."
> Patient: "$10 for your advice? Well, Doctor, here is $2. Take it, that's my advice."
> Doctor: "You cheap skate! You shnorrer, you low life, you racoon, you baboon!"
> Patient: "One more word from you, you'll only get $1."
> Doctor: "You . . ."
> Patient: "That's the word! Here's a dollar."[29]

Jews also put on burnt cork. Blacking their faces to impart their *shmaltz* (literally, chicken fat; figuratively, sentimentality bordering on bathos), Sophie Tucker, Al Jolson, George Jessel, and Eddie Cantor

---

27. Nahma Sandrow, "'A Little Letter to Mamma': Traditions in Yiddish Vaudeville," in Myron Matlaw, ed., *American Popular Entertainment* (Westport: Greenwood Press, 1979), 90.

28. Paul Antonie Distler, "Ethnic Comedy in Vaudeville and Burlesque," in ibid., 33–41.

29. Joe Smith, "Dr. Kronkhite Revisited," in ibid., 127–31.

became stars. Their black masks guaranteed freedom from conventional restraints. Perhaps the grimness of industrialization helps to explain the enormous popularity of Al Jolson, whose songs conjured up a mythical magnolia-scented South teeming with togetherness. If so, while Spenglerians were lamenting Western decadence, and poets in exile were raining metaphors of sterility on their respective wastelands, Jews were imitating the black libidinous style, and developing a coarse, vital humor with music to match.[30]

The Marx Brothers carried on the vaudeville tradition minus the minstrel masks. Fortified with S.J. Perelman scripts, they plunged into gleeful nihilism. Listen to Groucho, the "shnorrer" as explorer. "When I came to this country, I didn't have a nickel in my pocket. Now I have a nickel in my pocket." Resigning from the Friars Club, he explained: "I do not care to belong to a club that accepts people like me as members." Yet there were many more kicks for Groucho's straight-woman, Margaret Dumont. "That remark covers a lot of territory," he observed. "As a matter of fact, you cover a lot of territory. Is there any truth to the fact that they're going to tear you down and put up an office building?"[31] No one remained safe from Marx's demolition derby, least of all, Margaret Dumont, pillar of piety and symbol of WASP respectability.

Jack Benny, however, typified newer trends on radio. Born Benny Kubelski, he married Sadie Marks, who, like her husband, metamorphosed herself with a new nose and a new name into Mary Livingston. Ethnic humor issued only from the subsidiary characters in Benny's cast, like Eddie "Rochester" Anderson, Dennis Day, Messrs. Kitsel and Schlepperman, who presented stereotypes reminiscent of those on the vaudeville circuit. Vain, stingy, pompous, violinist *manqué* Benny played the butt and imparted his Jewish flavor almost subliminally. As Harry Popkin contends, the Hitler years constituted a period of relative silence on Jewish topics and actual desemitization. After World War II, however, defiant in the wake of the Holocaust and proud at Israel's

30. Ronald Sanders, "The American Popular Song," in Douglas Villiers, ed., *Next Year in Jerusalem* (New York: Viking Press, 1976), 197–98; Lewis A. Erenberg, *Steppin' Out: New York Night Life and the Transformation of American Culture 1890–1930* (Westport: Greenwood Press, 1981), 190–95; Stanley White, "The Burnt Cork Illusion of the 1920s in America: A Study in Nostalgia," *Journal of Popular Culture*, 5 (1971), 543.

31. Bier, *Rise*, 270–71; Altman, *Comic Image*, 188–89.

birth, Jewish comedians as well as Jewish writers emerged from the cultural closet. Among them Sid Caesar, Jack E. Leonard, Milton Berle, Mort Sahl, Lenny Bruce, Woody Allen, Mel Brooks, Saul Bellow, Bernard Malamud, and Philip Roth laughingly carried their low comedy into virtually every avenue of popular culture. They freshened up old stereotypes and injected doses of Jewish comic wisdom into American life. Their message was strong and clear: *mir zeinen doh* (we are here).[32]

Black comedians responded differently to the stresses affecting them than did their Jewish counterparts. True enough, blacks and Jews shared the humor of the oppressed. Inwardly masochistic, indeed tragic, externally aggressive, even acrimonious, their humor generated several distinctive forms of expression such as gallows humor, the ironic curse, double meanings, trickster tales, and retaliatory jokes.

Black humor's outstanding traits include its play quality, which seeks to ward off punishment and thus permits quick retaliation; its deep scrutiny; and a type of control humor which is vital for the maintenance of a highly attuned and carefully sensitized community.[33] Springing from its folk sources, Afro-American humor has proceeded mainly along two tracks destined to provoke laughter. Externally, it represents an accommodation to white society and functions as a mechanism for survival. Slaves used veiled humorous language to vent anger, just as they employed coded sayings to mask true feelings. The John-Master stories illuminate this process. John cusses out his massa whenever he pleases—whenever the massa is up at the big house and John is down in the field. John steals food and lies his way out of trouble by turning a pig into a baby and, when caught, reversing the magic. Slave stories featured outwardly docile subjects paying homage to their master as in this deathbed scene: "Farewell massa! Pleasant journey! You soon be dere, massa—[it's] all de way down hill!" Some slaves refused to be buried in the same gravesite with their masters for fear that the Devil,

32. Irving Howe, *World of Our Fathers* (New York: Harcourt Brace Jovanovich, 1976), 565–70; Wallace Markfield, "The Yiddishization of American Humor," *Esquire*, 64 (Oct. 1965), 114. For a succinct summary of this evaluation, consult Joseph Dorinson, "Jewish Humor: Mechanism for Defense, Weapon for Cultural Affirmation," *Journal of Psychohistory*, 8 (1981), 447–64.

33. Boskin, *Humor and Social Change*, 49–56.

"old Sam," might take the wrong body. Blacks chortled as they slipped past white scrutiny:

> I fooled Old Master seven years,
> Fooled the overseer three.
> Hand me down my banjo,
> And I'll tickle your bel-lee.[34]

John, the stereotype, epitomizes the rewards, the limits, and the hazards of the "trickster," wherein even verbal facility and skill in role playing were not enough. In one tale, John's absolute faith in prayer betrays him as the massa's cruel children prey on his gullibility and pelt him with "God's stones." To track the inner feelings of the Afro-American in servitude, one has to turn to the animal trickster. Rabbit is correctly identified with the slave, yet he also mirrors the oppressor's cruelty. Lawrence Levine cautions against simplistic equations. He prefers to view trickster tales as profound parodies of white society. Because the whites held such awesome power, their human chattels preferred to seek revenge disarmingly with guile and indirection. Even if the meek fail to inherit the earth, they might occasionally enjoy a last laugh. Slaves laughed "to keep down trouble and to keep our hearts from being broken." As John Little put it, "I have cut capers in chains."[35]

Folktales, in the useful paradigm of Arnez and Anthony, constitute "an oral tradition in which the group pokes fun at its customs, idioms . . . folkways." Such in-group humor fosters social cohesion. When black humor went public with burnt offerings, a ritual sacrifice oc-

---

34. Afro-American humor's twin tracks are charted in Joseph Boskin, "Goodby, Mr. Bones," *New York Times Magazine* (1 May 1966), 31. The roguish John stories are conveyed in a variety of sources: Daryl Cumber Dance, *Shuckin' and Jivin': Folklore from Contemporary Black Americans* (Bloomington: Indiana Univ. Press, 1978), 189–90; Richard Dorson, *American Folklore* (Chicago: Univ. of Chicago Press, 1959), 186–90; Norine Dresser, "The Metamorphosis of the Humor of the Black Man," *New York Folklore Quarterly*, 26 (1970), 216–19; Gil Osofsky, ed., *Puttin' on Ole Massa: The Slave Narratives of Henry Bibb, William Wells Brown, and Solomon Northrup* (New York: Harper and Row, 1969), 21–23; Harry Oster, "Negro Humor: John & Old Marster," in Alan Dundes, ed., *Mother Wit from the Laughing Barrel: Readings in the Interpretation of Afro-American Folklore* (Englewood Cliffs, N.J.: Prentice-Hall, 1973), 550–55. The "getting over" song is cited in Levine, *Black Culture*, 125.

35. Osofsky, *Puttin' on Ole Massa*, 39–40; Levine, *Black Culture*, 118–19.

curred. In American popular culture, the black as comic figure crept into our group fantasy as the smiling descendant of Pan. He lusted after chicken, watermelon, pig's feet, and white women. He feared ghosts (particularly in white sheets) and spoke in malapropisms. White performers Thomas Rice and Dan Emmett swooped down South in the wake of slavery to cannibalize black culture. Two blatant stereotypes surfaced, Jim Crow and Jim Dandy: the former, a rural, slow-witted buffoon; the latter, an urbane, effeminate city-slicker. Prodded by the upper-class, white-faced interlocutor, who played it straight, Crow and Dandy created havoc on stage. These types, contends Robert Bone, triggered laughter as audiences perceived the gap between affectation and reality. The travesty sought "to keep the pretender in his place."[36]

Sambo, Crow's cousin, a Darwinian loser and preindustrial primitive, became the nation's demeaned alterego or, in Bone's formulation, its anti-self. To whites he was

> slow-witted, loosely-shuffling, buttock-scratching, benignly-optimistic, superstitiously-frightened, childishly lazy, irresponsibly-carefree, rhythmically-gaited, pretentiously-intelligent, sexually-animated. His physical characteristics added to the jester's appearance: toothy-grinned, thick-lipped, nappy-haired, slack-jawed, round-eyed.[37]

Unlike Lear's fool, Ahab's Pip, or Bergen's McCarthy, our Sambo lacked wisdom. He was, in short, a buffoon.

The white performer who put on his blackface minstrel mask was performing a rite of exorcism. He was operating a safety valve for repressed emotions. The black persona he portrayed—indolent, inept, indulgent—embodied the anti-self and objectified the distance between social norms and man's instincts. Imparting a sense of freedom and inviting a return to childhood, minstrelsy answered deep psychic needs for white audiences, "the mammy for security and comfort; . . . the

36. Robert Bone, *Down Home: A History of Afro-American Short Fiction from Its Beginning to the End of the Harlem Renaissance* (New York: G. P. Putnam and Sons, 1975), 59, 60–61; Nancy Levi Arnez and Clara B. Anthony, "Contemporary Negro Humor as Social Satire," *Phylon*, 29 (1968), 339–40; Nathan I. Huggins, *Harlem Renaissance* (New York: Oxford Univ. Press, 1971), 261–83.

37. Joseph Boskin, "The Life and Death of Sambo: Overview of an Historical Hang-Up," *Journal of Popular Culture*, 4 (1971), 649.

Negro male for ridicule and jest."[38] For blacks themselves, this ridicule forged psychic chains: a bag for Uncle Ben, a box for Aunt Jemima, a cabin in the sky for Uncle Tom, a pancake restaurant chain for Sambo, and a joke for Rastus.

To survive, the black artist had to participate in self-caricature. To succeed, he had to perpetuate vile stereotypes. Billy Kersands juggled a cup and saucer in his mouth. Ernest Hogan, Ma Rainey, and Bert Williams donned the mask to conceal, as well as to express, true feelings. Williams, in fact, used two sets of jokes: one for white folks, the other for black. As "Jonah Man," Williams, helped and comforted by "Nobody," successfully pulled laughter from pain. Most of his peers, however, coupled their painful indignities with derisive laughter. Kersands and Hogan performed coon songs. Dunbar wrote them.[39]

Blacks' humor of accommodation was the only kind to which whites were ordinarily exposed until recently. To laugh openly at "the Man," "Mr. Charley," "Miss Ann," "pig," "honkey," "vanilla" was to invite certain punishment. Blacks, therefore, developed a gaming stance stoically laughing on the outside to cope with their pain inside. Black humor served many important functions including group survival, escape into pride and dignity, self-criticism, and the resolution of conflict.[40] Getting past society's censors, internal and external, as Freud maintained, brings pleasure even in the presence of pain, because a joke saves energy normally expended on upholding inhibitions or disguising aggression. Such jokes function, in fact, as miniatures of rebelliousness. In Daryl Dance's rich anthology of materials, which often pits the poor against those with power, one set of selections uses the Negro preacher as the target to expose vanity, ignorance, hypocrisy, lechery, alcoholism, gluttony, and materialism through his misadventures and misfortunes. For example:

38. White, "*Burnt Cork*," 543; Albert F. McClean, Jr., *American Vaudeville as Ritual* (Lexington: Univ. of Kentucky Press, 1965), 24–26; Robert Toll, *Blacking Up: The Minstrel Show in Nineteenth-Century America* (New York: Oxford Univ. Press, 1974), 29; Huggins, *Harlem Renaissance*, 260–74, offers a brilliant analysis of travesty.

39. Toll, *Blacking Up*, 245–48, 254–59, 262, 274; Robert Toll, *On with the Show: The First Century of Show Business in America* (New York: Oxford Univ. Press, 1976), 123; Morris Goldman, "The Sociology of Negro Humor," Diss. New School for Social Research 1960, iv, refers to the dual set of jokes used by Bert Williams.

40. Boskin, *Humor and Social Change*, 57; Robert Brake, "The Lion Act Is Over: Passive/Aggressive Patterns in American Negro Humor," *Journal of Popular Culture*, 9 (1975), 551–53.

The church people were having a party at which they served some punch, but the punch was so weak that, every time they got a chance, some of the men would sneak in a bottle and pour some whiskey into the punch. The Preacher enjoyed it so much, he just kept nipping. Later, when he was called to pray, he said: "God, bless the cow that gave this milk."[41]

When another minister and his son encountered a bear in the woods, the son urged, "Let us pray!" The minister responded: "Let us run. Son, prayers is all right in a prayer meetin' but they ain't no good in a bear meetin!"[42]

The elephant riddle-jokes, which achieved great popularity in the 1960s, frequently depicted the elephant as sexually superior, a crude disguising, in the suggestion of Abrahams and Dundes, for the stereotypical black male. Thus:

Why does the elephant have four feet?
It's better than six inches.

How do elephants make love in the water?
They take their trunks down.

In another cycle, the elephant is symbolically castrated!

How do you keep an elephant from charging?
Take away his credit card.

Before long, color riddles appeared as:

What's black and has a red cape?
Super Nigger.

What is black and white and rolls in the grass?
Integrated sex.

The prospects of black liberation often spurred anxiety among whites, triggering repressive responses in turn.[43] At times, in the great urban riots of the 1960s, the responses and counterresponses could erupt violently and self-destructively.

41. Dance, *Shuckin'*, 41–76; Levine, *Black Culture*, 321.
42. For the "bear meetin'" joke, see Mary Frances Berry and John Blassingame, *Long Memory: The Black Experience in America* (New York: Oxford Univ. Press, 1982), 102.
43. Roger D. Abrahams and Alan Dundes, "On Elephantasy and Elephanticide," *Psychoanalytic Review*, 56 (1969), 230, 231, 233, 237, 238–39.

Why then, was it that American audiences responded so favorably to black comedians in this period? Perhaps the answer lies in the role that standup comics play as cultural anthropologists. Lawrence Mintz's insight is crucial:

> As a licensed spokesman he is permitted to say things about our society that we want and need to have uttered publicly, but which would be too dangerous and too volatile if done so without the mediation of humor; and as a comic character he can represent, through caricature, those negative traits which we wish to hold up to ridicule, to feel superior to, and to renounce through laughter. Thus, for example, the blackfaced minstrels can be the objects of racist ridicule as a part of a ritualized experience in venting hostility and in defining socially undesirable behavior, yet at the same time they can function as positive, likeable spokesmen for topical satire. . . . Similarly the ethnic comedians could represent "greenhorns" to be laughed at for their ignorance, gullibility, poverty, and vulnerability, but laughed with for their street-wise insistence on survival and their ironic exposure of injustice. . . ."[44]

Stephanie Koziski has demonstrated that comedians can jar audiences into awareness of deeply buried cultural underpinnings. Like a Margaret Mead, the stand-up comedian "gets down" into primal roots. Comparable to the ancient storyteller in "primitive" cultures, he or she may also communicate shared values as well as the common knowledge.[45]

Building on folk sources and in-group banter, black comedians joined their Jewish and other ethnic counterparts in imparting cultural commentary and anthropological insight. Dick Gregory carried the ball directly into enemy territory in the early 1960s. As a civil rights activist-commentator, he repeatedly scored:

Restaurateur: "We don't serve Nigras!"
"That's cool. I don't eat them."

44. Lawrence E. Mintz, "The 'New Wave' of Standup Comedians: An Introduction," *American Humor*, 4 (Fall 1977), 1. The comedian who made the biggest waves is still mired in myth. See Joseph Dorinson, "Lenny Bruce, A Jewish Humorist in Babylon," *Jewish Currents*, 35 (Feb. 1981), 14–19, 31–32.

45. Stephanie Koziski, "The Standup Comedian as Anthropologist: Intentional Cultural Critic," paper presented at the Third International Conference on Humor, Aug. 1982, 8, 15, The Shoreham Hotel, Washington, D.C.

I sat in so long at lunch-counters. It took me ten years to discover that they didn't have what I wanted.

It's kinda sad, but my little girl doesn't believe in Santa Claus. She sees that white cat with the whiskers and even at two years old she know damn well that no white man coming to our neighborhood at midnight.

Makes you wonder . . . when I left St. Louis I was making $500 a week for saying the same thing loud that I used to say under my breath.

Wouldn't it be a hell of a thing if all this was burnt cork and you people were being tolerant for nothing?[46]

Godfrey Cambridge laughed at his wife's "Back to Africa" kick. "She did the bedroom in brown, the whole thing, drapes, ceiling, carpet, spread, pillow. One day she took a bath, came into the room and it took me three hours to find her." Cambridge roasted whites, too, with his "How to Hail a Taxi" routine and their concern over property values. "Do you realize," he asked, "the amount of havoc a Negro couple can cause just by walking down the street on a Sunday morning with a copy of the *New York Times* real-estate section under the man's arm?"[47]

Redd Foxx brandished his own weapons. He once threatened a less-than-enthusiastic, predominantly white audience with "Why should I be wasting time with you here when I could be knifing you in an alley?" He ruefully observed that the first black to receive an athletic scholarship from "Ole' Miss" was a javelin catcher. He parodied Tarzan of the Apes and derided Long Beach, California, blacks as "the ugliest Negroes I have ever seen." Foxx confessed the ambivalences inherent in mulatto-dom: "You wake up in the morning with a taste for . . . filet mignon with biscuits." Unmasking Sambo, Foxx confided that "'Boss' spelled backwards is double SOB."[48] He had come a long way from the restraints of minstrelsy.

46. Dick Gregory with Robert Lipsyte, *Nigger: An Autobiography* (New York: Pocket Books, 1970), 132; Dresser, "Metamorphosis," 226–27; William Schechter, *The History of Negro Humor* (New York: Fleet Press, 1970), 186–88, 189.

47. Ibid., 105–6, 192–94; Levine, *Black Culture*, 362; Mel Gussow, "Laugh at this Negro but Darkly,' *Esquire*, 62 (Nov. 1964), 94–95.

48. Redd Foxx-isms are found in Boskin, *Humor and Social Change*, 50–51; Levine, *Black Culture*, 361, 365; Schechter, *History*, 196; Redd Foxx and Norma Miller, *The Redd Foxx Encyclopedia of Black Humor* (Pasadena: Ward Ritchie Press, 1977), 234–56.

Jackie "Moms" Mabley and, more recently, Richard Pryor also found rich veins of humor in folk sources. Mabley's appearance, her references to soul food and her earthy wit established the appropriate image and tightened the bonds of kinship with her black audiences, while in comic reversals, she addressed powerful white men as "boy" and called prestigious white women "girl." Once she offered an account of a major United Nations conference:

> Aw, everbody was there. They had a ball. Yeah. All them men from the Congo, some of 'em was late getting there 'cause they had plane troubles, and they had to be grounded in Arkansas, Little Rock. One of them Congo men walked up to the desk in Little Rock and said, "I'd like to reserve a room, please." The man said, "We don't cater to your kind." He said, "No, you misunderstand me. I don't want it for myself. I want it for my wife. She's your kind."[49]

Such humor, as Dwight Macdonald once observed, is like guerrilla warfare. Success depends on traveling light, striking unexpectedly, and getting away fast.[50] Yet ethnic humor, because of its agitational elements, must return to the action repeatedly. Skirting the edge of gallows laughter, it cannot afford to escape into fatalism. Thus, in its quest for control over events and lives, ethnic behavior demonstrates that both oppressors and their adversaries use humor, but for strikingly different ends. The oppressors employ ridicule to maintain conformity to the status quo by adhering to iron-bound stereotypes. Ethnics in retaliation have created a world of internal joking where, in Langston Hughes's observation, "certain aspects of the humor of minority groups are so often inbred that they are not palatable for outside consumption."[51] Moreover, they often reverse roles and turn the tables on their adversaries by striving for a language of self-acceptance. Poet Marianne Moore perceptively noted that "one's sense of humor is a clue to the most serious part of one's nature." Mocking the features ascribed to

49. Arnez and Anthony, "Contemporary Negro Humor," 342; Levine, *Black Culture*, 363–66.

50. Dwight Macdonald, *On Movies* (Englewood Cliffs, N.J.: Prentice-Hall, 1969), 160–61.

51. Langston Hughes, "Jokes Negroes Tell on Themselves," *Negro Digest*, 9 (June 1951), 25.

them by outsiders has become one of the most effective ethnic infusions into national humor, particularly by Afro-Americans and Jews. Minority laughter affords insights into the constant and often undignified struggle of upwardly striving Americans to achieve positive definition and respectable status.

Humor and Gender Roles: The "Funny" Feminism of the Post-World War II Suburbs

NANCY WALKER

By now it is generally accepted that the women's movement of the 1960s did not come into being overnight. The publication of *The Feminine Mystique* in 1963 provides a convenient watershed event, but Betty Friedan's book documents the fact that women's discontent with their narrowly prescribed roles had been brewing for some time, and a variety of studies has provided evidence that all was far from bucolic in the postwar suburbs to which middle-class women were consigned by societal expectations.[1] Although many women did not participate in the "back-to-the-kitchen" movement of the late 1940s and early 1950s, the prevailing ethic stressed woman's fulfillment as wife and mother. Resis-

---

1. See, among others, Molly Haskell, *From Reverence to Rape: The Treatment of Women in the Movies* (Baltimore: Penguin, 1974); Elizabeth Janeway, *Man's World, Woman's Place* (New York: Delta, 1971); Douglas T. Miller and Marion Nowak, *The Fifties: The Way We Really Were* (Garden City, N.Y.: Doubleday, 1977); Janice Radway, "The Utopian Impulse in Popular Literature; Gothic Romances and 'Feminist' Protest," *American Quarterly*, 33 (1981), 140–62.

118

tance to this ethic found some overt expression in magazine articles,[2] but emerged more subtly in the popular art forms of the period, including film, fiction, and humor—particularly the humor created by popular women writers.

One study of the popular arts of the period is Brandon French's *On the Verge of Revolt* (1978), an analysis of the films of the 1950s. French points out that while the films of the World War II period reflected women's increased participation in the work force, those of the 1950s reinforced the image of woman as the guardian of the domestic comfort and tranquility that Americans sought after the horrors of international conflict. Yet French stresses that an underlying theme of these films is women's uneasiness with this image:

> On the surface, fifties films promoted women's domesticity and inequal- ity and sought easy, optimistic conclusions to any problems their fiction treated. But a significant number of movies simultaneously reflected, unconsciously or otherwise, the malaise of domesticity and the untena- bly narrow boundaries of the female role. By providing a double text, which contradicted itself without acknowledging any contradiction— that is, by imitating the culture's schizoid "double-think"—they docu- mented the practical, sexual, and emotional transition women were undergoing beneath the threshold of the contemporary audience's con- scious awareness.[3]

Another form of popular art that provides a contradictory "double text" for the postwar period is the domestic humor of American women. In popular humorous prose and light verse of the late 1940s and 1950s, writers such as Phyllis McGinley, Jean Kerr, Margaret Halsey, Betty MacDonald, and Shirley Jackson made comic material of

---

2. A fairly typical example is an article by Ann Leighton in a 1948 issue of *Harper's*, which begins:

> Kitchens, like wars, are planned around past crises, and men—never women— plan both. That men should plan wars, since they must be the first to go into them, is fair enough. Why they should also plan kitchens when they have no intention of entering them is not so clear. . . . Joy in a kitchen these days is as confined as the "matron" who cooks.

See "Back to *What* Kitchen?" *Harper's*, 196 (April 1948), 356.

3. Brandon French, *On the Verge of Revolt* (New York: Frederick Ungar, 1978), xxi.

ordinary domestic life. These writers treated the subject of women as wives and mothers in a lighthearted way that conveyed an acceptance of the domestic role—even, as in the case of McGinley, celebrated its joys and mishaps. The exploits of children, pets, husbands; the chores of the domestic routine; interactions with neighbors and community groups— all are elevated by humorous treatment to a level of ideality that suggests a blissful, if not precisely peaceful, accommodation to the domestic role. Yet it would be wrong to take this image as a faithful depiction of the reality of women's lives. Below the surface of the humor are significant signs of restlessness and unease.

An immediate problem, of course, is the extent to which these writers could have hoped to present "reality." There seems to be a paradox, if not a duplicity, in accepting women such as McGinley, Jackson, and Kerr as representative of typical American housewives of the postwar period: their successful careers as writers make them by definition atypical. It is impossible to know how many readers of McGinley's light verse in *Good Housekeeping* realized that a woman who wrote regularly for a mass-circulation magazine was intricately involved in a world beyond the supermarket and the PTA, and was therefore not affected to the same extent as they by isolation and unfulfilled dreams; but Friedan, in *The Feminine Mystique*, is acutely aware of the paradox. Calling these humorists the "Housewife Writers," Friedan chides them for denying, in their *personae* as housewives, the "lives they lead, not as housewives, but as individuals." Even more important, Friedan says, is the way in which they mislead "real" housewives:

> "Laugh," the Housewife Writers tell the real housewife, "if you are feeling desperate, empty, bored, trapped in the bed-making, chauffering [sic] and dishwashing details. Isn't it funny? We're all in the same trap." Do real housewives then dissipate in laughter their dreams and their sense of desperation? Do they think their frustrated abilities and their limited lives are a joke? Shirley Jackson makes the beds, loves and laughs at her son—and writes another book. Jean Kerr's plays are produced on Broadway. The joke is not on *them*.[4]

Though Friedan is correct in pointing out that the "Housewife Writers" could more easily afford to laugh than could their more restricted readers, she overlooks the fact that many of these writers struggled in

4. Betty Friedan, *The Feminine Mystique* (New York: Norton, 1963), 57.

both life and print with the tensions of career and home in ways that would have seemed quite familiar to many of their readers. Rather than telling the reader that her problems were not significant, these writers acknowledged them in both overt and covert ways in their humorous works. Perhaps the most succinct example of such acknowledgement in women's humor of the period occurs in Shirley Jackson's *Life Among the Savages* (1953). Entering the hospital for the birth of her third child, Jackson attempts to answer the receptionist's questions:

> "Age?" she asked. "Sex? Occupation?"
> "Writer," I said.
> "Housewife," she said.
> "Writer," I said.
> "I'll just put down housewife," she said.

At the end of the increasingly inane interrogation, the receptionist responds to Jackson's frustration by saying, "well, *really*, . . . You're *only* having a baby."[5] This single conversation includes challenges to the significance of both Jackson's career and her motherhood; the receptionist represents a world unwilling to accept the validity of woman's experience in either realm.

Just as women's experience has been frequently considered peripheral—even, often, by women themselves—so women's humor has seldom been studied for its underlying satiric intent. Scholars have acknowledged the sly, witty social satire of authors such as Jane Austen and Emily Dickinson, but the persistent distinction between "elite" and "popular" literature has precluded much study of social commentary in the work of writers whose apparent primary intention has been to amuse a mass audience of readers. In contrast to most of traditional (male) American humor, in which the central *persona* or narrator flaunts the standards of society—whether with ironic effect, like Huck Finn, or in fantasy, like the husband in Thurber's "The Unicorn in the Garden"—American women's humor commonly deals with the central (female) figure's attempt to meet or adhere to such standards. Whereas the male humorous figure, from Rip Van Winkle onward, seeks escape from the moral domination of women, the female figure in women's

---

5. Shirley Jackson, *Life Among the Savages* (New York: Farrar, Straus and Young, 1953), 67–68. Subsequent references will appear in the text.

humor struggles vainly to live up to expectations for her behavior emanating from a culture dominated by men. Alfred Habegger, in *Gender, Fantasy, and Realism in American Literature* (1982), puts the matter plainly:

> The prevailing view of American humor is that it developed out of a kind of border warfare between two cultures, vernacular and refined. I am proposing an additional dialectic—between male and female. The social basis of American humor may have been the staggering difference in our ideal gender roles.[6]

The target or object in women's domestic humor of midcentury is usually the speaker (and, by autobiographical implication, the author) herself. The agent causing her sense of inferiority is suggested rather than named; the humor is directed inward at the self, not outward at a specific social evil. However, a sensitive reading of these works makes it clear that there are specific causes for these women's feelings of inferiority and uneasiness, located in social norms and attitudes that decreed woman's separate sphere. Even the editors of a 1934 anthology of women's humor speak in a tone of resignation about the origins of the humor they have collected: " . . . the angle of vision from which women see a lack of balance, wrong proportions, disharmonies, and incongruities in life is a thing of their world as it must be—a world always a little apart."[7] Because such humor deals with the day-to-day realities of women's lives rather than with large targets such as political corruption or human hypocrisy, it engages the reader at a more personal level and produces a response that is initially more emotional than intellectual.

The response to domestic humor may be said to occur in three stages: *recognition, sympathy,* and *assent.* Because the situations depicted in these works are familiar ones to most female readers, the reader first recognizes her own experience in the writer's account, however exaggerated or otherwise distorted for the purposes of humor. When, for

6. Alfred Habegger, *Gender, Fantasy, and Realism in American Literature* (New York: Columbia Univ. Press, 1982), 125.

7. Martha Bensley Bruère and Mary Ritter Beard, *Laughing Their Way: Women's Humor in America* (New York: Macmillan, 1934), viii. As an indication of the scant attention traditionally paid to women's humor, this anthology is the most recent to have as its specific purpose making available work by women rarely included in anthologies of humor.

example, Betty MacDonald bemoans her inability to accomplish more than cooking three meals a day, or Margaret Halsey describes the top of her husband's dresser as looking like "a plate of scrambled eggs," the reader sees some aspect of her own experience reflected in the statement. Next, the humor itself invites sympathy: the writer's ability to make apparent fun of the situation engages the reader's respect and participation; humor becomes a strategy for coping with frustration, and the reader feels a bond with the writer who can simultaneously delineate and rise above a familiar, uncomfortable situation. Finally, and most importantly, the reader is subtly invited to agree with the writer about the source of the discomfort—to assent to the proposition that someone or something is at fault in a culture that isolates and trivializes women's experience. There is little way of knowing how actual readers of women's humor during the postwar period responded to either its overt or covert messages. It is safe to assume, however, that the primary readers were women rather than men—women who recognized the shape of their own daily lives in these accounts of domestic chaos and triviality. The apparent acceptance of such lives that is conveyed by the ability to laugh at their confusions lies thinly over a more meaningful subtext of protest. The necessity of the superficial geniality and the self-deprecation of such humor is illuminated by Martin Grotjahn in *Beyond Laughter*, written during this period:

> The woman of today is supposed to be warm, understanding, charming, attractive, passive, and accepting. She may show a sense of humor in her later years as a sign of maternal maturity; but she had better not show her wit too obviously if she is young and intelligent, for she will scare the contemporary male, who is easily frightened in his masculinity. She is permitted to have a sense of humor because it is an indication of her kindliness. Wit is decidedly not a sign of gentle love, but of undisguised hostility.[8]

The hostility in women's domestic humor is therefore muted, but it is undeniably present.

When we read women's humor of this era for both its explicit and implicit messages about women's role in society, we begin to see clearly the origins of some of the major themes of the women's movement of the 1960s. Despite their overt attempt to entertain the reader, women

8. Martin Grotjahn, *Beyond Laughter* (New York: McGraw-Hill, 1957), 52.

who wrote humor during this period made use of the various techniques of humor, including stereotype, hyperbole, deflation, and wit, to explore the problems of societal role definition. Underlying the cheerful surface of such popular works as MacDonald's *The Egg and I*, Kerr's *Please Don't Eat the Daisies*, and much of McGinley's verse is a contradictory current of uneasiness with the status quo—the isolation, the unrealistic expectations of women's lives, and male remoteness and domination.

The degree of the protest varies widely among these writers. MacDonald, in *The Egg and I*, openly deplores her situation as the wife of a would-be chicken rancher; at the other extreme is McGinley, whose *A Short Walk from the Station* is announced as a defense of the suburban housewife's way of life. Yet the theme of isolation—even in what McGinley cheerfully describes as the "village of women"—the stereotypical image of the submissive woman who seems content and accomplished in her role, and an attitude toward men that combines awe and condescension are common to all the major female writers of humor from 1945 to 1960.

A discussion of isolation as a theme in the subtext of women's humor in the postwar period necessarily begins with Betty MacDonald's 1945 bestseller, *The Egg and I*. Not only was MacDonald one of the most accomplished and popular humorists of the era—*The Egg and I* also reveals the force of the social conditioning that caused women to be isolated not merely geographically, but also from any sense of real achievement. MacDonald's first comic novel thus prefigures the themes and techniques of that genre.[9] The narrator (a thin mask for the author herself), following her mother's advice that "it is a wife's bounden duty to see that her husband is happy in his work," accompanies her chicken-rancher husband to "the Pacific Coast in the most untamed corner of

9. James D. Hart, in *The Popular Book* (Berkeley: Univ. of California Press, 1950), 267–68, attributes the overwhelming success of *The Egg and I* (more than a million copies were sold in the first two years) to a wave of late depression nostalgia for the rural life coupled with the book's reassuring message that "a return to nature could be even more irksome than an escape from it." This point is analogous to my contention that reading about the domestic trials of other women could make one's own complaints legitimate.

the United States, with a ten-gallon keg of good whiskey, . . . and hundreds and hundreds of most uninteresting chickens."[10] The geographical remoteness of MacDonald's life is both a reminder of such nineteenth-century works as Caroline Kirkland's *A New Home*[11] and a precursor of the suburban sterility described by the writers of the 1950s. An example of the discomfort of MacDonald's isolation is "knowing that if I forgot to order matches I would darn well have to learn to rub two sticks together or walk four miles on the loneliest road in the world to a neighbor." She struggles to be self-sufficient, but finds that

> after nine months spent mostly in the company of the mountains, trees, the rain, Stove and the chickens, I would have swooned with anticipation at the prospect of a visit. . . . And if the clawing hands of civilization could only have run a few telephone and light wires in there they could have had my self-sufficient right arm to chop up for insulators [91–92].

The isolation MacDonald describes is not only physical; more important is the emotional distance she feels from her husband, who has chosen this environment and who seems content with it. "He never seemed to be lonely, he enjoyed the work, he didn't make stupid blunders and then, of course, he wasn't pregnant" [93]. The understatement of "he wasn't pregnant" both amuses us and reminds us of the separate realities of men's and women's lives. *The Egg and I* describes a classic pattern: the husband who enjoys the challenge of his work while the wife is left to cope with the routine tasks of household and children.

This contrast between husband and wife is at once a major source of the humor—in Habbeger's terms, the "staggering difference in . . . gender roles"—and an index of the female narrator's dissatisfaction with her position. The humor is often self-deprecatory, as when MacDonald describes the narrator's inability to take an egg from under a hen—a task her husband handles with ease—without becoming "a bundle of chittering hysteria with the hens in complete command." Self-deprecation is a major subversive device of the domestic humor of the 1940s and 1950s. By denigrating her own ability to live up to societal

10. Betty MacDonald, *The Egg and I* (Philadelphia: Lippincott, 1945), 11–12. Subsequent references will appear in the text.
11. Caroline Kirkland, *A New Home—Who'll Follow? Glimpses of Western Life*, ed. William S. Osborne (1839; rpt. New Haven: College and University Press, 1965).

standards of domestic excellence, she appears to take the blame for her failure, and thus to accede to those standards; but the underlying message is that the standards—and those who seek to enforce them— are at fault. In the case of MacDonald's narrator, the agency of societal values has been transferred from her mother to her husband. In one passage in *The Egg and I* she describes the complete syndrome of the isolated wife. She begins with her excitement at her husband's return from town on Saturday afternoon, signaling the end of her lonely day. "How we reveled in those Saturday nights, smoking, eating, reading aloud and talking; unless, perhaps, as sometimes happened, I had forgotten to order kerosene." There follows the narrator's funny but frantic scramble to consolidate kerosene in one lamp and to coax light from the stubborn Stove (which is personified throughout to comic effect), but the scene ends on a sour note, thinly coated with wit:

> Bob was never one to scold, but he showed his disappointment in me by leaving the table still chewing his last bite and thrusting himself into bed, to dream, no doubt, of the good old days of wife beating [78].

The ultimate isolation is the silent disapproval, the mute renunciation of her efforts; and the hyperbole of "wife beating" at the end almost loses its comic force in the poignancy of the context.

In addition to the theme of isolation, *The Egg and I* also addresses the concept of woman's "proper role," both the subordination of female to male in the marital relationship and the gulf between the ideal of the perfect housewife and the frustrating reality of the individual woman's experience.[12] Surrounded by models of competence that she tries—and fails—to emulate, MacDonald's narrator is constantly aware that her being is defined by forces outside herself. The most immediate of these forces is her husband, whose exaggerated demands on her time and talents are treated with ironic humor. Early in their marriage, she realizes the limits of the role she is to play:

---

12. This theme later became the source of much of the humor in television situation comedy, notably in "I Love Lucy." Though the use of female incompetence as a staple of popular comedy has long made feminists uncomfortable, the motives for using it may vary widely. Whereas in situation comedies—until recently written and produced almost exclusively by men—the woman who cannot cope is a stock slapstick character, in women's humorous fiction, such as *The Egg and I*, the depiction embodies a rejection of rigid standards of performance.

"Who, me?" I asked when we were moving and Bob pointed casually to a large chest of drawers and said, "Carry that into the bedroom." "Who else?" he snapped and my lower lip began to tremble because I knew now that I was just a wife [50].

Yet instead of making the husband the object of the satire, MacDonald has her narrator respond to the realization that she is "just a wife" by attempting to become the perfect wife: "somewhere between a Grant Wood painting, an Old Dutch Cleanser advertisement and Mrs. Lincoln's cookbook" [71], but throughout *The Egg and I* MacDonald records the failure to live up to these ideals. The conditions of farm life are more primitive and rigorous than those of suburban existence, but in neither setting is there enough time to accomplish what seems required. Although Friedan stresses that housework expands to fill the time available for it, life on the farm, without suburban labor-saving devices, is truly demanding. Even so, MacDonald's narrator characteristically blames herself for never having enough time. "Obviously," she says, "something was wrong with my planning, for it took me sixteen hours a day to keep the stove going and three meals cooked." She continues:

I leaped out of bed at 4 a.m., took two sips of coffee and it was eleven and time for lunch. I washed the lunch dishes and pulled a dead leaf off my kitchen geranium and it was five o'clock and time for dinner [68].

Though faced with tasks that would have given any pioneer woman pause, she locates the problem in her own inability to conform to the ideal of the "perfect wife."

The combination of isolation and frustrated ambition leads to the most telling evidence of imminent rebellion in postwar domestic humor: resentment against men—typically husbands—who are not subject to the same restrictions. In *The Egg and I* this resentment is expressed more openly than it is in the humor of the 1950s, but it takes the same form: men are at once heroic and pitiable, capable of great feats and yet oddly childlike. The female narrator's distance from the actual lives of men—the rigid codifying of men's and women's separate responsibilities—causes her to regard her husband as an occasional visitor in her world: sometimes helpful, often merely annoying. Though Bob, the husband in *The Egg and I*, is not the absent and often nameless commuting businessman of suburban humor, his attitudes about "women's work" are similarly traditional in the extreme, and are exemplified by his insistence that she scrub the kitchen floor daily. "It was a badge of fine housekeeping," says the narrator with heavy irony, "a labor of love and a woman's duty to her husband" [75]. Not only does Bob think in such clichés about housework; he is also incapable of helping with it. When the narrator, for example, announces on Monday morning that she plans to do a "HUGE ENORMOUS washing," he obligingly goes to the spring for water and brings back "about four tablespoonfuls in the bottom of each bucket" [69]. The narrator's tone, here as elsewhere, is one of incredulity: Bob, in her view, becomes childishly inept when he enters her realm of household tasks.

By the end of *The Egg and I*, the serious rift between the narrator and her husband all but obscures the humor of their chicken-ranch experiences. They sit waiting for a babysitter, uneasy with their own silence, "like neighbors who suddenly find themselves in a hotel bedroom together" [285].[13] While this obvious marital tension is uncommon in domestic humor—precisely because its seriousness interferes with the light tone that such humor requires—MacDonald's acknowledgement of emotional distance, as well as her forthright complaints about the rigid role definition to which she is subject, provides more than a hint of dissatisfaction with being "just a wife." The feelings she expresses did not disappear as the postwar period continued; instead, they merely became more and more hidden beneath a humorous façade as the scene switched to the suburban version of the American Dream.

By the early 1950s, suburban existence had become an established fact of middle-class American life, and the voice of protest in women's humor became more subtle as larger numbers of women were persuaded that suburban living held the promise of the "good life." Between 1950 and 1960, the population in the suburbs surrounding America's major cities increased forty-seven percent, and in one study,

13. By the time of MacDonald's next book, *Anybody Can Do Anything* (Philadelphia: Lippincott, 1960), she is divorced from the "Bob" of *The Egg and I* and is making her way as a single woman with two children in Seattle. In this, an unfortunately neglected work by MacDonald, the latent feminist protest of *The Egg and I* becomes overt as she encounters sexist discrimination as a member of the work force.

women asked for their "principal aspiration" in moving to a suburban area responded overwhelmingly (seventy-eight percent) that they wished to improve the quality of their home lives; as one woman put it, to better fulfill the "normal family role, being a homemaker."[14] In keeping with the prevailing values of the day, Phyllis McGinley's sixth book of light verse, *A Short Walk From the Station* (1951), is ostensibly a defense of life—particularly women's lives—in Westchester County. She acknowledges that suburbia has already become a cliché for many writers:

> I have yet to read a book in which the suburban life was pictured as the good life or the commuter as a sympathetic figure. He is usually as much a stock character as the old stage Irishman: the man who "spends his life riding to and from his wife," the eternal Babbit who knows all about Buicks and nothing about Picasso, whose sanctuary is the club locker room, whose ideas spring ready-made from the illiberal newspapers. His wife plays politics at the P.T.A. and keeps up with the Joneses. Or . . . [she is] a restless baggage given to too many cocktails in the afternoon.[15]

McGinley's declared intention is to defend her world against those who see it as a "congregation of mindless housewives and amoral go-getters," particularly by detailing the accomplishments of her neighboring women: one is a novelist, one teaches ballet, another paints portraits. The unhappy women described by the suburban clichés may exist here, too, McGinley acknowledges, but she dismisses them: "Let them. Our orbits need not cross" [18–20]. At the same time, however, she describes the isolation of women's suburban life. "By day," she says, "it is a village of women. They trundle mobile baskets at the A & P, they sit under driers at the hairdressers, they sweep their porches and set out bulbs and stitch up slip-covers" [10]. The high point of the day is meeting the train from the city, a moment that is "delightfully ritualistic": "The women move over from the driver's seat, surrender the keys, and receive an absent-minded kiss." Skipping briskly through this language of submissiveness, McGinley remarks coyly, "It is the sort of picture that wakes John Marquand screaming from his sleep" [21].

14. Sheila M. Rothman, *Woman's Proper Place* (New York: Basic Books, 1978), 224–25.
15. Phyllis McGinley, *A Short Walk From the Station* (New York: Viking, 1951), 12–13. Subsequent references will appear in the text.

Yet many of the descriptions of women in *A Short Walk From the Station* depict satirically the pointlessness of women's isolated lives, and form a compelling subtext to McGinley's sturdy defense of the suburbs. In one poem after another she describes shallow, petty existences in the "village of women." In "Beauty Parlor," the women discuss operations, read movie magazines, and order sandwiches; the only decision one is confronted with is "whether to dapple/Her nails with Schoolhouse Red or Stolen Apple" [83]. In "Lending Library" a woman selects bestsellers not for their literary merit, but so that she may "join in without arrears/The literary prattle of her peers" [87]. The figure in "Hostess" is bent on keeping her guests busy with party games, lest "The scotched snake, Thought, should rear its venomed head" [98]. The most sharply satiric portrait of the isolated, unhappy woman is "Executive's Wife," which, after sketching the woman's affluent setting, ends with the lines:

> She often says she might have been a painter,
>   Or maybe writer; but she married young.
> She diets. And with Contract she delays
>   The encroaching desolation of her days [79].[16]

These sketches prove the existence of those women whose "orbits" McGinley has chosen not to cross; however content she may seem in Westchester County, her verse makes clear that she perceives women's discontent in their suburban remoteness. That McGinley herself may have experienced some isolation in the suburban setting that she overtly glorifies is strongly suggested by the tone of "The 5:32," a poem celebrating the arrival of husbands from the city. At "This hour best of all the hours I knew," she describes "a man coming toward me, smiling, the evening paper/Under his arm" [88]. It is clear that no matter how fulfilling McGinley would like to think the hours with hairdryers and slipcovers have been, only the eventual presence of men redeems the isolation of women in suburban settings.

If Phyllis McGinley reveals ambivalence about the suburbs as meaningful places for women to live, Margaret Halsey was far more convinced of their aridity. In the ironically titled *This Demi-Paradise: A Westchester Diary* (1960), Halsey uses the cover of humor to condemn

16. Perhaps significantly, the title of this poem was changed to the more general "Occupation: Housewife" in McGinley's selected poems. See *Times Three* (New York: Viking, 1961), 135.

the conformity and lack of purpose that she also treated seriously in several works of social criticism during the same period.[17] Halsey is the sort of neighbor McGinley would use as an example of the vital, engaged woman who disproves the suburban cliché; Halsey, in turn, feels remote from the women around her. At the supermarket she describes "the housewives of Suburbia . . . lined up like cows at milking time—patient, not visibly expectant, the carts with food piled in rounded pyramids suggesting udders upside down."[18] Intellectually and politically involved, she works with the PTA and the Brownies with more or less enthusiasm, but is always conscious of her difference from those around her. To the female members of the PTA program committee she is a "sort of 'clean' Vincent Van Gogh":

> Nobody entertains any serious apprehensions about my cutting off an ear; but the floors in my house are scuffed, stained and innocent of wax (they have carpets only in the center, and not always there) and I will tolerate anything on them except prostrate drunks. If that is not the sign of a mad genius, what is? [65–66].

When visited by a pollster who represents all that is standardized and unimaginative in the middle-class world, Halsey "felt that twinge of loneliness I get when I again become aware that the world is full of nothing but engineers and electronics experts—whereas I want it to be full of people who majored in English" [25]. Blandness extends even to the church she attends, a formerly "liberal" congregation now headed by a minister she calls "Dr. Aspirin," with a "low-calorie, salt-free, modern, liberal Sunday school" for her daughter. [11–13].

Halsey's stance as the remote, somewhat condescending intellectual living amidst dull mediocrity is quite different from McGinley's apparent defense of the suburban commitment to domesticity for women, and their differences place them at opposite ends of the spectrum of domestic humor. On a superficial level, McGinley endorses the majority view of women's "proper sphere": it is only in her satire that the specter

---

17. Margaret Halsey, *Some of My Best Friends Are Soldiers* (New York: Simon and Schuster, 1944); Halsey, *Color Blind: A White Woman Looks at the Negro* (New York: Simon and Schuster, 1946); Halsey, *The Folks at Home* (New York: Simon and Schuster, 1952); and Halsey, *The Pseudo-Ethic* (New York: Simon and Schuster, 1963).

18. Margaret Halsey, *This Demi-Paradise: A Westchester Diary* (New York: Simon and Schuster, 1960), 2. Subsequent references will appear in text.

of loneliness, of "desolation," emerges and the double message becomes clear.[19] Even in an apparently innocuous poem such as "P.T.A. Tea Party," McGinley describes a ritual that has become boring and meaningless. Instead of evincing an active concern for the education of their children, the women admire each others' hats and listen to listless reports. The teachers arrive apprehensively, expecting sharp questions, but find that the afternoon "droops/To smile and sip and talk of Hobby Groups" [77]. Even the eagerly awaited husbands can be disappointing. In "Country Club Sunday" McGinley describes another ritual, one which shows the very image of suburban life she has overtly rejected. In the midst of a bucolic scene, for which McGinley alters Wordsworth's line to create the initial irony—"It is a beautiful morning, calm and free"—the reality of male-female relationships emerges:

> Nothing remains of last night's Summer Formal
> Save palms and streamers and the wifely glance,
>   Directed with more watchfulness than normal,
> At listless mate who tugs his necktie loose,
> Moans, shuns the light, and gulps tomato juice [75].

Although Halsey is the more obvious satirist, she and McGinley share a basic perception that women's existence in the suburbs is arid and unfulfilling.

Further uniting the two writers, and forming a continuous thread in women's domestic humor, is their resistance to the ideal of the perfect wife and mother. The ideal is promulgated in part by the media—for example, MacDonald's Old Dutch Cleanser advertisement—and in part by the examples of other women: neighbors in *The Egg and I* and the committee women who disapprove of Halsey's scuffed floors. While Friedan blamed women's magazines for endorsing the image of the "Happy Housewife Heroine,"[20] the humorists of the postwar period concentrated their subversive attack on the women who represented perfection in the domestic role: neighbors, friends, or acquaintances

19. McGinley herself tired of the image of cozy domesticity her work so often conveyed. In a *Newsweek* interview in 1960, she said, "I'm so sick of this 'Phyllis McGinley, suburban housewife and mother of two.' . . . That's only an eighth or a tenth of my work. . . . There's a hell of a lot of straight social criticism." See "The Lady in Larchmont," *Newsweek*, 56 (26 Sept. 1960), 121.

20. Friedan, *The Feminine Mystique*.

who managed households and children with ease and equanimity are presented as more potent forces affecting women's sense of their proper function.[21] Halsey's next-door neighbor in *This Demi-Paradise* is reminiscent of MacDonald's Mrs. Hicks. She wears so tight a girdle that, "seen from the rear, she looks like a tongue depressor," and is "the kind of housekeeper who washes the mailbox and scrubs the outside of the front door" [81]. In Jean Kerr's *Please Don't Eat the Daisies* (1957), there is the woman "of unusually strong character who selected a college for her son in a single afternoon and who has always been able to plan a dinner for sixteen in five minutes."[22] These are the women against whom the domestic humorists measure themselves and find themselves wanting; they are regarded with envy and resentment because they embody the ideal of womanhood in the popular imagination.

Descriptions of the author's (or narrator's) own ineptitude in the domestic role constitute a substantial part of postwar domestic humor. It is here that the writer seeks identification with the reader, who feels reassured that one so famous as, say, Shirley Jackson occasionally makes a mess of things. Yet beneath the uproarious surface of domestic chaos—always stopping short of actual disaster or tragedy—is the suggestion that the repetition and trivialization of experience wear away at one's dignity. In *Life Among the Savages*, Shirley Jackson is openly defensive. Having detailed a morning spent washing diapers, cooking, and taking care of two small children, Jackson adds parenthetically, "and I don't care what *any*one says, that's a morning's work" [2]. The "anyone" here is one who would call her "just a housewife," as the hospital receptionist does; more frequently, the writer is comparing herself to the ideal housewife. In *The Snake Has All the Lines* (1960), Jean Kerr addresses this point hyperbolically when she cannot find anything suitable for her children's lunches:

> Another woman could make a tasty sandwich spread by mixing evaporated milk and mayonnaise with some curry powder. But I lack the dash for this kind of experimentation. For that matter I lack the curry

21. The choice of people rather than media as the target of satire depends also, of course, on their traditional potential for comic effect. We should not lose sight of the fact that Jackson, Kerr, and McGinley wrote for many of the major women's magazines during the period, and were unlikely to satirize their employers.

22. Jean Kerr, *Please Don't Eat the Daisies* (Garden City, N.Y.: Doubleday, 1957), 54.

powder, and—what is more to the point—I lack qualities of leadership. Yes, I do. I'm an unfit mother and a rotten housekeeper, as shiftless and improvident as a character out of *God's Little Acre*.[23]

Margaret Halsey, as "cookie chairman" of her daughter's Girl Scout troop, fantasizes about being unequal to the task and coming up short when the money is collected. "I could see the drumhead court-martial and the stern-faced women in field green. I could see the little back room where they left me with a revolver and a bottle of brandy" [57]. Domestic humor is filled with spilled milk, dripping faucets, measles, empty refrigerators—and with women who cannot cope with it all, whose distance from perfection leads them to the hyperbole of failure.

Nor are husbands much help. The typical husband in domestic humor is a somewhat remote figure who is involved only minimally in the day-to-day operation of the household. He is seen getting off a commuter train, puttering in the garden on weekends, and occasionally attending social functions. Relationships between husbands and wives vary widely in these works—Betty MacDonald's narrator and her husband are on the brink of divorce, while Margaret Halsey's husband is sometimes pictured as warmly supportive—but men are characteristically viewed as either distant gods or curiously inept children. The humorists adhere to clear, stereotypical distinctions between the talents of male and female, as in the following quatrain by McGinley:

A lady is smarter than a gentleman, maybe.
She can sew a fine seam, she can have a baby.
She can use her intuition instead of her brain.
But she can't fold a paper on a crowded train.[24]

On the surface, the poem is a tribute to the digital aptitude of the male of the species, coupled with an acknowledgement that the man's world is the world of travel, movement, and news. Yet on another level the message is heavily ironic: the act of folding a newspaper is clearly trivial compared to having a child or making a garment, and the male accomplishment is thus diminished. When men are viewed as having exceptional prowess, as is sometimes the case when machinery is in-

23. Jean Kerr, *The Snake Has All the Lines* (Garden City, N.Y.: Doubleday, 1960), 89.
24. McGinley, "Trial and Error," *A Short Walk From the Station*, 130.

volved, their apparent mastery is another occasion for women to exercise self-deprecation. Usually, as in the following excerpt from *Life Among the Savages*, the writer's hyperbole betrays the fact that she is writing for this effect:

> I am wholeheartedly afraid of fuses and motorcycles and floor plugs and lightning rods and electric drills and large animals and most particularly of furnaces. Laboriously, over the space of years of married life, my husband has taught me to use such hazardous appliances as a toaster and an electric coffee pot, but no one is ever going to get me to go down cellar and fool around with a furnace [148].

In "Apology for Husbands" McGinley says she is pleased that "He layeth rugs, he fixeth sockets,/ He payeth bills from both his pockets."

Yet the true tone of McGinley's "Apology"—and the dominant attitude toward men in domestic humor—is revealed in the final stanza:

> What gadget's useful as a spouse?
>   Considering that a minute,
> Confess that every proper house
>   Should have a husband in it.[25]

The concept of the husband as an object, a "gadget," is condescending in the extreme. This excerpt from Kerr's *The Snake Has All the Lines* is perhaps the most blunt of all:

> But, charming as men are, we can't sit here and pretend they're perfect. It wouldn't be good for them and it wouldn't be true. Marrying a man is like buying something you've been admiring for a long time in a shop window. You may love it when you get it home, but it doesn't always go with everything else in the house [121].

Kerr goes on to note that a man seems incapable of filling a salt shaker or remembering "a simple fact like what shirt size he takes, or what grade Gilbert is in" [122]. The husband's distance from the day-to-day operation of the household leads to his inability to be helpful or supportive in this realm. The wife must therefore take responsibility for all areas of household maintenance and child care, and her resentment toward this burden often causes her to view her husband as one more

25. McGinley, *Times Three*, 261.

child to be cared for. Even his accomplishments may be seen as those of a child. In "Volunteer Fireman," McGinley describes her husband as "A boy of forty who has skimmed the cream/From childhood's first and most enduring dream" [85].

This condescending attitude—similar, one must note, to the attitude toward women in much of male humor—seems almost certainly to be born of resentment. Isolated from much of the world and pressured to conform to ideal standards of domestic performance, the *personae* of postwar domestic humor adopt, for the purposes of humor, the stance of the cheerfully beleaguered. The overt message embodies acceptance of the role society has assigned; daily life is presented as an elaborate game with the woman as the perpetually amused loser—defeated, smiling, by a world that constantly demands more than she can handle. Yet beneath the façade of the humor is a serious challenge to societal expectations. The other half of the double text conveys severe discontent with the status quo, a discontent that emerges most clearly in the depiction of men. Men are not the enemy; the enemy, if there is one at all, is the woman who is apparently fulfilled by the domestic routine. Men are more nearly extraneous to the "real" lives of women; their experiences outside the home are so remote as to seem nonexistent, and their lives within the orbit of the home are trivial, insignificant, or mysterious. This complete separation of the lives of women and men might lead the writers to seek identity with other women, but when such closeness is effectively precluded by competition among women for societal sanction, the isolation is complete. In a telling passage in *This Demi-Paradise*, Margaret Halsey says:

> the thoughts of the housewife are long, long thoughts; and the lonely hours of cutting down bedspreads into cafe curtains or cooking up things for the freezer against company coming next week are often filled with fantasies and speculations. Some of these fantasies and speculations would cause the males of the society, could they know about them, considerable alarm in behalf of the status quo [179–80].

Although it would be far too strong to call the domestic humor of the 1950s a rallying cry for the feminist movement of the 1960s, it is safe to say that the female humorists of the period knew about—and often experienced—the sense of impotence and futility that pervaded women's lives. By treating these lives humorously, they were able to do two things. On a conscious level, they provided a safe, noncontroversial acknowledgment of the frustrations and limitations of the domestic experience for women, and thus provided readers with a safety valve for those feelings. Yet on a more important level, the humor expresses a hostility toward rigid role definition that prefigures the issues of the women's movement, and demonstrates once again that the movement was an inevitable part of a social continuum, with a broad base of support.

Despite the superficial approval that humor seems to bestow on its subject matter—in this case, the domestic lives of women in the postwar era—the principle of inversion on which humor works prompts us to consider the extent to which women's humor of this period provided an acceptable means of venting frustration for both writer and reader. Rather than, as Friedan suggests, offering merely a false panacea of laughter, women's domestic humor can be viewed as evidence of increasing hostility against social expectations. Seen in this way, the humor is subversive—even if not consciously so—and provides a text for the actual concerns of middle-class women during this period.

Richard Nixon
as a Comic Figure

STEPHEN J. WHITFIELD

In the entire span of American history, only two major party candidates have sought the presidency or vice presidency as often as five times. Both men were victorious four of those five times. One was Franklin D. Roosevelt. The other was Richard Nixon, who has been the most inescapable American politician of the era after the Second World War, virtually a serial character. If a voter had been forty-six years old or younger at the time of Nixon's resignation from office in 1974, in only one election was the opportunity to cast a ballot for or against him unavailable.

The purpose of the following remarks is not to analyze the contribution to issues and policies that Richard Nixon made as congressman, senator, vice president, and president. The agenda he advocated, the laws he helped write or sought to enforce, the actual impact he made upon the body politic are not discussed, nor is any depreciation intended of the criticism long uttered against his campaign tactics, his foreign policy in Vietnam and elsewhere, or his sense of social justice. Nothing in this essay is to be understood as minimizing the threat civil libertarians believed was the meaning of Watergate and its cognate crimes. Instead, I wish to draw attention to only one peculiar and distinctive facet of Richard Nixon's career: his status as a comic figure.

It is doubtful whether any postwar American politician, or even any chief executive in our history, ever evoked so much mirth—much of it angry—as he. Perhaps no other figure in our two centuries of experimentation in self-government tickled so extensively and so intensely the funny bones of the electorate. To be sure, he has enjoyed at least one advantage denied to presidents prior to the era of technically sophisticated mass entertainment. Humor is now a larger industry than it was in the nineteenth century, which is a statement of quantity, not quality. Radio, television, movies, photographs, and records have vastly extended the outlets through which comedy could flourish. Moreover, beginning in the 1960s, satire could become more direct, more savage, and more explicitly cruel, without fear of censorship, stigma, or punishment. Such openness also enlarged the possibilities of humor directed specifically against public servants. Yet these factors do not in themselves account for Nixon's special place in the history of political humor.

Franklin D. Roosevelt aroused intense hostility in certain quarters, especially among the upper class. Yet much of the viciousness that he inspired, and which took ostensibly humorous form (in doggerel, for example), could never surface on grounds of taste, and was expressed in whispering campaigns, in the conversation of *ressentiment* in parlors and cabanas. The satiric attacks on Lyndon B. Johnson, by contrast, were open, unabashed, often sadistic and scatalogical—and expressed with utter impunity. Performances of Barbara Garson's *MacBird*, with its insinuation that Johnson had conspired to assassinate his predecessor, were uninterrupted. In such a vitriolic atmosphere, with the shrapnel of satirists flying everywhere, restrictions on what constituted freedom of expression in humor or in dissent could no longer be imposed.

Nixon managed to stir at least as much animosity as Roosevelt and Johnson; and it is my argument that he provoked even more significant manifestations of satire and parody, jibes and jokes. Here a brief comparison can be made with Nixon's successor, who could never quite evade Johnson's description of him as unable to walk and chew gum simultaneously, or dodge Chevy Chase's buffoonery on *Saturday Night Live*. Yet unlike Roosevelt, Johnson, or Nixon, Gerald Ford was rarely perceived as threatening (indeed Vice President Rockefeller was located in one *Village Voice* headline as "only a banana peel away" from inheriting the presidency) and his national career was far too brief to challenge Nixon's preeminence as a comic figure. Indeed Nixon's own career was strangely entwined with the attacks of a political cartoonist and a satirist, in a way that no previous president's ever was.

The cartoonist who dogged him so tenaciously was, of course, Herbert Block. In 1948, two years after joining the *Washington Post*, Herblock drew Nixon for the first time, showing him with two other congressmen in Puritan costume, burning the Statue of Liberty as though she were a witch. By the 1952 campaign, Herblock was associating Nixon with Senator Joseph McCarthy, whom the cartoonist made eponymous by coining the term "McCarthyism." Herblock's ascription of guilt by association was so indignant that publisher Philip Graham refused to print the cartoons, using only reprints of Herblock's earlier work (though his material was syndicated in other newspapers throughout the campaign). Graham soon acknowledged, however, that Herblock was "the most gifted political cartoonist of our times," which meant restoration to the publisher's favor. During the 1954 campaign perhaps Herblock's most famous—or notorious—cartoon appeared, showing Nixon making a campaign stop by emerging from a sewer. The vice president himself cancelled his subscription to the *Post*, primarily— he later claimed—to spare the sensibilities of his daughters, who "were reaching an impressionable age."[1]

"In all of Nixon's career," the chief chronicler of the *Washington Post* has observed, "he probably never had a more implacable or more effective foe"; and indeed countless citizens probably formed their most lasting impression upon first looking into Herblock's Nixon, the dark jowls serving as the very image of the sinister. "I can't think of Nixon without thinking of Herblock," Ralph Nader once admitted; and Nixon himself, once asked about his newspaper-reading habits, confided that he "wouldn't start the morning by looking at Herblock," as though unconsciously echoing Boss Tweed's objections to "them damn pic-

1. Chalmers M. Roberts, *The Washington Post: The First 100 Years* (Boston: Houghton Mifflin, 1977), 275, 303, 326, 340; Herbert Block, *Herblock's Here and Now* (New York: Simon and Schuster, 1955), 45; Theodore H. White, *The Making of the President 1960* (New York: Atheneum, 1961), 266; Herbert G. Klein, *Making It Perfectly Clear* (Garden City, N.Y.: Doubleday, 1980), 240, 385; Richard M. Nixon, *RN: The Memoirs of Richard Nixon* (New York: Grosset and Dunlap, 1978), 163.

tures" by Thomas Nast. Like Herblock's depiction of McCarthy, like the monstrous figure of the atomic bomb that the cartoonist created, his Nixon always seemed in need of a shave. It is therefore possible to wonder if, in overcompensation, Nixon's appearance in the first debate in 1960 suffered due to his "Lazy Shave" powder streaked with perspiration, in contrast to Kennedy's grace under televised pressure. In any event, immediately after Nixon's electoral victory of 1968, Herblock did a cartoon showing his own office, with a barber's pole and shaving mug embossed with Presidential seal. A sign was also hung: "This Shop Gives to Every New President of the United States a Free Shave—H. Block, Proprietor."[2]

The proprietor believed that the president was entitled to only one, however. During the 1970 campaign, Nixon was shown giving directions to his vice president, who was about to descend into a sewer. (Spiro Agnew in fact made a speech denouncing Herblock as a "master of sick invective.") Nixon himself was less often depicted as a grimy dead-end kid, but increasingly as the incarnation—epaulettes and all—of the imperial presidency. Such portrayals of Nixon were at the center of an *oeuvre* that Stephen Becker, in his *Comic Art in America*, considered "the best . . . political cartoons that the country has ever seen."[3]

Nixon never did manage to elude the persistent question that was earnestly asked of him: "Would you buy a used car from this man?" Its source is obscure, but it has often been attributed to Mort Sahl, who sprinkled paprika on the timorous tradition of political satire he had inherited in the 1950s. The line itself became so celebrated that variations on it seemed effortless, as in Dick Gregory's description of the other major candidates of 1968: Hubert Humphrey looked like the sort of man who would actually buy a used car from Nixon, Wallace like the sort of man who was about to steal it. By 1968 Sahl himself had tired of humor; and as political life seemed to become more phantasmagoric than ever, he could no longer summon his formidable resources of wit. The presidencies of Johnson and Nixon struck him as too gruesome for

2. Roberts, *Washington Post*, 399–400; Nixon quoted in Stefan Kanfer, "Editorial Cartoons: Capturing the Essence," *Time*, 105 (3 Feb. 1975), 63; Herbert Block, *Herblock's State of the Union* (New York: Grossman, 1974), 98.

3. Block, *State of the Union*, 104; Agnew quoted in Roberts, *Washington Post*, 412; Stephen Becker, *Comic Art in America* (New York: Simon and Schuster, 1959), 334.

humor. While Nixon was president, Sahl commented, "it only hurt when *he* laughed" (emphasis added).[4]

Sahl was undoubtedly alluding to the Dubious Achievement Awards, which *Esquire* Magazine presented annually beginning in 1961. These photos and captions and squibs were largely the creation of staffer David Newman (later the co-scenarist of *Bonnie and Clyde* [1967] and *Superman* [1978]) and art director Robert Benton (the other author of *Bonnie and Clyde*, as well as the future director of *Kramer v. Kramer* [1980]). In the subsequent two dozen years of the Dubious Achievement Awards, the most popular target for *Esquire*'s satirists has been Nixon, about whom readers are usually asked to wonder: "Why Is This Man Laughing?" In the total number of appearances in this annual feature, only Elizabeth Taylor has come close—and she of course had to share billing with her husbands and reputed lovers.[5]

Yet all those photographs of Nixon's face creased in grins and guffaws cannot disguise a paradox in his status as a comic figure. It is widely conceded that Nixon himself does not overflow with wit, and no etymologists have claimed that the phrase *joie de vivre* was invented to describe his personality. The number of jokes about him vastly outstrips the number attributed to him. Unlike Calvin Coolidge, for example, Nixon at least tried to exude an air of joviality; and, perhaps before the carapace of statesmanship fully enveloped him, he was funnier. In the early years of their marriage, Pat Nixon has recalled,

> none of us had much money . . . so we would just meet at someone's house after skating and have food . . . and then we would sit around and tell stories and laugh. Dick was always the highlight of the party because he has a wonderful sense of humor. He would keep everybody in stitches. Sometimes we would even act out parts. I will never forget one night when we did "Beauty and the Beast." Dick was the Beast, and one of the other men dressed up like Beauty. This sounds rather silly to be telling it now, but in those days we were all very young. . . . It was good, clean fun, and we had loads of laughs.[6]

4. Joseph Boskin, *Humor and Social Change in Twentieth-Century America* (Boston: Boston Public Library, 1979), 96; Mort Sahl, *Heartland* (New York: Harcourt Brace Jovanovich, 1976), 99–100, 143.

5. Phillip Moffitt, "Twenty-one Dubious Years," *Esquire*, 97 (Jan. 1982), 7.

6. Patricia R. Nixon quoted in Joe McGinniss, *The Selling of the President 1968* (New York: Trident, 1969), 7.

Here the public has had to take Mrs. Nixon's word for it; few others have been privileged to discern her husband's antic disposition. Kennedy's flashing wit erupted so naturally, his perspective on life was so tinged with detached irony, that Bill Adler could bottle it and market it in a post-assassination anthology, *The Kennedy Wit* (1964). Its bestselling success made such volumes *de rigueur* thereafter. In the last couple of decades in particular, politicians have been expected to amuse even if they could not inspire, leading Adler to claim that even Nixon's career revealed "a delightful sense of humor, a sharp wit and a unique ability to bring laughter to audiences and friends." Yet when Adler felt obliged to edit *The Wit and Humor of Richard Nixon* (1969), its thinness was not even measurably helped by the inclusion of Nixon's acceptance of the 1968 GOP nomination—a speech not memorable for its abundant one-liners.[7] As though in compensation, Garry Wills's insightful and underrated study of *The Kennedy Imprisonment* (1982) is as glum and remorseless as his earlier *Nixon Agonistes* (1970) is packed with sardonic thrusts. In the later work, Wills recounts an incident that almost sank Nixon's candidacy in 1960. Asked at a press conference to list particular contributions the vice president had made to the administration, Eisenhower begged for a week to think of something. Nixon attempted to repair the damage by suggesting that the president was "probably" being "facetious," to which Wills jibed: "Quite a card, that Ike." (The scholar of Hebrew might add that the biblical root of "Ike"—Isaac—means "he shall laugh.") Yet generally the comic spirit has seemed so inaccessible to Nixon that Hunter S. Thompson, the *enfant sauvage* of political journalism, could not "imagine him laughing at anything except maybe a paraplegic who wanted to vote Democratic but couldn't quite reach the lever on the voting machine."[8] Asking "Sock it to me?" in a celebrated segment of *Laugh-In* in 1968 was therefore hailed as an epiphany, a refreshing revelation that Nixon could make fun of himself.

Here the impact he exerted on the nation's stockpile of humor can best be understood by distinguishing Nixon from two of his predeces-

---

7. Bill Adler, *The Wit and Humor of Richard Nixon* (New York: Popular Library, 1969), 7, 109–28.

8. Garry Wills, *Nixon Agonistes: The Crisis of the Self-Made Man* (Boston: Houghton Mifflin, 1970), 123–24; Hunter S. Thompson, *The Great Shark Hunt: Strange Tales from a Strange Time* (New York: Summit, 1979), 185.

sors. Abraham Lincoln and Lyndon Johnson probably provoked more ribaldry than anyone before Nixon in large part because of their ungainly appearance, their gawkiness and homeliness. Both were depicted as rather fantastic creatures of regional folklore, and the backwoodsman from Illinois and the cowboy from Texas were either relished or found repellent because of their western coarseness. The careers of both were indelibly stamped with the agony of the warfare over which they presided, sometimes lending a tragic or venomous edge to the humor they invoked. Lincoln of course was not only an avid consumer of jokes, but an effective joke teller as well; and perhaps of no other president could an exhaustive biography devote an entire chapter to limning the comic spirit Lincoln embodied, as Carl Sandburg did in *Abraham Lincoln: The War Years* (1939). Lincoln's lanky frame and striking features were the delight of caricaturists. Yet it is too easily forgotten, not only in the bitter wake of the Vietnam War but also because of Johnson's oleaginous piety on television, how scatalogically funny he could be out of camera range. (Some examples are recorded in David Halberstam's *The Best and the Brightest* [1972]). His features seemed so easy to caricature, while his policy in Indochina provoked such unprecedented outrage and appeared cloaked in such deviousness, that in 1968 Jules Feiffer could speak for his fellow cartoonists: "These are the best days since Boss Tweed."[9]

Such exhilaration was somewhat premature, however; the best was yet to come. Yet Nixon himself at first glance might have seemed an implausible candidate for ridicule. Unlike Lincoln or Johnson, he was not associated with regional folklore or humor. The way a Johnson or a Jimmy Carter talked struck many Americans as amusing; and even Kennedy's Boston accent, as Vaughn Meader demonstrated in his album, *The First Family* (1962), could be made risible. Yet Nixon did not betray any regional peculiarities; and a persona so bereft of local color pungency made him the supreme challenge for impressionist David Frye. "It took me a long time to get Nixon," he once remarked, "but it took the *country* a long time to get Nixon." Frye's own acts of impersonation have generally begun with the voice. This was especially difficult with Nixon, who "has a radio announcer's evenness of speech, very well modulated, and you can't pick out any highs and lows. If I

9. Jules Feiffer, Introd., to *LBJ Lampooned: Cartoon Criticism of Lyndon B. Johnson*, eds. Sig Rosenblum and Charles Antin (New York: Cobble Hill Press, 1968), 10.

hadn't had to do him, I wouldn't have tried." The voice level Frye reached turned out to be the same as the one he used for Gregory Peck and Martin Luther King, requiring Frye to concoct other characteristics to make Nixon distinctive—not only recognizable but also devilishly funny.[10]

Nixon defied lampooning by his very blandness. It might not have been easy to mock a politician who struck many observers as without style or soul, his forced geniality camouflaging a suspected emptiness within, the eagerness of the "chronic campaigner" coinciding with an icy ambition. Consider, for instance, the following descriptive passages:

> [Nixon seems] the kind of kid who always carried a bookbag. Who was 42 years old the day he was born. . . . Other kids got footballs for Christmas, Nixon got a briefcase and he loved it. He'd always have his homework done and he'd never let you copy. . . . He looks like somebody hung him in a closet overnight and he jumps out in the morning with his suit all bunched up and starts running around saying, "I want to be President."

And here is a second opinion:

> Nixon used to look, on clasping his hands in front of him, like a church usher (of the variety who would twist a boy's ear after removing him from church).[11]

The first of these passages is an observation by Roger Ailes, who helped conceive and execute the Nixon television campaign of 1968. The second bastinado—barely distinguishable in tone or perspective— is from an opponent, Norman Mailer, who once commented on the idiom of the astronauts that they appeared resolved "not under any circumstances [to] say anything more interesting than Richard Nixon would say in the same situation."[12] Nixon seemed to exude a priggishness and stiffness that invited deflation. His foes regarded his utterances as a touchstone of tediousness, so devoid of the sparkle of personality

10. Roy Bongartz, "Deformità perfetta of Richard Nixon, Lyndon Johnson and Other Heroes," *Esquire*, 75 (Feb. 1971), 74.

11. Roger Ailes quoted in McGinness, *Selling of the President*, 103, 108; Norman Mailer, *Miami and the Siege of Chicago* (New York: Signet, 1968), 44.

12. Norman Mailer, *Of a Fire on the Moon* (New York: Signet, 1971), 109.

that his conversation would, in H.L. Mencken's phrase, "make a barber beg for mercy."

Such dullness, which would not have defeated Sinclair Lewis, torpedoed a play like *An Evening with Richard Nixon* (1972), which presented its subject not as a kind of Babbitt redux but as a cynical, hypocritical hustler. Perhaps sensing how banal Nixon's words actually were, dramatist Gore Vidal encased them within a setting involving Presidents Washington, Eisenhower, and Kennedy to suggest not only the declension of the Republic but also to suggest how fully Nixon's character and tactics typified contemporary political conduct. The form of *An Evening with Richard Nixon* is not entirely unlike various one-man shows that have become popular in recent years, in which the wisdom, charm, and wit of certain distinguished Americans are dramatized through extended soliloquys. Yet Vidal's play, drawn largely though not entirely from the historical record, differs from Hal Holbrook's Mark Twain, or Henry Fonda's Clarence Darrow, or James Earl Jones's Paul Robeson, or James Whitmore's Theodore Roosevelt, in that it is grounded in what Murray Chotiner would immediately have recognized as "the denigrative method." Its aim is not to inspire admiration but to arouse ridicule and disgust. By attempting to demonstrate that Nixon had hardly been unique in his shadiness, by spoofing the pieties that seemed to have marked his career, Vidal was showing the political system itself as sanctimoniously sordid and unworthy. This playwright sought no sobriquet of patriotic Gore. Yet at least the significance, if not the artistic merit or historical weight, of his work should be noted. Neither before nor after *An Evening with Richard Nixon* has a reputable dramatist sought to use a documentary approach to a presidential career for purposes of derision rather than uplift.[13]

Like Vidal, the documentary filmmaker Emile de Antonio provided no ruffles and flourishes in his exhumation of Nixon's career in *Millhouse: A White Comedy* (1971). It too tries to barbecue Nixon in his own words and actions (by depicting his clumsiness). Its release again reveals the singularity of Nixon's appeal as an object of satire, in that documentary films about presidential careers are ordinarily hagiographic and are shown at adulatory nominating conventions or preserved in presidential libraries. Here the news footage is edited to expose

13. See also Amram M. Ducovny, ed., *I Want to Make One Thing Perfectly Clear: The Illuminations of Richard Nixon* (New York: Ballantine, 1971).

Nixon in his most disturbing moments, but the effect is somewhat numbing. He turns out to be not quite as oafish or foolish as Antonio appears to believe, nor as sinister as the senatorial subject of the filmmaker's earlier documentary on the Army-McCarthy hearings, *Point of Order* (1964). The relentless fidelity of recording Nixon's slips of the tongue may even be cruel enough to elicit sympathy.

Millhouse takes for granted Nixon's unattractiveness of personality, his absence of magnetism and redeeming personal traits. This too is a noteworthy feature of the humor he has inspired, and a paradox of his career. For so successful a politician, it is remarkable how little affection he generated even among his associates and admirers. Nixon has seemed ill suited for his work; on the basis of personality alone, he could hardly have expected that the electorate would promise him a Rose Garden. For American politics has typically been a contact sport, bearing a special kinship to professional wrestling, with much grunting and screaming and heaving, but nobody really getting hurt. Its players have understood it as a game—sometimes even a con game—in which genuine hostility and unappeasable rancor are usually futile and dysfunctional, since the players will be back next time and perhaps some sides will be switched. Politics has therefore rarely attracted to its ranks those who seethe with ideological or personal hatreds, with take-no-prisoners virulence. The muckraker Lincoln Steffens, for example, was charmed by the roguish bosses whom he wished to expel from city halls. In fact he liked them better than the reformers who were his allies, but who rarely included affability in their repertoire.

Nixon has therefore been rather uncommon among American politicians, for he was a "loner" whose sensibility at worst seemed "black Irish," atrabilious. When G. Gordon Liddy came out of an early meeting impressed by his *capo's* "personal warmth,"[14] that should not be accepted as a credible portrait of the president but taken rather as proof (if any were necessary) of Liddy's own bizarre nature. For all the viciousness Franklin Roosevelt unleashed among the wealthy, he evoked far greater affection and even adulation in other precincts. Nixon never commanded such personal loyalty, however, and it may not be too daring to suspect that his lack of "personal warmth" has helped to ensure that the comic attacks on him would be unrestrained.

14. G. Gordon Liddy, *Will: The Autobiography of G. Gordon Liddy* (New York: St. Martin's Press, 1980), 125.

David Levine, who may well be one of the most talented caricaturists who has ever lived, has made it a practice not to meet his subjects out of fear of liking them ("I lose my act that way"). That worry may have been unwarranted in this particular instance, but in any event a special animus was injected into his spitting images of Nixon. Levine's lampoons of Johnson shedding crocodile tears, and then of a crocodile shedding LBJ tears, may be better known than his impressions of Nixon, but his drawings of Johnson's successor are nevertheless executed with such demonic energy that there is something exhilarating about such indignation. Like all caricaturists, Levine has built upon the exaggeration of certain features. As Roy Bongartz has pointed out, Levine's Nixon is marked by "a darkened shading of the lower face, and especially by small, hooded eyes. He comes over as especially heartless by the addition of teeth that Levine makes a bit sharper and more pointed than normal teeth."[15] The incisors make Nixon look especially maleficent (not the case with Johnson); the ski-jump nose is also disproportionate; and sometimes the eyes are not even visible. Even if one knew little about Nixon's policies, there would be something scary about Levine's drawings of him.

The most effective cartoons of Nixon, however, have been generated by presidential policies and actions. During the national boycott of grapes in support of the United Farm Workers campaign, the Department of Defense increased its purchases of nonunion grapes. Levine showed Nixon gorging himself with the fruit, next to a pig whose mouth is also stuffed with grapes. After the National Guard killed four students at Kent State and Nixon denounced "bums" who protested violently on college campuses, the cartoonist depicted him leading a firing squad, hissing the word "bums." During a major antiwar demonstration, he pointedly refused to meet with its representatives, watching a football game on television instead. Levine drew Nixon and Agnew watching it, surrounded by toy buses, while behind the television set was a huge mound of corpses and coffins.[16]

The darkness of the lower face, the thickness of the eyebrows over the piercing, threatening eyes seemed to become heightened with Watergate. Levine portrayed him as the protagonist in *The Exorcist* (1973),

15. Bongartz, "Deformità perfetta," 74, 75.
16. David Levine, *No Known Survivors: David Levine's Political Plank* (Boston: Gambit, 1970), 8, 11, 16–17.

tied to his bed, foully screaming as a figure is expelled from his mouth; the figure is a spooky mini-Nixon. He gloatingly plunges a bomb into the breast of a female figure symbolizing the republic, the sharkish grin still on his face. Dollar bills float from his eyes and mouth, as though Levine had taken the advice that "Deep Throat" gave to Bob Woodward to "follow the money." The President is shown as Marlon Brando in *The Godfather* (1972). He is shown as Captain Queeg in *The Caine Mutiny* (1951), nervously fingering the steel balls in his left hand while testifying on the witness stand to his loss of command. After the presidential resignation, Levine superimposed on the otherwise benign and open face of Nixon's successor the familiar scowl and surliness. One caricature has Nixon petulantly stamping his foot—a gesture Levine has acknowledged taking from Adolf Hitler, whom the cartoonist has depicted without exaggeration because the truly monstrous is not rendered more so through techniques of inflation.[17] That may be scant comfort to Nixon.

Levine's caricatures of many other politicians have been so lethal that his editors, principally at the *New York Review of Books*, should have been prepared to notify next of kin. Nixon made himself conspicuous within a much wider field of targets. Yet he was also fated to attract the interest of someone whose fame was exclusively based on harassing Nixon's campaigns. The merry pranks of Dick Tuck became legendary, beginning in 1950, when he positioned himself as an advance man in the senatorial campaign against Helen Gahagan Douglas. Tuck was, of course, a mole. He organized a rally at the University of California campus at Santa Barbara, picking a day and a time of maximal inconvenience to students and commandeering the largest auditorium on campus (seating capacity 4400). Forty students showed up to hear Tuck himself deliver some rambling, intentionally narcoleptic opening remarks that also raised questions about his candidate's reputation for rock-'em, sock-'em tactics against Representative Jerry Voorhis. Finally Tuck introduced the speaker by announcing that Nixon would address the topic of the International Monetary Fund.[18]

Tuck continued to devote himself to impeding Nixon campaigns—for example, by posing as a fire marshall to provide low estimates of the

17. David Levine, *The Arts of David Levine* (New York: Alfred A. Knopf, 1978), x, 196–200; Bongartz, "Deformità perfetta," 71.

18. David Felton, "The Bugging of Mack the Knife," *Rolling Stone* (11 Oct. 1973), 29.

size of rallies. (Gauging crowds is admittedly an imprecise art anyway; the Kennedy camp jokingly counted the nuns and multiplied by a hundred.) Tuck would whisper to bandleaders at Republican rallies that the candidate's favorite song was "Mack the Knife," so that Nixon's entrance would be greeted with lyrics describing the pearly teeth of a shark who's back in town. In 1962 the Republican gubernatorial candidate went into the Chinatown section of Los Angeles, where he was faced with a sign that proclaimed in English: "Welcome Nixon." Yet in Chinese ideograms the sign asked: "What about the Hughes loan?" (a reference to the loan that the multimillionaire had given Nixon's brother Donald). So formidable had Tuck's reputation for pranks become that, when a huge shipment of buttons arrived for a 1968 ethnic rally in New York urging in several languages a vote for Nixon, the nearby presence of the puckish Tuck caused Herbert Klein to order their destruction. Unable to read Greek or Chinese or Italian, the candidate's press secretary decided not to take any chances—though in this instance Tuck was quite innocent.[19]

Nixon tried to get even at the Press Club in Los Angeles by remarking that the last time he had seen Tuck, he had been wearing a Nixonette dress. Yet Nixon, feckless as ever at badinage, was topped by Tuck's repartee that his lips were forever sealed. He promised never to disclose how Nixon found out that it was indeed Tuck inside the Nixonette costume. Another form of retaliation was a kind of imitation: the employment during the Democratic primary campaigns of 1972 of Donald Segretti (the Italian word for "secrets"). Segretti's credentials had consisted of disrupting opposition campaigns in the campus politics of the University of Southern California. Segretti's 1972 fakes and forgeries included letters to newspapers imputing sexual misconduct to Hubert Humphrey and Henry Jackson. Such nasty variations on Tuck's themes resulted in a jail sentence for conspiracy and for distributing false campaign literature.[20]

Nixon's persona of stuffiness and sanctimoniousness invited ridicule; the rigidity of his public character was like a magnetic field that attracted the darts of deflation. Tuck was a symbiotic jester who virtually

19. Ibid., 30, 31; Benjamin C. Bradlee, *Conversations with Kennedy* (New York: Pocket Books, 1976), 19; William Safire, *Safire's Political Dictionary* (New York: Random House, 1978), 296.
20. Felton, "Bugging of Mack the Knife," 32; Carl Bernstein and Bob Woodward, *All the President's Men* (New York: Simon and Schuster, 1974), 126–27, 149, 152–53.

made a career out of twitting Nixon. For Abbie Hoffman, so blithe a spirit that at the conclusion of the Chicago Seven conspiracy trial he received a twenty-one-day prison sentence for laughing, teasing Nixon was a natural extension of his daily activities. When Hoffman's wife gave birth to a son they named 'america,' the happy couple sent a birth announcement to the White House, in the name of Mr. and Mrs. A. H. Hoffman. An embossed card came back: "President and Pat Nixon wish to congratulate you on the birth of your new baby." After Hoffman informed the Associated Press of the First Family's good wishes, Press Secretary Ron Ziegler denied the claim. Hoffman, whom a government psychological study concluded was an exhibitionist, then brandished the White House card in front of reporters and declared: "This is not the first time that bastard's told a lie."[21]

That reputation for prevarication was a mere prelude to the extraordinary phenomenon known as Watergate, commonly described as a "caper." The illegal entry and bugging of Democratic headquarters, the cover-up that followed, and the rest of the "White House horrors" that were revealed or intimated ensured that the politician nicknamed Tricky Dick would henceforth be known primarily for the "dirty tricks" associated with Watergate. It also meant that satire was not something that would close Saturday night but would run through the Final Days and thereafter. So farfetched were the events as they unraveled that the creativity of even the most far-out, off-the-wall comedians was dwarfed.

A couple of generations earlier, Will Rogers could modestly assert that "there is no credit in being a comedian when you have the whole government working for you."[22] Yet even he was handicapped by not having on his payroll Alexander Haig, who speculated that the eighteen-minute gap on a crucial White House tape was due to "some sinister force" (perhaps a veiled allusion to his Commander in Chief after all), or the tabulators of an "enemies list" that included Barbra Streisand and Joe Namath (whom the gridiron experts in the Nixon entourage identified as a quarterback for the New York Giants), or Billy Graham, who explained that the crimes of Watergate occured because Christian Americans had not prayed enough. It seemed too fantastic for even the most inventive satirists to have concocted. P.J. O'Rourke of

21. Abbie Hoffman, *Soon To Be a Major Motion Picture* (New York: G.P. Putnam's Son's, 1980), 222, 262.

22. Rogers quoted in "The Third Campaign," *Time*, 76 (15 Aug. 1960), 42.

the *National Lampoon* had therefore shown much foresight in having voted for Nixon in 1972, asserting without shame: "My livelihood was at stake." Art Buchwald beamed long after Watergate that "Nixon was my Camelot. Every day was something new," he reminisced. "I'd wake up in the morning, see something in the paper like the 18-minute tape gap, and write my column without even going to the office. I'd be on the tennis court by 10 o'clock. It was beautiful—it ran for a year, and you didn't have to make anything up." Mark Russell, whose reputation for satire was until 1973 largely confined to patrons of Washington's Shoreham Hotel, has recalled: "The day Richard Nixon resigned, I wept. I had to go back to writing my own material." A Feiffer cartoon from 1973 showed an urbanite plagued by anonymity and disesteem, whose life brightens only at night when, snuggled in front of his television set, he can have the waves of Watergate revelations lap over him.[23] Feiffer was not only depicting the citizenry. He was also representing the nation's satirists, for whom (in Wallace Stevens's formulation) "in the presence of extraordinary actuality, consciousness takes the place of imagination."

Yet even reality, no matter how improbable, cannot be apprehended as without form, without a framework of preconceptions and emotions already shaped by a combination of values and experience. What did Nixon in, and sent some, if not all, the president's men to jail without passing go, was not the actual break-in at the headquarters of the opposition, nor the assorted violations of civil liberties, nor policies such as the illegal and secret bombing of Cambodia. It was the enormous effort expended to lie about such deeds. Had Nixon and his aides not attempted to "cap the bottle," but instead had admitted wrongdoing, had the president himself expressed contrition for the illegal acts of the plumbers and their superiors, it is widely conceded that the public outcry might have subsided; Nixon would have remained in office. Likewise, had the tapes been destroyed so that the cover-up could not have been proven, the web of lies that the White House had spun would not have ensnared him. More fateful than the illegal acts

23. O'Rourke quoted in Franz Lidz, "Winning Through Denigration," *Johns Hopkins Magazine*, 31 (June 1980), 16; Buchwald quoted in Jim Ball, "Buchwald: 600-Word Cartoons," *Boston Phoenix*, 9 (30 Sept. 1980), 15; Russell quoted in William Gildea, "That Capitol Comic, Mark Russell!" *Town and Country*, 135 (Nov. 1981), 244, 344; Jules Feiffer, *Feiffer on Nixon: The Cartoon Presidency* (New York: Random House, 1974), n.p.

themselves, the mendacity that surrounded them—summarized in the term "Watergate"—proved to be devastating to the president's tenure in office and to the authority of his leadership in a presumably open society.

Watergate could be widely perceived—and satirized—in terms of truth decay because of the reputation for sneakiness and hypocrisy that long dogged Nixon's political life. Never at wit's end, Adlai Stevenson once observed that "Nixon is the kind of politician who would cut down a redwood tree, then mount the stump for a speech on conservation." Soon thereafter an even more partisan Democrat, Harry Truman, told Merle Miller more bluntly that "Nixon is a shifty-eyed, goddamn liar, and people know it. . . . I can't see how the son of a bitch even carried one state" in 1960, since "he doesn't know how to tell the truth. I don't think the son of a bitch knows the difference between telling the truth and lying." Nixon, who was one of the only two American politicians whom Truman genuinely and vehemently despised, had promised during the 1960 television debates with Kennedy to ban such language from the White House if he were elected.[24] Even with expletives deleted, the White House tapes of the Watergate era showed how poorly that particular promise had been kept.

A British journalist quipped that it had taken the Americans about two hundred years to get from a president who could not tell a lie to a president who could not tell the truth. A couple of years after the Bicentennial, Johnny Carson joked that "whenever anyone in the White House tells a lie, Nixon gets a royalty."[25] One need not believe that the fall of man occurred at the time of Nixon's first inaugural in January, 1969, or that candor and honesty had been universally respected in the White House until then, to acknowledge the power of the comic thrusts at the dishonesty of the Nixon administration. Indeed, the notion of Nixon honestly accepting his own responsibility and complicity seemed so incongruous that the *National Lampoon's* album, *The Missing White House Tapes* (1974), elicits laughter when the actor impersonating Nixon admits, "I *am* a crook." Even the classical logical conundrum—

24. Stevenson quoted in Leon A. Harris, ed., *The Fine Art of Political Wit* (New York: E. P. Dutton, 1966), 240; Merle Miller, *Plain Speaking: An Oral Biography of Harry S. Truman* (New York: Berkley, 1974), 135, 178, 335; Roberts, *Washington Post*, 326.

25. Carson quoted in Kenneth Tynan, *Show People: Profiles in Entertainment* (New York: Simon and Schuster, 1979), 187.

what happens if a Cretan says that all Cretans are liars?—was short-circuited when one of the president's pistoleros took the witness stand in 1973 before Senator Sam Ervin's committee. To the routine preparatory question ("Do you solemnly swear to tell the truth, the whole truth and nothing but the truth, so help you God?"), Gordon Liddy gave an answer that was not routine: "No."[26] Such implausible exchanges were the stuff of comic extravaganza.

If "satire is a lesson," Vladimir Nabokov once announced, "parody is a game." In *Our Gang* (*Starring Tricky and His Friends*), published in 1971, Philip Roth offered both. Aside from the artistically negligible *MacBird*, no other work has subjected an American president to so scalding a satiric assault. In provoking the indignation of a National Book Award-winning novelist, Nixon demonstrated his distinctive flair for galvanizing comic currents. *Our Gang* has a lunatic logic all its own, which was triggered by a San Clemente statement firmly opposing abortion in the name of "the sanctity of human life." At about the same time, while the warfare was occurring in Vietnam, Nixon was showing very casual tolerance for Lieutenant William Calley, convicted by his fellow officers of murdering civilians at My Lai. Roth seized upon such moral incongruity to make Trick E. Dixon cynical and duplicitous, and to make the supporting cast—from an alliterative vice president to the Reverend Billy Cupcake—into grotesques. In the course of the novel, Trick E. Dixon invades Denmark, considers admitting to homosexuality, is assassinated (the Boy Scouts are among the suspects), and makes a speech in Hell, where he is a candidate for the top slot against Satan himself. There is an acetylene fury to *Our Gang*, but it is not an artistically searing and fulfilling work of literature. The wildness of Roth's philippic lacks shape and weight; its humor provides few shocks of recognition. Nixon's resilience and eagerness to manipulate the electorate are effectively rendered; but, a bit like its subject, *Our Gang* is something of an elaborate wind-up mechanism, which proves to be rather affectless—and unaffecting.[27]

Its most hilarious section skewers an Agnew who rages with metronomic alliteration against the "revolutionaries" of the 1960s. Yet the most cogent criticism in the novel spins off from Nixon's rhetorical style. This is not surprising, given Roth's own verbal virtuosity. As he

26. "Watergate's Sphinx Speaks," *Time*, 115 (21 April 1980), 58.

27. Philip Roth, *Our Gang* (*Starring Tricky and His Friends*) (New York: Random House, 1971).

would write in *The Ghost Writer* (1979), an author's most crucial instrument is a distinctive voice, "something that begins at about the back of the knees and reaches well above the head." *Our Gang* is a neat trick of ventriloquism—capturing what Roth depicts as Nixon's unctuous premium on "sincerity," his entangled effort to make his views "perfectly clear," his desire to have it both ways, and above all his smirking effort to do the politically expedient thing while smoothly claiming that it is a politically unpopular (hence courageous) service to the nation. Herblock hit most of these notes himself, in a more concise parody of a Nixon speech (burlesquing Churchill), in his *State of the Union* (1974). Yet *Our Gang* can also be considered the literary equivalent—with much greater resonance but also more obvious flaws—of David Frye's impersonation of Nixon: eyes darting back and forth in nervous anticipation of possible detection, tongue pushing against cheeks and then drawing back, and jerky body language betraying both a desire to put something over and an uncertainty whether his audience will buy it.[28] That sort of tension Frye deftly captured in an album entitled *Richard Nixon: A Fantasy* (1973), in which self-control is rapidly forfeited, as Nixon turns into Humphrey Bogart as Captain Queeg, blaming Haldeman, Erlichman, and Dean for the theft of the strawberries on the ship of state.

More so than most politicians, Nixon's career encouraged speculation on the intangibles of identity itself. Showing so few regional stigmata, he has appeared especially displaced. Trying to please so many, he risked being no one himself. During the 1960 campaign, Kennedy privately predicted that Nixon would tire himself out, because he did not know who he was: and such a struggle to find himself would prove exhausting. Nixon seemed to project the fear that there was no "there" there, which in his worst critics inspired a manic loathing. Hunter Thompson labeled Nixon "a foul caricature of himself; a man with no inner convictions, with the integrity of a hyena and the style of a poison toad." Even the milder assessments and assaults have not triumphed over the enigma of Nixon's identity. Feiffer and Frye both specialized in lampooning Nixon's uncertainty that he was indeed in the White House.[29] It was as if he had to reassure himself. The pious and

28. Block, *State of the Union*, 7; Bongartz, "Deformità perfetta," 74.
29. Henry Kissinger, *Years of Upheaval* (Boston: Little, Brown, 1982), 1181–87; Thompson, *Great Shark Hunt*, 185; Feiffer, *Cartoon Presidency*, n.p.; David Frye, *I Am the President* (Electra Records, 1969).

patriotic assertiveness was meant to ward off the suspicion of phoniness, and the solemnity and sobriety became an overcompensation for a certain lack of *gravitas.*

The piety and patriotism that Nixon so unabashedly advocated did much to set his opponents to pawing the ground and snorting. His immersion in the purification rites of nationalist sentiment and sanctity annoyed liberals in particular. "Nixon's farm policy is vague," Stevenson once complained, "but he is going a long way toward solving the corn surplus by his speeches." This facet of Nixon's persona was underlined in "The Politics of Woody Allen," a Public Broadcasting System program taped in December, 1971, but never aired. Allen wrote and directed it, and played a character modeled on Henry Kissinger, a former political science major whose heroes at Harvard had been Aaron Burr and the Kaiser. This advisor recalls helping Nixon stage the Checkers speech: "We needed some symbol to wipe out any notion the public might have that wasn't 100% wholesome. . . . He wanted to have a Miss America contest going on in the background. . . . [Nixon] also thought perhaps if he were dressed in an Uncle Sam suit . . . red, white and blue . . . with the beard. . . . a rented beard. . . . Then I hit on the idea of telling America he owned a dog—a spaniel." The Woody Allen character adds that Nixon objected at first: "He thought if maybe he came out dressed like a little boy with Dwight Eisenhower holding his hand—they could perhaps do an endearing little thing but—er. . . . I persuaded him that all he really needed was to talk about Checkers."[30] The script also included more conventional jokes about Nelson Rockefeller's wealth, as well as the more typical Allen humor appropriate to a recidivist prisoner of sex. Nevertheless the treatment of Nixon showed an indulgence in satire—rather than Allen's customary farce or parody—that is again an index of Nixon's singularity.

Another ironic assault on the star-spangled themes that have attracted Nixon is Robert Coover's *The Public Burning* (1977). It was highly praised upon publication for its comic audacity and richness. Yet the jollity of the novel is so forced and willed, the flotsam of memories of mass entertainment so overwhelming, that it is hard to believe that too many readers plowed through its 661 pages with consistent attentiveness and pleasure. Coover's novel is historical in its recreation of the

30. Stevenson quoted in Harris, ed., *Political Wit,* 240; Eric Lax, *On Being Funny: Woody Allen and Comedy* (New York: Charterhouse, 1975), 201–6.

politics and popular culture of the 1940s and 1950s. Yet history is fictionalized to alter the site of the execution of Julius and Ethel Rosenberg to Times Square, where political dignitaries and mass entertainers have gathered for the patriotic carnival. Thus Brother Milton Eisenhower and "Uncle Miltie" Berle are invited to the same party. Yet by telling much of the frenetic narrative from the perspective of an intelligent, devious, and industrious Nixon, *The Public Burning* has a goy-meets-Berle incongruity and inconsistency. The long sections devoted to Nixon are by no means unsympathetic, however, since he is not a maniac like others on the anti-Communist stage. As the three-day narrative builds toward the climactic public execution, Nixon passionately embraces Ethel Rosenberg in Sing Sing. The vice president then shows up on the Times Square stage with his pants falling down, exposing a rear end on which the words "I am a scamp" have been written in lipstick. Such humiliation greatly diverts the audience. At the end of Coover's novel, following the capital punishment in the entertainment capital of the East Coast, the exuberant figure of Uncle Sam sodomizes Nixon, who thereupon confesses his love to the embodiment of patriotic fervor.[31] Such scenes are supposed to be amusing.

How could Nixon have animated such fantasies of humiliation, have stimulated such dark and degraded humor? How could a leader who could inspire such virulence also be the demiurge of so much material classified as comedy? For Freud of course the correlation between hostility and humor was no coincidence. Much of the satire that Nixon generated was too base to have been transmuted into liberating laughter, and was about as subtle as short-sheeting, but it does serve as an illustration of Freud's theory of jokes. The defeated gubernatorial candidate himself inadvertently suggested as much in his "last press conference," November 8, 1962: "And I say as I leave the press, all I can say is this: For sixteen years, ever since the Hiss case, you've had a lot of—a lot of fun—that you've had an opportunity to attack me."[32] A study of the aggravated assault inflicted on Nixon would indeed appear to be just what the doctor ordered in *Wit and Its Relation to the Unconscious*.

Yet it is doubtful that the extent of Nixon's lying, or the drabness and

---

31. Robert Coover, *The Public Burning* (New York: Bantam, 1978), 536–52, 580–81, 586, 658–61.

32. Nixon quoted in Wills, *Nixon Agonistes*, 414–15.

dourness of his personality, could add up to such intensity of antagonism, however. Watergate proved to be more than a third-rate burglary,
but it was less than subversion of the structure of the republic. Its
impact was astonishing. It came to outweigh the dramatic successes the
administration claimed in foreign affairs. It discredited the office of the
presidency so much that, in Louis Auchincloss's novel, *The House of
the Prophet* (1980), the character loosely based on Walter Lippmann is
taken to be sliding into senility because he has written a pro-Nixon
column.[33] (In a minor but representative incident reported in *Time*
magazine, the prize for most frightening costume at a 1973 Halloween
party in New York was awarded to a child wearing a Nixon mask.)
Given the pall Nixon managed to cast, it deepens the paradox to recall
how successful he was as a politician—and to wonder how so insecure a
man could fancy himself one. In 1960 Nixon lost by the thinnest
popular margin in the century to the debonair candidate of the dominant political party; and in 1972 he won the most impressive mandate in
the twentieth century to date, losing fewer states than Roosevelt did in
1936 or Johnson in 1964. Yet Nixon also seemed to remind many
liberals and intellectuals of an inept dentist, compulsively striking a raw
nerve again and again. Why?

Perhaps the most convincing explanation, though it was composed as
an answer to a rather different question, can be found in Wills's *Nixon
Agonistes*. Its argument is that Nixon has truly been the man of the
center who, far from acting from a protean flexibility and expediency,
has believed in certain axial principles of American society that are not
yet invalidated. Despite the hairpin turns in his career, Nixon has stood
for something other than tactical advantage. According to Wills, he has
remained faithful to the ideal of a competitive society, based on equality
of opportunity and nurturing the value of success bestowed on the self-
made, upwardly mobile man. In Nixon's belief in the primacy of work
and of struggle, in his assumption of the sufficiency of capitalism, he
has been—in the nineteenth-century sense—a liberal, and has adhered
to that earlier ethos without irony or detachment. Nixon has not
questioned the authenticity and desirability of that primary strain in the
American heritage, and in this respect he has been alien to the project of
modern thought which, from Nietzsche to Nozick, has attempted to

33. Louis Auchincloss, *The House of the Prophet* (Boston: Houghton Mifflin,
1980), 14–16.

formulate social values in a godless world. To those, especially liberals, whose lives have been corroded by what Lippmann called "the acids of modernity," Nixon was bound to come across as unsophisticated, priggish, hopelessly square.

His old-fashioned prissiness was too tempting for many satirists to skip, but Nixon's character reflected a solidity and rigidity, an adherence to the reality principle rather than the pleasure principle suggestive of an earlier America. The nation is now too diverse and kaleidoscopic to be personified by any one politician, but Nixon has come close to incarnating the legacy of nineteenth-century Protestantism and liberalism. "I believe in the American dream, I believe in it because I have seen it come true in my own life," Nixon avers in Coover's novel. "*Time* has said that I've had 'a Horatio Alger-like career,' but not even Horatio Alger could have dreamed up a life so American—in the best sense—as mine." *The Public Burning* has Nixon engaging in Alger fantasies, beginning with a "log-cabin starting line."[34]

This vein is mined in other works as well. Kurt Vonnegut's *Jailbird* (1979) incorporates Nixon on the periphery of the life of Walter Starbuck, the Algeresque antihero who is the narrator of the novel. Grilled by Congressman Nixon during a HUAC hearing, Starbuck innocently names someone sent to prison for perjury, and later President Nixon makes Starbuck his "special advisor on youth affairs"—about which he knows nothing. When the plumbers stash an illegal one-million-dollar campaign contribution in his obscure office and he refuses to identify them, Starbuck is sent to prison himself. *Jailbird* thus reworks the typical Alger plot, in which the hero rises after recovering a millionaire's strongbox from thieves. Such myths are mocked as well in David Frye's album, *Richard Nixon Superstar* (1972), and especially in John Seelye's parodistic *Dirty Tricks* (1974), which follows the rise of a "likely lad" named Nick Noxin. "I am guilty," Noxin admits, "guilty of abiding faith in the American system of free enterprise."[35] Yet neither work is successful. Frye's splendid gifts of mimicry outshine the rather tiresome and uninventive material with which his writers supplied him, and Seelye's contrived application of the Alger fable is well below the inspired standard he set in *The True Adventures of Huckleberry Finn*

---

34. Coover, *Public Burning*, 366, 383–84, 427.
35. Kurt Vonnegut, *Jailbird* (New York: Dell, 1979), 56, 58, 85, 95; John D. Seelye, *Dirty Tricks, or Nick Noxin's Natural Nobility* (New York: Liveright, 1973), 148.

(1970). Yet the line between Ragged Dick and Tricky Dick is one which, however sinuous, was eminently worth tracing.

Even if Garry Wills overstated the consistency of Nixon's nineteenth-century liberalism, there is no other locus to discover whatever political principles have studded his career. Since discrepancy is pivotal to comedy, the juxtaposition of the nineteenth-century ethos and its manifestation in Nixon may have instigated many of the chuckles he provoked. Wills wrote, in the very last sentence of his book, that "Nixon, by embodying that creed, by trying to bring it back to life, has at last reduced it to absurdity."[36] In calling him "the last liberal," Garry Wills was premature, since the discovery by Frank Wills—Watergate's guard of honor—did not mark a discontinuity in the American political tradition. In their various ways, Nixon's successors have accepted the nineteenth-century faith as well. Yet *Nixon Agonistes* does identify the public culture that might ignite sparks of laughter, when so problematic a personality as Nixon nominated himself as its advocate.

His proximity to the central tradition of American individualism made his own emotional inadequacies and moral failures more disturbing, more challenging than might otherwise have been the case. Writing under a pseudonym a decade before Watergate, John Kenneth Galbraith calculated—rather gently—how low Nixon ranked on a "McLandress coefficient": a mock social scientific measurement of the number of seconds a person can think of any topic other than himself. Among public officials, Nixon ranked lowest.[37] Yet worse was to come. The flag pin in Nixon's lapel proved to be no evidence of virtue, and offered no immunity against corruption; the White House prayer breakfasts did not purify the language or the sentiments on the telltale tapes; the appeal for law and order did not disguise the betrayal of the public trust. The hypocrisy appeared so dramatic, because the pitch Nixon made was so exalted. The journalists could follow the money, from the Hughes loan to Hugh Sloan; and the humorists could take the rest of the afternoon off. In the desperation of an appeal to authority that Nixon and his staff themselves did so much to undermine, in insisting on executive privilege or asking for respect for the office of the presidency, the Nixon administration's pleas were (in the phrase of the

36. Wills, *Nixon Agonistes*, 602.
37. Mark Epernay (pseud. John Kenneth Galbraith), *The McLandress Dimension* (Boston: Houghton Mifflin, 1963), 2–3, 13, 14.

Viennese satirist Karl Kraus) like prescriptions written by patients. In invoking the tradition of individualism, Nixon was inadvertently calling attention to his own character, whose flaws do not of course thereby make him a tragic hero. Yet because his grip on his own self was usually too tight and his dislike of his foes too intense, he could in many precincts be regarded as a comic figure.

It is a critical commonplace that the tragic hero recognizes his own complicity in his downfall, perceives how his own character and conduct have resulted in his destruction. Without such self-knowledge, there cannot be tragedy, though there may be pathos, as when Senator Thomas Eagleton—a midwesterner with a secret locked in his past— told Mailer in 1972 that one of his favorite books was *The Great Gatsby*. Without such self-knowledge, there may also be comedy, as in both David Frye's and David Levine's eerie portrayals of Nixon as Captain Queeg. Neither comic artist could have known that the president's favorite novelist was Herman Wouk, the inventor of a naval officer who forfeits his leadership because of excessive zeal in asserting his authority, and who defeats himself by doubting and then undermining the loyalty of others.[38]

38. Norman Mailer, *St. George and the Godfather* (New York: Signet, 1972), 100; William Safire, *Before the Fall: An Inside View of the Pre-Watergate White House* (Garden City, N.Y.: Doubleday, 1975), 564.